The First to Speak

The First to Speak

. . . . .

A WOMAN OF COLOR
INSIDE THE WHITE HOUSE

. . . . .

Kristin Clark Taylor

DOUBLEDAY

New York · London · Toronto
Sydney · Auckland

PUBLISHED BY DOUBLEDAY
a division of Bantam Doubleday Dell Publishing Group, Inc.
1540 Broadway, New York, NY 10036

DOUBLEDAY and the portrayal of an anchor with a dolphin are
trademarks of Doubleday, a division of Bantam Doubleday Dell
Publishing Group, Inc.

"I, Too" from *Selected Poems* by Langston Hughes, copyright 1926
by Alfred A. Knopf, Inc. and renewed 1954 by Langston Hughes.
Reprinted by permission of the publisher.

Designed by Nancy Field

Library of Congress Cataloging-in-Publication Data

Taylor, Kristin Clark.
      The first to speak : a woman of color inside the White
   House / Kristin Clark Taylor. —1st ed.
         p.   cm.
      1. Taylor, Kristin Clark. 2. Presidents—United States—Staff
   —Biography. 3. Afro-American women public relations
   personnel—Washington (D.C.)—Biography. 4. Public relations
   personnel—Washington (D.C.)—Biography. I. Title.
   E840.8.T39A3   1993
   973.928'092—dc20
   [B]   92-42475
                                                          CIP

ISBN 0-385-42510-4

To my parents,
James W. Clark and Mary Elizabeth Clark,

who gave their seven children
a head start in the world
and steered us, always,
toward the light.

ACKNOWLEDGMENTS

Many people put their energy and spirit into the creation of this book. I especially want to thank those who took the time to sit down with me and reflect: President George Bush, General Colin Powell, Marlin Fitzwater, David Bates, Roger Ailes, Peter Teeley, Rich Bond, Allen H. Neuharth, Peter Prichard, Ron Martin, Joseph Watkins, Stephen Hart, Reid Detchon, Maria Sheehan, Barrie Tron, Chriss Winston, Sean Walsh, Lisa Battaglia, Bob Ellison, Maryann Stevens, Anna Perez, Sally McElroy, Shirley Green, Curt Smith, Doug Wead, and Rev. Dr. Leonard Smith of Mt. Zion Baptist Church in Arlington, Virginia. My gratitude extends also to the people behind those names who helped make many of these meetings happen: Kathy Super, Laura Melillo, Carolyn Piper, B. J. Cooper, and Tracy Quinn. Special thanks to Joyce Campbell, Carol B. Aarthus, and Joyce Naltchayan for their logistical help from within the White House.

I praise God for the families in my life, beginning with my own: My husband, soul mate, and best friend, Lonnie, for his spiritual support, his strong embrace, and his constant, unconditional encouragement. With the pride and passion which only a mother can feel for her children, I thank my two babies, Lonnie Paul and Mary Elizabeth, who were patient right up until the very last word was written. Bless you, my babies, for bringing your blankets downstairs some nights to stay close while Mommy wrote.

To my father, James W. Clark, and the memory of my mother, Mary Elizabeth Clark, both of whom kept me energized and fortified throughout this project. And to my beautiful sisters and my brother, the ones who surrounded me with love and laughter at the beginning of my life and ever since, I also give profound thanks: Joann Clark Anderson, Ingrid Lisbeth Draper, Noelle Clark, Donald Jose Clark, Tanya Renee Clark, and Nikki Clark Ferguson. Our closeness keeps me warm; I will wear it wrapped around me always, like a protective cloak. Individually and collectively, you are extraordinary. I am proud to be a part of your legacy.

I am indebted also to my mother-in-law, Magdalene Sturges Taylor, for bringing her third son (and my husband) into the world, and for her quiet, gentle words of wisdom and encouragement. She is a remarkable woman, the mother of eleven bright, beautiful children—all of whom, without exception, rallied close around me while I wrote. The Taylor troop helped keep me buoyant: Sarah Sturges, Leroy and Cammille Taylor, Maggie Taylor, Theodora Taylor, David Taylor, Magdalene Taylor, DeAnder Taylor, Rita Taylor, Martin Taylor, and Zandria Taylor Scott. I am truly blessed and tremendously strengthened by having not just one but *three* remarkable family networks interwoven so beautifully into the fabric of my life.

I couldn't have finished this project without the emotional

nourishment from my loving, literate, lifelong sister-friend, Novellia "Cookie" Jones, and my office assistant and friend, Valry Fetrow, both of whom rode the waves of my moodiness with style and grace as I struggled through the final stages of my manuscript. To my editor, Casey Fuetsch, who called me on the phone one gray, cloudy afternoon to welcome me to the Doubleday family, and who nudged me along with the same determination and resolve that I would expect from one of my own sisters: Thank you for believing in my story and breathing life into the manuscript. To my agent, Jane Dystel, as tough and sassy as I one day hope to become, who listened to me after our first meeting and said, simply, "I believe in you. Let's do it."

Much appreciation to my resourceful, tenacious re-searcher, Sam Silverstein, and to the people who reviewed my final manuscript and offered valuable feedback: Celeste James, my sister-friend with the huge heart and the beautiful smile, and Fred Fetrow, whose literary background and knowledge helped my story shine. To those at BellSouth Corporation— John Clendenin, Raymond "Mickey" McGuire, and C. Rich-ard Yarbrough—who gave me the emotional space and support I needed to write this book and work simultaneously.

I often think of the handful of people who made a pro-found impact on my life early in my career, many of whom I haven't seen in years. Each of you, in different ways, played a role in helping me with this book, for without you there wouldn't have been a story to tell: Ken Seigneurie, Ben John-son, Joe Stroud, and John Seigenthaler. Thanks also to Tom Gibson for reaching out and being the first to bring me into the political fold, and to so many of my other friends who rallied close: Cheryl Kienel Jackson, Holly Williamson, Schelly Reid, Carlos Jones, Wallace Terry, Karen Gaddis, André Latham, and Charlie Miles.

And finally, ultimately, thanks be to God, who guided my hands as I wrote and lifted my spirit when I wanted to put down my pen and rest. It was His path that I followed daily, hourly; it was His goodness which kept me anchored and directed. Thank You for Your infinite glory, goodness, and beauty. You are the river that runs through me always. Thank You for steering me through.

Contents

The First
to Speak

CHAPTER 1

. . . . .

Between
Two Worlds

. . . . .

T HE SUN STREAMED into the Oval Office, bouncing off my
patent leather pumps and warming my arms. I sat in a
straight-back chair immediately across from the President. Bush
glanced through the index cards which held the opening remarks he was about to make to a group of out-of-town reporters and editors. I watched him bite the inside of his lower lip as
he read, his eyebrows slightly furrowed, long legs crossed, shoes
freshly polished.

Several other aides in the room sat at silent attention,
ready to launch into graceful, succinct clarification of any question that came from the President's lips, on any issue. Pick a
subject. Any subject. If an answer existed anywhere in the
world, these men would know it. They're who I called the
President's Gray Matter Men: brainy, smooth, and highly intel-

1

lectual, but bland and somewhat one-dimensional, like a slab of gray marble. These people who sat in this oval room—all white males, except for me—were the best and the brightest. I wondered if their whirring brains prevented them from hearing the sparrows and chickadees singing just outside the window or from feeling the warmth of the sun through their Brooks Brothers suits.

Slightly behind me, on the two white sofas in front of the fireplace, sat Marlin Fitzwater, the President's press secretary, and Brent Scowcroft, national security advisor. Also present were Richard Darman, budget director; Roger Porter, domestic policy advisor; and my boss, David Demarest, White House communications director. White House Chief of Staff John Sununu sat on the arm of the sofa, looking rumpled and reflective. (Something about his presence and posture reminded me of the Pillsbury Doughboy—except for the fact that he didn't giggle like that crazy Doughboy, and Lord knows he didn't dance silly jigs on people's kitchen countertops. No, sir. Giggles and jigs were definitely not what John Sununu was about.)

I had planned this media event from A to Z, interacting with the out-of-town reporters for weeks in preparation for this luncheon and press conference. I knew their concerns, their pet peeves, some of their children's names. I also knew that at least one of the networks was going live with the President's remarks and would need a two-minute warning before interrupting their regularly scheduled programming. We were running short on time. The moment the President looked up from his cards, I took my cue, cleared my throat, and began to speak.

"Mr. President, we're about to move to the State Dining Room for a regional press briefing and luncheon with members of the press. After lunch, you'll make brief remarks, expected to last about four and a half minutes, then open the floor to questions."

I felt my baby stretch and strain inside of me, groping around for more space inside the cramped quarters of my stomach, but I didn't miss a beat.

"Everything's on the record, of course," I continued. "Even your casual luncheon conversation. At least one of the networks is going live, so we'd better try to stay on schedule. Mrs. Bush is expected to join you for lunch and—"

"Do you think they're going to back me into a corner and ask me about Neil?" Bush interrupted, directing the question to no one in particular and everyone in general. He'd been preoccupied and publicly testy with the media about questions concerning his son Neil, who was then under fire for his dealings with the Silverado Banking Savings and Loan Association in Colorado. It was the President's hot spot, and we all knew it. Marlin moved first, predicting aloud—and, as it turned out, correctly—that the media firestorm surrounding Neil had finally begun to die down. Demarest and I echoed our agreement.

We ran through about ten possible questions I had prepared early that morning on a range of issues, and Bush tried his hand at answering them all, his six Wise Men and one Very Pregnant Woman listening intently and adding tidbits and clarifications whenever necessary. These prebriefings were like superpower dress rehearsals.

As the President finished his last question, the door opened, and his personal steward, Domingo Quicho, moved quietly into the room, slightly bent at the waist, carrying a glass of orange juice. After placing it on a napkin on the President's

3

desk, he turned to leave. I studied the lines on his face, as I had many times in the past. Domingo had come to learn the President's ways. Sometimes without even being told, he could sense when the President preferred juice or simply sparkling water instead of hot tea or soda.

My baby lurched inside me again, bouncing on my bladder, this time forcefully enough for it to show on my face.

"You okay, Kristin?" The President had noticed. I felt embarrassed and out of place. A seersucker suit rustled in a chair beside me.

"I'm fine, thank you, Mr. President. Just an unexpected twinge. If we're finished here, gentlemen, we should—"

"This little bambino's not going to arrive early, is it?" he asked. He wouldn't let go. There was a hint of a smile on his face, but I could tell he was genuinely concerned and expected an answer.

Voila! Bingo! I never thought it would be possible, but the President had finally, *finally,* asked a question which his Gray Matter Men couldn't answer. And there was no figuring this one out. No tidy, prepackaged, calculated predictions; no neat hypotheses. My pregnancy definitely did not lend itself to the precision of White House politics.

"I'm fine, Mr. President. There won't be any early deliveries around here, I promise." To the sound of relieved laughter, we all rose along with the President, I secretly hoping that my water wouldn't break all over the beautiful Oval Office rug. I'd have been embarrassed enough to die a thousand deaths.

Still chuckling lightly, we began moving through the White House complex, past the Rose Garden and through the East Corridor en route to the State Dining Room and the anxiously awaiting reporters.

Fluidly, like mercury, two Secret Service agents slipped into place to form a protective shield around the President as he walked; we had learned instinctively to give the agents the room they needed. Their "ring" wasn't quite as tight when we moved within the complex. This was the President's home, and it was neither fitting nor necessary to crowd him too tightly here. Tim McBride, the President's personal assistant—always pressed, perfect, and personable—fell gracefully into ranks as we moved, as did the White House photographer, David Valdez. We all matched the President's pace, like a tiny herd of gazelle following their male leader. Always the gentleman, Bush deliberately kept his long strides slower than usual so that I could lumber along at as dignified a pace as I could muster. I said a silent prayer of thanks to the Lord for making Bush an experienced, empathetic father.

"Timberwolf" was en route, one agent whispered into his wrist. (This was the code name given the President by the Secret Service.) Estimated time of arrival: two minutes. A member of my staff, Maria Sheehan, was already positioned in the dining room beside an agent. The agent nodded his head slightly, the cue that the President was en route. The awaiting guests sensed that Bush's arrival was imminent. Ties were adjusted. Hair was patted into place.

Perfect precision was the name of the game in the White House—language and movement crisp and efficient, every watch synchronized. At this stage in my pregnancy, not only were my physical movements inefficient, they seemed gawky and exaggerated, as though I were moving through water or Jell-O in slow motion. And as for synchronization, my wrists were too puffy from pregnancy for me to even think about a watch. My father, wise from having helped bring seven children into the world (six girls at that), had mailed my maternal grandfather's pocket watch for me to use until my swelling subsided. My little gold pocket watch, I was pleased to admit, was synchronized with everyone else's.

I remembered my grandfather whenever I looked at the watch, always wearing colorful plaid shirts, smelling like mothballs and Mentholatum Deep Heating Rub, his hair soft and white as a dandelion. Grandpa drove a big, pale green fish-tail Cadillac and would always toss me quarters, saying in a soft voice, "Run down the street, pigtail, and buy yourself some cream. And look both ways before you cross that street. If anything happened to you, your mother would kill me and you both." I saved his quarters in an old sock in my dresser drawer; I still have them today.

I glanced across the table at the President to gauge how we were doing on time. Surrounded by reporters, he was chatting comfortably about sports and local politics. He was obviously enjoying himself. Everyone cued off of the President. Even the waiters watched attentively to assess his progress; they would serve his dessert once he looked as though he was comfortably ready. We were like a finely tuned dance troupe or musicians in a symphony orchestra; without precise cooperation and interaction, our collective mission would fail.

Through my small talk, I glanced casually around the room. One reporter, to my horror, had stuffed his cloth napkin deep into his shirt, and looked as though he was about to pick up his finger bowl and drink from it. Rather than embarrass him by leaning over and whispering the proper social instructions ("Listen, you moron. That bowl's for finger dipping, not drinking. Get a grip! You're sitting in the White House in the same room with the President of the United States!"), I imme-

6

diately plunged my fingers into the bowl, wiggling them around delicately. Fortunately he spied me and followed suit, plunging his own fingers in as well and glancing around the table with a look of relief. He'd been pulled from the brink. (If he'd actually taken a sip, my guess was that Bush would have had a good chuckle about it later.)

I studied the waiters who moved throughout the room. Many of them were elderly black men with slightly stooped backs and kind, tired faces. They were a hairbreadth away from actually being "old"; their hands would be even more wrinkled by the time my baby was born.

Sitting in the State Dining Room under the beautifully shimmering chandeliers, I felt the familiar words of poet Langston Hughes slapping softly at the nape of my neck:

> I, too, sing America.
> I am the darker brother.
> They send me to eat in the kitchen
> When company comes,
> But I laugh,
> And eat well,
> And grow strong.

These men in this room are indeed my "darker brothers," I thought. They are my brothers, my grandfathers, my kinfolk who walked these halls long before I was even born. I came from them; they are my history. They have served elegant, sumptuous meals to generations of diplomats and dignitaries, toiling in the White House kitchens for longer than I am old. They are slow, dignified, and deliberate in their every movement. And they are beautiful.

I somehow always felt ashamed when these proud men

served me. The scene seemed slightly off-balance, improper. My grandfathers shouldn't have to mop up my gravy spills or brush the crumbs from my table. Let someone else do it. If they'd been hip, young black men wearing tight pants and sexy smiles, I realized, it wouldn't have been quite as unsettling. But these were older men who were serving me—my grandfathers, all of them, with slow-moving hands and wise eyes. What indignities had they suffered during their lifetimes? What injustices had they known in their youth? My mother spoke once of trying on a hat in a downtown department store only to have the manager approach her and demand that she purchase the hat, because Negro women weren't allowed to try on the merchandise. "You try, you buy" was the store's policy toward Negro women. And my great-great grandmother, while playing on the banks of a Richmond river as a young child, was kidnapped by paddyrollers, stolen away forever. Two white men took her away in a covered wagon and traveled to Bessemer, Alabama, where they resold her into slavery, clearing a handsome profit for themselves but completely transplanting our family roots. In one afternoon, my family's history was changed forever. And all because my great-great grandmother chose the wrong moment to play in the sun.

Surely these men who were serving me must be more intimately familiar with injustices such as these. Certainly they, too, must have stories to tell and tragedies to try to forget.

Sitting under the huge, dark portrait of President Lincoln, Bush leaned back in his chair and joked with one of the waiters, calling him by his first name.

I always wanted to slide under the table when he did that. I knew Bush meant no disrespect, but my grandmother would never have tolerated such a thing. Had I been disrespectful

8

enough to call any of my elders by his or her first name, she would have marched me outside to pick the longest branch from the forsythia bush in the backyard. She'd deftly remove the yellow leaves by running her thumb and forefinger from the base of the branch all the way to the tip, leaving the branch bare and evil-looking.

"Whipping sticks," she'd call them. Those whipping sticks would whisk lightly across my bare brown legs with blinding speed. And as strong-willed as my grandmother had been in her heyday, she probably would have lit heartily into Bush's legs, too, had she heard him call these proud old men by their "familiar" names.

Perhaps this show of humility and respect toward the elderly was culturally unique to my people, or even individually unique to me. But everyone I knew—especially black people—never called their elders by their first names, and we certainly didn't have them serving us food and cleaning up behind us. This smacked too much of Mint Julep in the Big House—too *Gone With the Wind*-ish for me. I knew what I was experiencing was "culture clash," when my two converging worlds—one steeped in the rich, familiar history of the black experience, the other nestled comfortably in the powerful, white, insular world of the White House—collided. I was protective of the pride of my people, and of the memories of my predecessors.

But something stirred somewhere in the back of my mind that afternoon at lunch. Something told me to recognize and even find pride in the symbolism of the moment. There I sat in the shining splendor of the State Dining Room, having coordinated this entire media event, while directly across the same table from me sat the President of the United States, and a few feet above him hung a portrait of President Abraham Lincoln, assessing me from above the grand fireplace.

I was the first woman of color to be appointed to this position. I was well respected by my peers and by the President. I was young, intelligent, happily married, and about to give birth to my second child. I realized with a pang that feeling guilty and embarrassed about having the waiters serve me was actually condescending.

I was simply struggling to assimilate my two dramatically different cultures into one world, to merge my past into my present—sometimes like trying to fit round pegs into square holes.

I wasn't brought up being served by old black men or sharing meals with presidents. I was brought up on summer evenings spent sitting on the front porch with my family, whispering into the night until the porch lights flickered on; I was brought up chasing the ice cream man down the street and watching, mesmerized, as my older sisters applied their makeup in our crowded, bustling upstairs bathroom.

Mine was a bicultural balancing act. I was straddling two worlds—trying hard to make sense of them both.

CHAPTER 2

. . . . .

Brown
Venus

. . . . .

Ivy LEAGUE, BUTTONED-UP, aristocratic types have never
really been my cup of tea. Fortunately, the key people with
whom I interacted when I first arrived at the White House—
namely Craig Fuller, chief of staff to Vice President George
Bush, and indeed Bush himself—were real-life, down-to-earth
people, comfortable with themselves and with their places in
the world. Unlike so many others around them, they refused to
be steeped in the rigid formality and picture-perfect protocol
of the White House.

Both Bush and Fuller were unpretentious and plain-
spoken, with a naturalness about them that immediately put
people at ease. I could visualize the two of them sitting at
someone's kitchen table, cracking open peanuts and popping

11

them into their mouths as they talked. It'd have to be a pretty high-class kitchen, mind you, with marble floors rather than linoleum, and fine silk wallpaper rather than a slapped-on coat of Sherwin-Williams paint, but their images could fit comfortably and quite naturally into someone's kitchen nonetheless. The "kitchen test" has become my secret, reflexive measurement for gauging people's down-to-earth qualities and the believability of their character: How comfortable would they actually feel (and look) sitting at someone's kitchen table?

I couldn't imagine Nancy Reagan, for example, sitting at *anyone's* kitchen table—not even her own. One of the cleaning ladies in the White House once pointed out to me (I never found out if this was entirely accurate) that you can see a tiny part of the First Family's kitchen if you look out of the Indian Treaty Room in the Old Executive Office Building toward the West Wing complex. Sometimes at night, back when Reagan was still in office, I'd strain my eyes to see any signs of life—a shadow, a flicker of movement, a refrigerator door opening, anything. But no luck. Ronald and Nancy Reagan were not kitchen types. They both failed my kitchen nutcracking test miserably.

With Bush and Fuller, what you saw was what you got. And although they both hailed from the insulated world of power and political prestige, it never showed in how they regarded those around them. Their down-to-earth qualities made my transition into the White House much easier; for, unlike them, I did not hail from the ivy-covered world of power and privilege.

· · · · ·

I AM NOT THE PRODUCT of a wealthy family. I didn't grow up in a mansion. Never had a maid to wash my clothes or a cook to prepare my food. Never rode in a limousine (and certainly not an armored car) until I started working for George Bush. As a child, and especially as the youngest child, I had more than I needed—but I always recognized and appreciated the sacrifices my parents made to make it possible.

My father, James W. Clark, worked nights as a foreman at a large tire company downtown near the Detroit River. My mother, Mary Elizabeth Clark, was a schoolteacher. Together they instilled in us an insatiable hunger for knowledge and an unquenchable thirst for personal and professional achievement. Like many parents, they wanted their children to have more than they had, in the same way I now look at my own children and wish the same for them.

All six of my siblings and I grew up on the north end of Detroit, right off of Woodward Avenue, in the heart of the city. Mother and Daddy purchased the home in 1941, after years of scrimping and saving. The eldest child, Joann, seventeen years my senior, was only months old when they moved in. But Mother and Daddy were meticulous planners, methodical in their approach to creating a family and purposeful in their mission to nurture us in a safe and loving environment. They moved into the five-bedroom house knowing they wanted a large family later on, so they pinched here and scraped there to finally purchase their dream house. They also knew exactly how they wanted to raise the children they would eventually have: in a comfortable, stimulating environment with easy, direct access to the best public resources available—particularly schools. Back then, the neighborhood was predominantly white. We were the second black family to move onto our comfortable, tree-lined street.

Gradually, as the neighborhood became more integrated over the years, our social contact with other black families became more frequent. Relationships and interpersonal dynamics began to shift: My older sisters began to venture out more freely into their neighborhood, exploring their newly claimed territory.

And the community grew closer. Everyone knew each other; every mother watched out for every other mother's child. Kids played outdoors well into the summer nights while their fathers, watching absently, sat on lawn chairs on the front porch, listening to the Tigers' game on the radio. Growing up felt good. Mud pies lined the steps of our back porch. Summer breezes slammed bedroom doors shut. The tinkling, broken-sounding melody of ice cream trucks sent all of us scrambling for somebody's pocket. Clothes smelled like the outdoors. I'd sit on the stoop with my best friend and next-door neighbor, Cookie, talking and giggling until the streetlights came on. We'd finish our conversations in our pajamas, whispering through our open second-floor bathroom windows until our parents finally ordered us to bed.

And always, the sounds.

Sounds are some of my richest childhood memories. There were the smooth-talking local deejays who came to be our heroes, crooning their smooth, mysterious magic into our world on Woodland Street—Donnie "The Luvv Bug" Simpson, silkier and sexier in every young black girl's eyes than Elvis ever hoped to be; "Martha Jean the Queen," as dignified as the Queen Mother herself, with twenty times as much soul. And always, always, there were the sweet, soulful sounds of Motown

—perfect, passionate mood-setting music for those blue-light-bulb basement parties where teenagers (my older sisters among them) would slow-dance to the tunes of Smokey and Stevie and Aretha and Diana.

The sounds were some of my warmest memories: Mother's lilting voice as she spoke to and laughed with "Mama Lilly," our beautiful, gray-haired grandmother, on the telephone; neighborhood friends laughing and screaming in the alley out back; and, through my afternoon nap, the sound of lawnmowers droning somewhere down the block or around the corner. This is what carried me into adulthood, creating in me a healthy, renewable reservoir that, even today, keeps me strong and buoyant.

The members of my family drew strength from their relationships with each other, and from our sheer number. As the baby, I was thrust happily into the middle of the chaos, accustomed to and fully expectant of the affection and warmth that was heaped upon me from all sides. Even when I wasn't the family's center of attention, I always yearned to be close to them, in the thick of it all.

My older sisters were mesmerizing. In our basement, they'd choreograph elaborate lip-synching routines with the Supremes (Joann would always get to be Diana. As the oldest, it was her prerogative.) Or Martha and the Vandellas. They were amazing—graceful and as beautiful as African queens. Their laughter was infectious. Sometimes during those Motown gigs they'd even cajole my brother Don into being Smokey or Stevie. Don was always quiet and reserved (who could blame him, really, with six highly opinionated, domineering sisters?), but most times he'd allow himself to be dragged, reluctantly at first, into the fun.

Even Mother and Daddy would sometimes come down to watch as my sisters brought the sights and sounds of Motown into our home with dances like the Temptation Walk, the Jerk, the Hully Gully, the Mashed Potatoes, the Slop, and the Watussi. Motown hadn't turned into a national legacy yet. It hadn't yet metamorphosed into one of the most nostalgic periods of American history. Joann, Ingrid, and Noelle went to high school with Diana Ross. Diana lived downtown in the Brewster Projects, a rough, ragged area where we were never allowed to venture. Aretha Franklin lived near La Salle Boulevard, Stevie Wonder on the northwest side. On any warm summer evening, from any house or street corner, you could hear "The Fabulous Four Tops" or "The Tempting Temps"—if not crooning on the radio, then in the voices of the black teenage men singing a cappella on the street corners in small clusters, trying to strike that same sweet, soulful harmony.

Years later, when movies like *American Graffiti* and *Grease* came out—nostalgic movies that tried to re-create some of the soulful sounds of the fifties and sixties (sounds which were largely created by black musicians and songwriters)—I could never understand why the scripts were almost totally void of black roles. We were the heart and soul of the sound itself. For us, it was far more than just "music." It was our culture, a way of living that we ourselves had created.

Ours was an orderly, purposeful, reaffirming world, full of all the things my parents worked so hard to convey to their children—civility, compassion, intelligence, love of music and creative arts, and, perhaps the most important element of all, thirst for educational achievement and excellence.

Mother and Daddy considered the education of their seven children their highest priority. Joann, Ingrid, and Noelle

—the three oldest children—were all raised during the 1950s, when the schools in our neighborhood were either predominantly white or on the verge of becoming integrated. Back then, the public schools were excellent and the resources plentiful. They all enjoyed the benefits of a sound, solid education.

It was the good Lord who protected my older sisters from the outward ravages of racism—God, of course, and Mother. The more subtle elements of racism and prejudice picked at them occasionally—sometimes so subtly even they themselves couldn't immediately feel its effects or intentions—but if Mother were anywhere close enough to see it happen, her protective shroud would cover us completely, softening the blows.

Once in grade school, Joann brought home a book from the school library, *Little Black Sambo*. Calmly and without overt anger—and in the dead of winter, no less—Mother put on her coat and walked the eight blocks to the school. She told the teacher and the principal that no child of hers could *possibly* be exposed to such negative, degrading images of the Negro race; that her child's self-esteem would not be weakened now, not as she and Daddy were fighting so hard to build it up. She could never, ever tolerate such destructive images being conveyed to her daughter. I can imagine her now, issuing her simple directive: "I'm sorry, but we just can't have this. Figure out what you need to do, but get that book out of this school." She and Daddy attended a school meeting several days later. After the meeting, Mother casually found her way to the library. The book had been removed from the shelves. Mission accomplished.

But by the time I reached school age in the mid–sixties, the patterns had begun to change. The riots had white folks packing up and moving out of the inner city in a contemporary version of a wagon train, fleeing to the outlying suburbs— Birmingham, Oak Park, Southfield, Ferndale—and as a result, the city's once strong tax base began eroding like the rust-eaten paint on our family station wagon. Things began to change. Newly built freeways, designed, ironically, with the intention of stimulating "urban development," actually sliced inner-city black neighborhoods completely apart, destroying communities that were once close-knit and strangling small black businesses that were once prosperous. Neighborhoods like ours, once quietly tucked away from the urban blight, were gradually becoming mean city streets. Resources were dwindling; race relations deteriorating rapidly. Communities were coming unglued. The land shifted beneath our feet: What was once our comfortable north-end neighborhood became the "inner city"—to some, the "ghetto" even. And as public resources dwindled, to my parents' deep disappointment, so, too, did the quality of public school education.

Although it represented a substantial financial sacrifice at that time, Mother and Daddy decided to send me to a private school. All the rest of their children had benefited from good, solid public school education. Nothing would deter them from making sure their baby girl, their last child, also received the best available education. Nothing—not shifting socioeconomic trends, or changing demographics, or "white flight" into the suburbs—would deter them from their mission.

· · · · ·

I STARTED ROEPER at age five, in kindergarten, and stayed for ten years. Founded by a progressive German immigrant couple,

18

Roeper was a posh private school in Bloomfield Hills, one of
Michigan's wealthiest suburbs. The school was created specifically for "gifted" and talented (and wealthy) students. It was a
sprawling campus that felt more like college than kindergarten:
soft, rolling hills, swimming pools, and acres of uninterrupted
space. The Upper School was a refurbished mansion which sat,
quite majestically, high on top of a hill. We held our assemblies
in the great dining room; the master bedrooms and suites were
our classrooms; what was once some millionaire's attic had
been magically, charmingly transformed into the Upper School
art department. For ten years of my young life, I commuted the
forty-odd miles every day. I sometimes felt like Alice, having
stumbled and fallen down into another world—a magical, wintry-white Wonderland.

I was one of the first of a small wave of black students to
integrate Roeper's exclusive, handpicked, lily-white student
body. I never rode the school bus during all those years, even
though I secretly wanted to. Roeper buses weaved their way
through the exclusive enclaves of the very wealthy. They didn't
venture deep enough into the inner city to pick me up. Instead,
one of the school cooks, a cheerful black woman with sparkling
eyes who always hummed quietly to herself, picked me up
every morning on her way in and dropped me off in the late
afternoons. Although a part of me wanted to experience the
excitement of the bus ride, I was secretly a little relieved that
that big, yellow Roeper school bus, chock-full of curious white
kids, didn't come down my street. Julia's car was unobtrusive. I
could almost slip in and out of the neighborhood unnoticed,
incognito. Because of the long commute, I had to leave my
house very early, long before my neighborhood friends even
rose from their beds to prepare for school. And I'd arrive home

late in the afternoons, while many of them were usually outside playing. To the kids in my neighborhood, Roeper was a world away, another planet. "You go to *what* school?" they'd sometimes taunt. "Why you got to go so far to go to school, girl? You got somethin' wrong with you?"

Every weekday morning for ten years, Julia would honk her horn once and I'd scramble out the door with a piece of toast in one hand and my little attaché case in the other. Not a bookbag or a knapsack—an attaché case, filled with my completed homework assignments from the previous day. My neighborhood friends teased me mercilessly about that attaché. Something was wrong with the picture. But my friend Cookie would always say, "Go 'head, girl. Learn all they can teach you. You know you're doin' the right thing. I'll be waitin' for you when you get back." Cookie was never judgmental, never cynical. We took what we gave each other as a prized possession. And from it grew a lifelong, unconditional friendship.

I don't remember whether the school required that each child carry an attaché or whether Mother conceived the idea herself. But she loved it. Even when she and Daddy visited me in Washington, D.C. decades later, she'd rise early just to watch me leave the house, attaché case in hand, en route to my real-life, grown-up office. Mother and Daddy found great joy and gratification in admiring and fussing over the fruits of all their labor.

My entire world changed when I entered Roeper. At five years of age, a pattern was established which would follow me for the rest of my days. It represented the very first of the delicate balancing acts I would have to perform like a skilled high-wire artist in the circus: being the singular black voice in the midst of a white, powerful, status-conscious plurality. Even at age five, I tried mightily to integrate my two separate and distinct worlds—the world of Roeper and the world of Woodland Street—into one cohesive movement. It was to be the beginning of a lifelong effort to converge my two worlds—to weave my competing cultures into one whole cloth.

I struggled with feelings of alienation and isolation at being one of the few black children in the entire school. The only other black folks I came into contact with at Roeper besides my few black friends were the cooks, the domestic workers, and the drivers. They were warm and giving, and they always seemed to watch over me with an extra-careful eye; they'd always put an extra helping of macaroni and cheese onto my plate because they knew it was my favorite. I sensed that they wanted to take special care of me while I was in that place, and I will never forget their kindness and generosity.

But even with the feeling of isolation always lingering along the fringes of everything I did, I was happy to be part of the Roeper family. It, too, was a positive, close-knit environment, and I developed many strong, meaningful friendships. I relished the luxurious, sprawling beauty of the campus, and I considered myself blessed to have been afforded the opportunity to attend such a special school. I fully recognized and appreciated the sacrifices my parents made to send me there.

But Roeper was an environment completely different from anything I'd ever known. Straddling the trappings of the privileged, powerful upper class by day and the comfortable, familiar ethnicity of my family and neighborhood friends by night began to take on a ring of cultural schizophrenia. The contrasts became dizzying and disorienting—almost surreal. It was hard to keep a solid footing.

Eventually, the ground beneath me began to slip. Being so

far removed from my own people at such a young age, and for so many years, began to do strange things to my "blackness," to my racial identity. Perhaps I started Roeper too young, before I was strong enough to sustain pride in who I was and where I came from. I began to find myself daydreaming about what it would feel like to have lighter skin and longer, straighter hair. I wanted to be more like my white friends. I was appalled and horrified at myself for feeling so ashamed, and I knew my family—Mother especially—would have been outraged and unforgiving of my emotional weakness and complete loss of dignity. But I had been drawn into a different world to which none of them could relate. Rather than finding pride in being different, I sought refuge in trying to become the same.

In my eyes, which I kept shamefully downcast, my blackness had gradually become a disease. At school, I felt ashamed of being black. At home, I felt ashamed of myself for being ashamed. I knew that I was a sinner, and that God would never forgive me for not loving myself. As if having an out-of-body experience, I'd watch myself standing at the bathroom sink, scrubbing my hands until they were raw, subconsciously trying to make my beautiful brown skin become lighter. I refused to hold hands with my white girlfriends because the very sight of my dark color against their lily-white skin was too startling and ugly a contrast. It looked wrong, out of synch, unsightly. I sometimes even wore a hairpiece to school—straight and full, falling just above my shoulders. I explained to Mother that I *just had to have one* because it was the latest fashion craze, and that Tanya, another of my older sisters, occasionally wore one to high school, *so why couldn't I?* My parents never suspected that the real reason I wanted that hairpiece was borne out of

22

my sense of shame. Although it was a temporary phase (I probably wore it a total of ten times), I still burn with embarrassment and anger when I remember that I took such drastic, deliberate steps to hide my own natural hair. How could this have happened to me? I was raised in a houseful of strong, proud black women who shied away from absolutely nothing and no one. They knew exactly who they were and where they came from, and, unlike me, they grew stronger with the knowledge and appreciation of their ancestry and origin.

I'd pray in church every Sunday for the Lord to deliver me from myself—to bring me back into focus and help me come to realize the error and shamefulness of my ways. I'm convinced that it was His divine intervention that led me, one afternoon, out of my own dark shadows of shame. I'll always consider the moment—or more appropriately, the revelation—a gift from the Lord. It was His way of telling me that my prayers had been heard and answered, and that I was ready to be placed back on the right track. That one moment, on that one afternoon, changed forever how I regarded myself.

I was eight years old. It was several days before Halloween, and I was in our attic, searching for my costume—an old Hawaiian grass skirt. My sister Nikki was going to take me trick-or-treating. I was always a little frightened of our attic and rarely ventured up into it alone, but on this day Nikki refused to accompany me.

She spoke sternly: "You can find the skirt yourself. It's in the box right near the front window," she said. I made furious mental notes because I didn't want to be up there long. "Always rely on *yourself* to get the job done—not on others," she said. This was no time for teaching me the lessons of life, I thought. I sometimes grew tired of my sisters always trying to teach me practical lessons about life and living. She meant well, but damn. All I wanted to do was go trick-or-treating!

After rummaging through several boxes, I finally found the skirt, orange and wrinkled. As I folded the box flaps back down, my eyes caught something else inside: a scrapbook, thick with paper; yellowed and disintegrating with age.

Everything in me said to turn and leave right then, to run back downstairs to the safety of my sister. The air in the attic was thick and dusty, and I was scared up there by myself. But something stronger seemed to hold me there. I stood motionless, peering down into the box. Finally, I reached in and pulled it out.

Inside, there were several dried flowers, mums probably, decades old and colorless with age. Two or three faded satin ribbons were inside too, the inscriptions barely visible. One read, "Charter Member, St. Philips Lutheran Church." That must have been Mama Lilly's from many decades earlier. She and a handful of other black women founded our family's church—where all of us were baptized and raised, where my own children would come to be baptized. There were faded photos of unidentified people: three little girls on swings; a smiling black woman holding a baby on someone's front porch; a small black boy standing by a raggedy wire fence; other vague, nameless images which I could guess at but could not identify. I kept looking, intrigued.

And then I saw it: a front-page newspaper article from the *Pittsburgh Courier,* banner headline 'BROWN VENUS' IS CARNEGIE TECH MODEL, and then the subhead HAS POSED AT YALE, HARVARD. The profile was unmistakable, the posture intimately familiar. There stood the most beautiful woman I'd ever seen,

24

probably in her late teens or early twenties, draped in a dark velvet wrap which flowed off of her bare shoulders and rested in a graceful pool at her feet. She was indeed a "Brown Venus." She was beautiful. There she stood, in a graceful, languid pose, small, perfect hands held as delicately as a china doll's, surrounded by art students, all white, from Harvard and Yale, who were trying to copy her graceful poise onto their easels. It was Mother.

I flipped through other articles in the album. Mother's face and figure appeared everywhere. I had heard my sisters speak vaguely and briefly about Mother's "modeling days in college," but never did their conversations have the impact that that photo album had on me in the attic that afternoon.

"Sepia Siren," the article called her. "The world's most perfect face and figure." Her image was everywhere.

The articles described Mother as a rare jewel, as an intelligent, articulate Negro woman who worked as a professional model to put herself through her first few years of college at the University of Michigan. (She attended the University of Michigan in Ann Arbor before transferring to Wayne State University in Detroit.) She posed for art students at Harvard, Yale, and the Museum of Fine Arts in Boston; she modeled in major department stores and at exclusive art shows. Even today, several portraits of her hang in art museums and galleries. It is said that a sculpture still stands of her today in one of the exclusive private boarding schools in Michigan.

As I peered more closely at these images of Mother, my own shame and embarrassment slid away forever, like the old, useless skin of a snake.

This young Negro woman had had to push away the same cobwebs of racial alienation and isolation in her day that I was now battling with in my own. She, too, must have felt misplaced and alone, struggling to keep a grip on her identity as she moved within an all-white, upper-crust environment of privilege and wealth. The only difference—and it was a major difference—was that her deep brown skin shone with pride; her every movement, her every pose, even the way she held her hands conveyed a powerful sense of self-worth born out of generations of graceful dignity. Mother's beauty, pride, and sense of self were strong enough to make heads turn, alluring enough to make people want to capture her image on film and on canvas.

Something deep inside me had been ignited. I stood to leave. Without realizing it, and without ever knowing of my self-imposed indignity, Mother had rescued me from myself. From that afternoon in the attic and ever since, I've felt proud to be a black woman from a fine family, and I've been thoroughly comfortable with my own tenacity and self-sufficiency. I have my mother to thank for washing away all the vestiges of my misplaced shame and self-pity. In me, she had cemented hope, pride, and a newfound, reinvigorated self-esteem in a way that she never even knew.

· · · · ·

ALMOST IMMEDIATELY THEREAFTER, like a chain reaction, several events unfolded which helped guide me back onto more solid footing. I was coming to like who I was again. My prayers were being answered. And strangely enough, the answers were born out of turmoil and suffering.

The answers, for me, came in the form of the burgeoning civil rights movement, the deafening scream of national black pride, and the rousing rhythm of black self-awareness. They came with the sudden, tragic assassinations of Robert Kennedy and Dr. Martin Luther King, and with the 1967 race riots which tore our city apart.

I was eight-going-on-nine when the riots started, a young black girl with pigtails, skinny legs, and dusty saddle shoes. I watched from the safety of my parents' bedroom in confusion and dismay as a procession of U.S. Army tanks crept slowly down our narrow alley—down the same alley where my friends and I only days before had romped and played in the summer sunlight. I remember looking up at the summer sky, which was smoldering a strange orange color from the fires that raged throughout the city. A powdery, grayish film of cinders and ashes blanketed everything—our station wagon, our front-yard bushes, even our lawn, which Daddy had just mowed that afternoon.

Was all this craziness happening to my school friends in posh Bloomfield Hills, I wondered? Would they be surprised when I told them the things that went on? What was happening to our world?

Some evenings I'd sit with my family in silent horror, watching live television news reports of German shepherd police dogs mauling black protestors; of powerful fire hoses flattening grown men and women against the walls of buildings like so many pesty insects; of the jeering, hateful white faces pushed up close into the cameras, mouthing "Dirty rotten nigger" and spitting into the faces of the brave men and women who refused to be treated like dirt.

Such injustice and inequity triggered a deep, visceral reaction. I realized, years later, that I'd actually *wanted* to maintain and feed that anger—that I'd deliberately encouraged my rage

27

and bitterness to fester like an open sore in hopes that it would sharpen my vision and redirect me toward the racial pride and dignity that I felt growing within me.

By the time I entered my tenth year at Roeper, I considered myself a junior revolutionary, a radical of the highest order, full of myself and my beautiful blackness. I still loved Roeper and the relationships I'd developed over the years, but I no longer wanted to remain in that racially imbalanced environment. I had reached a crossroads. I yearned to be with my own people again. I felt suffocated, thirsty, incomplete. But it wasn't so much a feeling of racial victimization as it was a feeling of loneliness, pure and simple.

I finally decided, on my own volition, to leave the rolling hills of Roeper and complete my education in a public high school in downtown Detroit. It was then, and remains now, one of the most important decisions I've ever made in my life: to abandon the luxurious lifeline of my posh, protected school —an environment that I had known all of my young life—and reattach myself, like a severed limb, to my black culture. I prayed that the transplant would be successful. I saw it as my last chance to live and learn among my own people. I could feel that part of me was still taking shape. And I knew that I wanted my own culture and ethnicity to be a complete part of who I was to become. That I had actually allowed myself to daydream about being white had thrown me into a tailspin. It was almost incomprehensible. I took it as a signal that something in me had slipped terribly out of kilter. And I knew that if I didn't make my move then, it would be too late.

Mother and Daddy were, as always, comforting and supportive. They were proud of my maturity. They, too, recognized the magnitude of my decision. I wasn't just a student transferring to a new high school. I was a young black woman struggling to grasp her own culture before the opportunity slipped away from her forever. Some of my friends at Roeper, both black and white, tried desperately to dissuade me. "If you go to a public school," they warned, "you'll never make it to the Ivies. You can kiss Harvard and Yale goodbye. You won't survive. You'll be another black face in a sea of black faces. You'll never amount to anything much." I decided to take my chances and bid ten years' worth of friendships goodbye. I managed to maintain one or two former friendships, but I slowly dropped off of Roeper's radar screen and began moving in a different, dynamic world.

But in many ways, Roeper had also been a beautiful blessing.

From it, I had learned lessons far beyond my years, lessons many people don't learn for a lifetime. Roeper had played a critical role in the professional achievements I would enjoy later in life. By the time I was six years old, I had learned to move comfortably in and around the white power structure, to interact with people and cultures different from my own. I had been a part of the Anglo-American upper-class world for too many years to feel intimidated or threatened by it. Unlike many black urban-dwelling children, I didn't see white America, the "establishment" if you will, as foreign and far removed. My reason for leaving was pure and simple: I felt incomplete, imbalanced, as though I was missing out on too much of the vital, enriching cultural experiences of my own people. My "black experience" had been reduced to a part-time, short-term gig.

Although I was blessed to have strong, steady anchors throughout my childhood and early adolescence, I overcompensated. By the time I left Roeper and entered Cass Technical

High School, I was publicly espousing the teachings of Marcus Garvey and his black separatist philosophy. I hadn't yet found my happy medium. During part of my sophomore year in high school I wore an African turban, wrapped tight and tall around my head. I was now a proud African sister who studied Swahili and spent my weekly allowance on beaded Kenyan bracelets and T-shirts which read, "Back to Africa." I painted the black nationalist flag of red, black, and green onto my school locker and was called to the principal's office for defacing public property.

Gradually, as I adapted to my new surroundings and became more comfortable with my environment, the rage within me began to extinguish itself. I still clung like a drowning person to my racial and cultural identity, but I had become more introspective, philosophical. I removed my African turbans and cut my beautiful hair almost bald. I wanted to wear a supershort cropped "Afro" like the poetess Nikki Giovanni, my new black heroine. I tucked my Marcus Garvey books into the corner of our den and began memorizing and reciting every poem that Nikki Giovanni ever wrote. My bookshelves now were filled with black literature, poetry, and ancient philosophy. Langston Hughes. Kahlil Gibran. Aristotle. Maya Angelou. Imamu Amiri Baraka. And always, always Nikki Giovanni, talking about sexy black men in tight pants and the majestic beauty of the Nile River.

I became less angry, more mainstream, and I finally allowed the boys to court me. I basked in the beauty and pride which Mother helped me discover that afternoon in the attic, years earlier. I regarded myself as a second-generation Brown Venus. I began wearing makeup, accompanying my girlfriends to Big Boy after school for hamburgers and chocolate shakes, and borrowing my sister Noelle's bright yellow two-seater sports car to simply sit out in front of the school, looking cool with my homegirls. At sixteen, I formally learned the practice of Transcendental Meditation (TM) and became a vegetarian, cleansing both my mind and my body. (Both TM and vegetarianism were direct influences of my family. My brother Don had been a vegetarian years before it even became fashionable. Mother and Noelle had learned to meditate several years earlier, and they enthusiastically embraced my desire to learn.)

Over the course of several years, I had come full circle: from the shoulder-length, straight-haired hairpiece I'd wear occasionally at Roeper, to the tall African turban, to the huge, round Afro reminiscent of the Angela Davis days, to, finally, the short-cropped Afro. Through all of the philosophies and beliefs in between. Through all of the daishikis, the earth shoes, and the tie-dyed T-shirts—even through the platform shoes and "windowpane" blue jeans of my more fashionable, mainstream senior year. By the time I graduated from Cass, my intricate, tangled web had somehow straightened itself out. By my senior year, I was doing normal things like running for homecoming queen (I lost) and being nominated for "Class Cute" (I won). I was fairly popular, had a steady boyfriend who didn't look like Marcus Garvey, and had developed one or two close friendships (crazy, bubbly Karen Gaddis and quiet, spiritual André Johnson, with whom I'd laugh and act high school silly in the halls).

Finding myself during my early adolescence and teenage years was an exhilarating, tumultuous process. And it was tiring. My psyche had grown a little weary. But through it all, I was blessed with several constants in my life, constants which have remained true and strong today: a loving, supportive family; a small, close network of friends; and an unwavering belief in a gracious, giving God.

The early years of my life, every tumultuous phase I experienced, had strengthened and fortified me in ways I would never even realize or appreciate until later—until, for instance, I moved into the no-nonsense, rough-and-tumble world of White House politics.

CHAPTER 3

· · · · ·

The Call

· · · · ·

I HALFWAY IMAGINED that being hired for a job at the White House involved discreet discussion in the secluded corner of a mahogany-paneled drawing room, behind thick menus, heavy dark velvet curtains, and double martinis; perhaps seated with a blue-blooded, blow-dried Ivy Leaguer wearing presidential cufflinks and tasseled loafers so clean you could see yourself in their shiny leather.

Instead, I was standing at my kitchen sink giving my newborn baby a bath.

It was August 1987, and I was home on maternity leave from *USA Today* when a call came from Tom Gibson, my good friend and former colleague who had once worked with me on the newspaper's editorial page. Gibson had left *USA Today* to become White House associate director of cabinet affairs for President Reagan. George Herbert Walker Bush was weeks away from formally announcing his candidacy for President,

33

and his chief of staff, Craig Fuller, ever the quiet, methodical organizer, wanted as many people as possible placed in key posts on his White House staff before the announcement.

I had been home with our firstborn son, Lonnie Paul, for five months. Admittedly, my interest in politics during that time was limited to the twenty or thirty minutes of news we might (or might not) have time to watch every evening after dinner, between feedings, burpings, and the horrible gas pains which made my son yelp like a puppy in pain.

On the afternoon Gibson called, my most pressing concern was why the diaper man was late with his afternoon delivery. I was also wondering whether I'd pumped enough of my breast milk earlier that morning to last for two hours' worth of a lightning-fast trip into Georgetown to shop for a new tent-sized dress to cover my now more than ample hips. I needed to get out of the house, if only for a two-hour reprieve. George Bush, while I respected his politics and admired his seemingly solid, gentle character, was absolutely the last person on my mind.

My mother and I were in the kitchen struggling at the sink, trying to bathe my screaming, squirming brown baby boy, when the phone rang. My nerves already jangled, I picked up the receiver with soapy hands.

"The VP is looking for an assistant press secretary," Gibson said. Tom never was one for lengthy salutations, but the earsplitting screams in the background must have jarred something in his memory: "Oh," he said seconds later. "How's that bambino of yours doing?"

I looked at my mother bent over the sink—one small hand expertly holding both of Lonnie Paul's squirming feet as if she were preparing to stuff a Thanksgiving turkey, the other hand smoothing his chest with warm, soapy lather. Lonnie Paul was as slippery as a baby seal, and the prospect of being held down against his will had him thoroughly enraged.

Before Lonnie Paul actually developed a genuine liking for the water, I'd challenge myself to fly through bathtime ordeals within thirty seconds or less. I always played a variation of "Beat the Clock" at our kitchen sink; the goal was whatever the hell I could accomplish in the allotted time—take it or leave it. Ears still dirty? Too bad. Dried milk still caked around his tiny, perfect little lips? Oh well. His screams made me feel guilty. They frightened me, too. I brought him into the world, and I certainly didn't want to be the source of his discomfort. Not even for a minute.

My mother's approach, however, was how she approached everything in her life: purposefully, gracefully, and with total, unshakable confidence. Lord knows she had grasped her share of squirming feet in her lifetime. To her ears, Lonnie Paul's screams were no more bloodcurdling than mine (or those of any of my six older siblings) were at that age. It wasn't my mother's nature to impose time limits. I don't think I ever saw my mother hurry through anything. If she had a job to do, she took her time to get it exactly right. My hands raced over my son's body like greased lightning. Her hands—beautiful, deeply veined hands that could comfort and cool a fevered forehead within seconds—would glide leisurely, confidently, over rounded buttocks, behind ears, probing gently in between folds of skin.

I knew Mother could easily finish the task if I had wanted to continue my conversation with Gibson. Still, it wasn't a great time to launch into a serious telephone call.

"George Bush is going to win this election," Tom continued, undaunted by either my initial reservation or the hysterical screams in the background. "He's a man who could use your talent."

I was vaguely interested as Gibson spoke, and I was flattered that he had thought of me as a possible candidate. But something larger reminded me that this would not be a good match. Politics was never really my game. I considered myself a serious journalist with a promising future. During the summer of 1982, fresh out of college and halfway through an internship at the *Detroit Free Press,* I had been recruited by Gannett Company executives to help launch *USA Today.* The position sounded too good to be true: a full editorial board member on what would eventually become one of the nation's largest newspapers; only one of a handful of young black women in similar positions throughout the country. I was twenty-three years old when I took the job and moved to Washington, D.C. It was my first permanent full-time job out of college—not all bad, as a friend reminded me at the time, for a first-time gig.

Now, at age twenty-eight, I had settled comfortably into a satisfying life at *USA Today.* I was a respected and vocal member of the paper's editorial board, one of only two or three original remaining members who had helped design the paper's opinion page. I had expanded far beyond my daily editorial page feature—"Voices from Across the USA," a vox-pop series of people-on-the-street interviews that gauged reactions to daily editorial issues—and I was regularly publishing bylined interviews and an occasional column or editorial. Being a part of such an exciting project—helping design and launch a splashy, successful national newspaper—had already invigorated not only my spirit, but my career path.

I was receiving all the right signals from Gannett's senior

36

executives, and my hard work was beginning to pay off: The handwritten thank-you notes for a job well done by Gannett's chairman and USA Today founder, Al Neuharth; the increasing responsibility and visibility afforded me by the paper's editorial director, John Seigenthaler, the Gannett executive who personally and aggressively recruited me from Detroit. It was a comfortable life and a great first job, and my colleagues on the board fast became my friends.

Largely because of Neuharth's strong personal commitment to bring more minorities and women into the nation's newsrooms, Gannett had been identified as a progressive, color-blind corporation that went the extra mile to hire and keep qualified minorities within its ranks.

My niche at the paper felt secure, with plenty of room for growth. It was a dynamic environment, and in it I found a certain comfortable security that contrasted with the White House job Gibson was describing.

"They're looking for some new blood on the staff and some fresh talent," Tom continued. "I already sang your praises to Craig Fuller, Bush's chief of staff. He wants to talk."

Pans clattered and smashed to the floor. Lonnie Paul had triumphantly pulled one leg free from my mother's vise-like grip and kicked over a pan of marinating steak. For a split second, there was dead silence. The war had escalated; the battle lines were drawn. Lonnie Paul 1, Mother 0. I saw my quick afternoon trip into Georgetown dissolving before my very eyes. My anxiety level ratcheted up a few notches. For an instant I remembered the television commercial with the frazzled housewife pulling her hair out at the sounds of the baby crying, the dog barking, and the phone ringing: "Calgon, take me *away!!*" she screams, and instantly and magically ends up in a beautiful, quiet bathroom in a tubful of bubbles. That's just what I needed, I thought, fantasizing: a serious Calgon moment.

"What the hell is happening over there?" Tom finally asked. "It sounds like you're in the middle of a combat zone. Look, find the baby some formula," he suggested. "Then get your keister over here and start talking to some people. You're good, Taylor, but so are a lot of other people who are seriously bucking for this position. This job isn't going to wait around until you decide whether you want it or not."

The hard sell now, the final pitch: "You owe it to yourself to at least check it out."

Ol' Tom really knew how to push the right buttons. He was the ultimate politician and one of the brightest, most committed ideologues in the Reagan White House: "At least check it out." His words rang in my head. Small sparks of excitement flickered, but something inside me still resisted.

A part of me actually relished the thought jumping back into the swim: conversing with stimulating, intelligent people over six months old in words of more than one syllable, and becoming more familiar, again, with Mikhail Gorbachev's reign of power than Dr. Seuss's *Green Eggs & Ham*. But another part—larger than I cared to admit at the time—was deeply troubled at the prospect of walking away from my baby.

I'd given birth to Lonnie Paul almost six weeks prematurely. He went into fetal distress while I was in labor, and my doctors immediately recommended—and proceeded with—an emergency caesarean. It was traumatic and unsettling—the first real emotional challenge of our marriage—but we weathered the storm, and our firstborn son had rebounded heartily. But even though his recovery was now complete, I still felt as if I were abandoning my helpless offspring, snipping the umbilical cord before either one of us was fully and emotionally prepared for the separation. Not only the extenuating circumstances surrounding his birth but his very arrival—this little person suddenly insinuating himself so dramatically into our lives—greatly influenced how I approached even the prospect of returning to the *USA Today* headquarters. It was harder still to imagine me leaving my son only to face the rigors of a new, pressure-packed environment like the White House.

Through all the deliberation, through all the quiet nighttime conversations with my husband Lonnie after we'd put the baby to sleep, I never once doubted whether I was capable of performing the job. Competence, to me, was never the issue. Like my mother and her mother before her, I had been instilled with a strong sense of confidence and self-worth. I knew then, as I know today, that no task is insurmountable, no challenge impossible to meet head-on. The strong black women in my bloodline, in whose footsteps I was now walking, had worked hard to lay for me the strongest of all foundations. They had left behind something tangible and transferable: Their confidence in who they were and what they knew they could achieve. My five older sisters and older brother had passed on the mantle to me with pride, loving encouragement, and—perhaps most important of all—the fullest expectation for me to achieve.

Growing up the youngest in a houseful of ambitious, intelligent black women, I had learned almost instinctively how to not only survive but thrive in a highly competitive environment. The seven Clark children hold seventeen university degrees—three doctorates, a law degree, six master's, and seven bachelor's. With only an undergraduate diploma, I am by far the Clark child with the least amount of formal education. I'm not bothered by it; in fact, we laugh about it sometimes when we all come together.

Even my mother, busy trying with Daddy to nurture her seven children through varying stages of adolescence and early adulthood, received, after more than ten years of trying, her undergraduate and graduate degrees. Mother's timing was always impeccable: At quite a late age—far beyond a woman's traditional childbearing years, especially back then—she gave birth to me, the last of her progeny, during her spring semester break at Wayne State University in Detroit. And, weeks later, when classes resumed after the break, she, too, was back in school with her fellow students, all of whom were decades younger than she.

Mother was the only graduate—male or female, black or white, young or old—who walked across the stage on graduation day to the applause of a cheering section that was made up of her own seven children and one wonderfully supportive husband. Shortly thereafter, the *Detroit Free Press, Jet* magazine, and several other publications ran articles about the Clark family and about Mother's amazing accomplishment. It was recognition well deserved.

It was clear that the outside world really did see us as something of an anomaly. And it wasn't until much later—not until I started having children of my own, really—that I realized how hard my parents worked at the balancing act that ultimately cemented my own self-worth. Our family was always taught to view outstanding achievement as the norm. We were never allowed, nor did we ever want, to rest on our laurels for too long. We knew that doing so was unproductive. We knew that it could lead to stagnation—to intellectual paralysis.

So, if such a thing is possible, my self-esteem and pride had been nurtured long before even I myself had been created. Surmounting—and surpassing—challenges was a part of my history. I had been exposed to nothing else.

Still, as I considered the White House position, I remained vaguely aware that many of my journalist colleagues rather cynically regarded the slick wizardry of political public relations with a wary eye. "All form and no substance" was their usual charge.

Lonnie, six feet tall and as solid as my grandmother's backyard oak tree, sensed my heightened interest. He nudged me gently: "You're bright and beautiful and talented. For now at least, time is on our side. We're in our twenties! Fifteen years from now, neither of us will be as resilient, or in as much demand. My God, we'll be middle-aged! At least get with Fuller's people and talk some specifics."

Lonnie was my rational voice, my sense of calmed reason. He had a demanding job on Capitol Hill as a senior political aide to Republican U.S. Senator Arlen Specter of Pennsylvania. He was finishing his freshman year at Georgetown Law School in the evenings—dashing to class at the close of the day, cramming for exams into the wee hours of the morning, and somehow, through it all, handsomely and effortlessly fulfilling his role as husband, father, and best friend. He was my Rock of Gibraltar.

Mother, who could read my emotions like no other human on earth, encouraged me to pursue the job.

"Why not just shoot for the heaven and the stars?" she said to me over the phone as we discussed the position. "You know you'd do a beautiful job!" Mother's own personal

41

strength buoyed and inspired me. She taught me, by using herself as a real-life example, that there were no limits beyond those which we impose on ourselves. She was my guiding light.

I had heard Lonnie's voice and Mother's. Now it was time to listen carefully to my own. I looked lovingly at my brown baby as he slept, remembering all we'd been through at the beginning. I knew in my heart that our crisis with his premature birth was over. He was getting plump and gregarious, eager to jump headlong into his new life. I could clearly see that he had made the transition into his new world quite well.

It was now time to make my own.

Excited but still a bit hesitant, I called Craig Fuller's office and made an appointment with him that same week. That I was able to get an appointment with Fuller so quickly, sight unseen, was unusual in itself. A man as busy and "politically significant" as Fuller must have had lines a mile long outside of his office—old friends wanting favors, prospective job candidates, seasoned politicians seeking advice. He was a major power player and a respected, formidable presence on the national political scene. Ol' Gibson must have really given him the old earful. I felt grateful toward my friend for his faith in me.

· · · · ·

Fuller was not at all as I'd envisioned a chief of staff. His manner was easy, his smile quick. If it hadn't been for the secure phone on his desk—reserved exclusively for conversations with the President and the Vice President—he could have just as easily been a mortgage banker or a corporate lawyer.

Okay, so his suit, an expensive dark blue wool pinstripe, was probably made by one of the Brooks Brothers. But at least I couldn't see my image reflected in his shoes. And thank the good Lord God he wasn't wearing those crazy tasseled loafers that every pseudopolitician in Washington was wearing at that time, or the yellow "power" tie and matching suspenders that were then the current craze. Fuller was much too powerful and too comfortable with himself to follow fashion trends. And he was much too wise to even want to. He was approachable and relaxed, but very, very shrewd. There was something seasoned in his eyes; his instincts were as sharp as a cat's.

Fuller's office was spacious but unpretentious. He shared a suite with Vice President Bush, whose office was eight or nine steps across the hall. Model planes were scattered throughout the room. Pictures of B-52 bombers and Air Force fighter planes adorned his walls. Like Bush, Fuller was an accomplished pilot. Flying was still his hobby. That's one way he and Tom Gibson became good friends: They were both recreational pilots and flew together often. I was to discover later that Fuller approached crises from a pilot's vantage point: Once a problem presented itself, he'd target it carefully, lock it into his radar screen with his sophisticated homing device, then blast it out of the sky.

"Here's the job, as I'll explain it," he began in a soft voice. No banal questions like "So why do you want to work in the White House?" or "What do you see yourself doing ten years from now?" The immediacy of a presidential campaign was upon him. He wanted to find the right person for the job and move on to the other important matters—like getting his boss elected the next President of the United States.

43

"We're looking for someone who knows how the media works, who's had the experience," he said. "Tell me how you know the media."

"Well, Craig, I *am* the media," I answered, hoping I didn't sound too cocky or self-assured. Not until I answered his questions did I realize I'd ever be able to use the mild disdain some journalists feel for public relations types to my own advantage. Although I didn't really include myself among them, many journalists seemed to regard media relations people as probing, prohibitive gatekeepers. My personal impression, overall, was that they seemed a somewhat uninspired group, but I harbored no resentment toward them. I saw them as necessary functionaries, trying the best way they knew how to get their job done: writing press releases, issuing soundbites, trying to be the most efficient spin doctors they could be for whatever person or product they represented.

"You know as well as I do that many reporters regard press secretaries as a necessary evil," I said, holding his steady gaze. "They're irked by the presence of a third party, and they don't like to be spoon-fed select bits of information. They generally regard PR professionals as unwanted filters that prevent them from going directly to the source. They like dealing with their own kind."

Fuller leaned forward in his chair, picking at his thumbnail. A tiny tuft of hair stood up at the back of his head. I sensed that he was at least interested, perhaps even pleased, so I continued.

"I take pride in the fact that I would be joining the Vice President's White House staff from a major national newspaper," I said. "I am not a closeted public relations staffer or a corporate speechwriter who's never seen the inside of a newsroom—although if you look at my resume you'll see that I have held those types of positions, too," I reminded him. (In an effort to broaden my scope and perhaps groom myself for bigger and better things, I'd accepted two temporary assignments just before I'd left to give birth to Lonnie Paul, as a public affairs officer on the corporate side of the company and as a temporary business correspondent and occasional feature writer for the company's news service.)

"I understand the media," I continued, "and I know how to anticipate their needs. The ability to predict a preemptive strike is just as important as being able to defend yourself against one once it hits," I said.

And then, as a final appeal to his probable discomfort with —or at least apprehension toward—the media, I delivered the coup d'état: "I know what whips these guys into a feeding frenzy, and I know how to keep the waters calm during a storm."

The shark/piranha reference was somewhat of a cheap trick designed to appeal to his fear rather than his intellect, and it made me feel as though I was selling out my colleagues and my chosen field, but the job interested me, plain and simple.

I suddenly wanted the interview to be over. I was still nursing and needed to get home to feed Lonnie Paul. But Fuller continued, watching my reaction, "Obviously you know there are many other candidates we are seriously considering." I didn't flinch—didn't miss a beat.

"But none who would bring my talent and background to the job. I'm a skilled writer. Calm during times of crisis, with sharp instincts. There's no one else who would work as hard to get George Bush elected in 1988. I can guarantee you that," I answered back quietly.

Better slow your buggy down, Miss Saditty, I thought to myself. You're beginning to sound like a used-car salesman. You're also beginning to sound like you really, really want this job, when only last week you were telling Tom Gibson to go jump in a lake. It was true. I had come full circle: I was now determined to snag this job—not simply for the thrill of the hunt (although that was, indeed, an element), but because I sensed the challenge and had decided that I was up for it. I wanted to do my part to serve my country and help get George Bush elected.

The White House had a distinctive feel to it. Maybe it was the sheer, unadorned power of the Executive Office, or the strong sense of history. Perhaps it was the sight of the national security offices with digital combinations on all of the doors, or the sound of that tall-backed, burgundy leather chair squeaking from across the hall—a chair that you knew had to be filled by none other than George H. W. Bush himself. It was a powerful draw, like the current of the ocean. I made up my mind. I wanted the job.

Fuller and I talked about the tremendous, sometimes inordinate power of the press, the personality of George Bush, the responsibilities of the job, the success story that USA Today had become, and my role in the newspaper's actual launch. I told Fuller at the outset that I wasn't interested in traveling with Bush regularly because of my need to spend evenings with my five-month-old son. He smiled, assuring me that that would probably work out well because they were looking for someone to run the press office while the acting press secretary was on the road with Bush, which would be often.

He rose from his chair, effectively ending the interview. I

stood up with him, hoping that my bra shields, made especially for nursing mothers, had stayed in place.

"I'd like for you to sit down and chat with Steve Hart next, the VP's acting press secretary," Fuller said casually. I knew that was a good sign. Fuller was much too busy for platitudes or flattery. If I hadn't impressed him, he would have politely ushered me to the door with a vague "We'll be getting back to you."

I met with Steve several days later. He was only a year or two older than me, but already more buttoned up and formal than Fuller. He seemed almost too serious—particularly for his young age. And unlike Fuller, who sat beside me in a chair during our interview, Steve sat behind his desk. Not that it mattered much, but it did create a gap of sorts.

"So, why do you want to work at the White House?" Steve asked. There it was. I knew it had to surface at some point: the banal question over which Fuller had so expertly leapfrogged.

I took a deep breath: "Because I want to help George Bush get elected. Because I know I can make a difference," I answered. Weak. Cliché-ridden. I might as well have said something inane like "Because I want to work for my country." Steve tapped his pencil on his desk. I felt a run begin in my nylons and work its way down my thigh. Damn.

"What did you do before *USA Today?*" he asked, staring hard. He really was too intense for his age. I wondered if he had an ulcer.

"I was a summer intern at the *Detroit Free Press,*" I answered, trying to sound dignified rather than defensive.

"And before that?" he pushed.

"I was in college. Undergraduate."

Was he trying to embarrass me? Hadn't he even taken the time to read the resume I'd sent him?

I recrossed my legs and realized I had better smooth my feathers a bit. My hackles were beginning to rise. I felt like Mariel Hemingway playing Woody Allen's appallingly young girlfriend in the movie *Manhattan:* In one memorable scene, a friend of Allen's, the overeducated Diane Keaton, asks, "And what do you do, dear?"

"I go to high school," replied Hemingway, as innocent as a fawn.

The chemistry between Steve Hart and me continued to clash. But somehow, as time went on, both of us somehow began to lower our guard. Steve was intelligent and quick-witted, but overpolished, like floors that are beautifully waxed but perilous to walk on.

A few days after my interview with Steve, I received a call from Fuller's office. They had narrowed the field to three final-ists, and I was among them. He wanted to talk "one more time," as his assistant explained, before they made the decision. I returned to Fuller's office, and we talked for several minutes about things like salary ranges and specific job responsibilities.

"When will you make your decision?" I asked.

"Within the next week," Fuller responded crisply. "We need to get this finished so we can move on to other things." He was a man who didn't tarry.

Several days after that second meeting, I was in the nurs-ery changing Lonnie Paul's diaper when the phone rang. I answered, thinking it would be the diaper delivery service. I remember being slightly agitated because the service had missed the weekly pickup date *again* and my son's hamper was full of soiled, stinky diapers.

"Yes?" I said with exasperation in my voice.

"Ms. Taylor? Please hold for Mr. Fuller."

Seconds passed. Lonnie Paul squirmed in my arms. Finally, someone picked up the line. "You've got the job if you want it," Fuller said. I visualized him sitting at his desk, surrounded by airplanes, talking into a secure phone, maybe picking at his thumbnail.

I squeezed Lonnie Paul so tightly and so suddenly that the poor child peed onto my terry-cloth bathrobe. Yes, I wanted it. I really wanted it!

I hung up the receiver. I was in. I'd made it. I got down on my knees in our living room, gently laying Lonnie Paul on the floor beside me, and said a prayer of thanks.

No matter how much I had pushed for that job, I knew it wouldn't have happened if the Lord God hadn't meant for it to be. I thanked Him for guiding me down this new career path, and I beseeched Him to walk with me as I launched into yet another new, exciting experience.

Then I picked up my son, nuzzled my face into his silky brown hair, and finished changing his diaper.

. . . . .

CHAPTER 4

Welcome to the White House

. . . . .

I SPENT MY ENTIRE FIRST DAY at the White House feeling as if something were about to go wrong.

As I organized my desk that October morning in 1987, the image of Lonnie Paul tugged relentlessly at my heart. I unpacked my framed photos, flipping his pictures face downward on my desk. So soon after I'd left him for what would be the first full day, his photos would prove more of a painful distraction than a source of comfort. Part of me wanted to say, "Damn feminism and the eighties working woman. Kick this superwoman stuff to the curb. I want to be home with my baby." I had to force myself to brush away the feelings of maternal inadequacy, so I turned instead toward the subject files left in the office by my predecessor. I needed the distraction.

The emotional struggle I felt on that first day was more difficult than I had anticipated. The fear of the unknown made me anxious. And in this job, there were several unknowns: whether Bush would actually win the election, whether a newly aligned career was the right move, and what this new, looming "thing" in my life called the White House was really going to mean. Would the rumors about cutthroat, backstabbing political animals prove to be true? Did White House staffers actually scurry to position themselves within the President's line of vision when he walked into a room? Did they grovel and grope to touch the hem of his garment? Was it a mean place? Would I be welcome? What, exactly, went on behind those black iron gates?

Thankfully, a week before I started my job, I had discovered a wonderful place of spiritual and emotional refuge: a small, yellow church with green doors, just across the street from the White House, on the other side of Lafayette Park. The church (also known as "The Church of the Presidents" because every President who had ever occupied the White House had worshipped there at some point) was called St. John's. If I hadn't turned to look at the antinuclear protests across the street in Lafayette Park, I might have overlooked it completely. But something seemed to draw me toward it. Something about it beckoned me to enter. So I did.

Inside, everything was still. The smell of mildew hung heavily in the air, taking me back to my childhood, to the strong attic smell in my house and the memory of Mother squinting into the shafts of sunlight at the dust particles dancing in the air.

As I moved deeper inside the chapel, the wooden floors

creaked and groaned softly beneath my feet. I knelt in a pew. Closing my eyes, I found my center and whispered a deep, silent prayer of thanks for this exciting opportunity. I prayed for guidance and strength, and for a smooth transition into this challenging new phase of my life.

Emerging minutes later, I gazed across the park at the White House and smiled. There it stood, dignified and glorious. But it no longer seemed overwhelming or intimidating. It had been gracefully reduced to its simplest terms: It was indeed beautiful, regal even, but it was only a house inhabited by another living, breathing human being, by another person whose heart beat roughly the same number of times per minute as mine, who shivered in the cold and perspired in the heat, just like me. The storm clouds that had been gathering in the dark corners of my mind had been gently blown away.

I didn't realize until the moment I walked out of the sanctuary that I hadn't simply been anxious about the new challenge; I had been frightened. It also hit me, at that moment, that Mother and Daddy's love, nurturing, and spiritual guidance had become more a part of me than I ever realized. Throughout my life—and with such a strong but gentle touch —they had nudged me toward excellence and taught me to meet challenge head-on. But as I stepped out of the church, I felt more pride than intimidation; I was going to serve my country and my President. I was going to become a tiny part of history. I somehow knew then that whatever was to come during my tenure in this new place, and in everything that I did, I would be all right.

A week later, I was sitting in my small new office. Praise the good Lord. I began to glance through some files.

A press aide poked his head into the door and told me I had a phone call. My heart lifted immediately. I knew it was Lonnie, calling to wish me a good first day.

"It's the FBI," he said wryly. "Welcome to the White House."

They summoned me to the fourth floor.

When I reached the small fourth-floor office, a bland and balding man motioned for me to sit. He was wearing a polyester suit jacket and a brown plaid tie that must have been the only one of its kind in the world. I considered making a small joke—to kind of break the ice—but he didn't look as though he had much of a sense of humor. Those FBI types never really do.

"We need to review several items concerning your investigation," he said. He rolled his chair back from his desk. "Would you mind waiting here momentarily? I need to retrieve a few more items."

I waited in the cramped office alone, legs crossed, trying to look like an assistant press secretary to the Vice President of the United States. Two minutes passed. Four. I wondered if they'd found out about my revolutionary, Angela Davis–angry, turban-wearing high school days. Would the fact that I was once a self-proclaimed teenage black nationalist in the tenth grade represent a clear and present danger to the President of the United States? All kinds of crazy things went through my mind. I didn't know whether to turn myself in or bolt out of the door.

After a few minutes the agent returned with another file in his hand. "We're not yet finished with your investigation," he assured me. "But I have to ask these questions on your first day as routine procedure."

The words "routine procedure" helped calm my rattled nerves. I put the handcuffs out of my mind.

"Have you ever done anything that would seriously embarrass the President or the Administration in any way?" he asked without looking up from his file. Here was a man who'd asked this question thousands of times. I wondered if he enjoyed his job. After a time, he looked up to hear my response.

"No, definitely not," I answered somberly.

"Ever done anything for which you suspect you could be blackmailed?" he continued. "No, certainly not," I answered confidently.

"Any outstanding credit card bills, overdue student loans, you know—anything of that nature?" he inquired.

Not many people in the world begin their first day on a new job by being called in and questioned by the FBI. I suppose I should have expected as much. But it still felt like an intrusion, albeit a necessary one.

After my release from the Big House, I cruised the halls for a few minutes. I wanted to get a feel for the staff and their patterns. Who were these people who moved within this place that many referred to as "the most powerful address in the world"?

This world, as I could see even on my first day, was full of muted, I'm-an-insider-Republican White House staffers trying to get and keep that special "look." Although most of Vice President Bush's staff, too, represented that slice of privilege and power, they somehow seemed less formal than Reagan's—not buttoned quite as far up to the neck. The imperial feel of the Reagan White House hadn't yet seemed to trickle down onto the Bush staffers. The "Bushies" carried about them a certain air of formality and conformity, but they also seemed more laid-back and less anal-retentive than the Reagan types I'd heard about. Over the next few weeks, the visual patterns became clear and predictable.

For the women: cute bob haircut, preferably one that bounced slightly when the wearer walked. Black velvet headband or bow. Expensive, heavy gold jewelry, simply designed (usually somebody's grandmother's or great-aunt's, passed down as an heirloom). Christian Dior "Alabaster" ultrasheer hosiery (nude heel, and never, ever flesh-colored; flesh-colored hosiery was the ultimate in tacky). The classic, low-heeled Ferragamo pump with the flat bow in the center (preferably black patent leather), or, for those whose wallets would allow, the Bruno Magli slingback. And never, ever anything higher than an inch-and-a-quarter heel. Lots and lots of crisp linen in the summer. Dark paislies and houndstooth in the fall and winter. No frills, lace, polyester, press-on nails, hair weaves, cornrows, or stiletto heels.

"The look" was understated, borderline bland—not anywhere near as provocative as a *Cosmo* cover, but perhaps a short step away from being as staid and sterile as *Town & Country*. I often thought that if I saw one more Ferragamo pump peeking from the neighboring bathroom stall in the ladies' room, I'd scream.

For the men: starched, plain white shirts with French cuffs (the better to wear the much coveted presidential cufflinks on special occasions). Wool pants with a three-quarter-inch break at the cuff. Black tasseled loafers, always spit-shine clean. Lots and lots of expensive black and dark blue suits—never, ever double-breasted. No natty tweeds, Old Spice cologne, dusty shoes, shiny suits, ponytails, pocket protectors, short-sleeve shirts, or rubber galoshes.

Later, on Bush's presidential staff, I would come to see some of the younger, hipper men—like my boss, Communications Director David Demarest—break the mold and sport a pair of Gucci loafers occasionally. Sig Rogich, President Bush's "special events" man in charge of staging presidential events, had the most fashion chutzpah of all. Staffers would watch with envy and admiration as he broke every dreary White House fashion mold: expensive suede Italian slip-ons, the dreaded double-breasted suits, $30 socks emblazoned with funky designs, alligator belts worth more than the cost of a tune-up for our car. Rogich was a trailblazer—cocky as all get-out, but refreshingly unencumbered by White House fashion dictates.

Coming from a family of fiercely independent, frustratingly stubborn women, I planned never to make any attempt to conform. If there was a mold, I didn't want to fit into it. Never mind the fact that my hair was too short for velvet headbands, and those Dior pantyhose would always run the moment I put them on (and at about five or six dollars a pop, it wasn't worth the effort). I don't own one pinstripe suit, and I've never really liked paisley.

My patterns and preferences are a little different: I like rich, royal purple silks, sun-splashed yellows, dramatic winter whites. I like a heel with a little height, to show off my legs. Earrings that dangle, to offset the roundness of my face. Golden and rust-colored silk blouses and suits that shimmer and dance under the right light, to highlight and glorify the pure, God-given brownness of my skin. What I like are super-super-ultra-super-sheer black pantyhose, thank you, simply because they look so good covering mocha chocolate brown legs.

Once, while attending a two-day college job fair in Washington, D.C., my assigned roommate, a heavyset girl named

Myra, admonished me for wearing a linen pantsuit. "Girl, how you think you gon' get a job when you graduate wearing all that linen stuff and dangling earrings?" she asked, clearly disgusted. "This ain't no disco; it's the real world. And if you want to land a responsible, well-paying job when you graduate, you better find yourself a pinstripe suit and get with the ways of the world." Poor Myra meant well, but she didn't have a clue about individual taste and personal preference. But she'd helped me more than she knew: I decided, as she spoke, never to buy a pinstripe suit simply for the sake of having it in my closet. After the job fair, I never saw Myra again.

Later on, as I would survey my colleagues during White House planning meetings or strategy sessions, it felt as if I were gazing into the eye of a dark, overcast thunderstorm. Meetings were a field of grays and blacks and Brooks Brothers blues. In the White House, not only was I one of the only women *of* color, I was quite often one of the only women *in* color as well.

After I'd had my fill of the White House fashion extravaganza, I returned to my office. It was about the size of Lonnie Paul's nursery but not as bright and cheerful. Heavy, beige drapes covered the window, which overlooked the parking lot that was reserved for the White House motor pool. Across the hall was Mrs. Bush's staff; down the corridor were the Vice President's counsel and his offices of domestic policy, foreign policy, and national security. I could get comfortable here, I thought to myself. After a minute or two, the aide poked his head in again.

"Administration wants to see you now."

Several offices down the hall, a woman named Vickers Bryan, just about my age, ushered me in. After a cool welcome and a quick lecture on how using the White House stationery for personal use constituted a criminal offense, she whipped out a yellow marking pen and a White House staff list. Here was a woman who was definitely ready to get down to the nitty-gritty. It was time to talk some serious turkey.

"There are obviously certain people on the White House staff whose names you better commit to memory starting today, if you don't know them already," she warned. "I'll do you a favor and go through the list and highlight the most important names. It really is in your best interest to remember these."

I wondered if Vickers had a husband or a family. I wondered if they liked her much. "Craig Fuller is chief of staff," she said, drawing a thick yellow line through Craig's name and enunciating her words slowly, as if I might not comprehend otherwise. She was a tad condescending, and more abrasive than I was accustomed to.

"Thanks, I know," I answered back, sugar sweet. "He's the one who brought me into the White House." Don't get petty now, girl, I thought to myself. No catfights allowed on the first day.

"Susan Porter Rose is Mrs. Bush's chief of staff and, I should add, her longtime friend," she continued, pursing her lips and highlighting the name in yellow as she spoke. "Very important. Understand?"

Was she serious? What was I, an assistant press secretary or a telephone receptionist?

"Tim McBride and Patty Presock are on the Vice President's personal staff. A call from them is like a call from the VP himself.

"And," she concluded, running a hand through her curly

perm, "I shouldn't have to tell you that *everyone* from the President's staff who calls deserves an immediate response. *Everyone.* Especially names like Duberstein. Fitzwater. Culvahouse. Chances are they won't be calling you at all. But you need to learn real fast the way things work around here. Who's in and who's out can change with the light of day."

For the rest of the day, as Steve Hart introduced me to various members of the staff, I kept wondering to myself, Are you a yellow highlight, or not? (Every time I see Susan Porter Rose or hear her name—in fact, even to this day—I think of yellow marking pens.)

The White House was a very status-conscious place indeed, and power came in varying gradations. Not just everyone merited a yellow highlight.

I called Mother later that evening. She'd been waiting by the phone to hear about my first day. I could envision her sitting in our kitchen in Detroit, legs crossed, waving to Daddy to go upstairs and pick up the other extension so that he, too, could hear about the excitement.

"Are the people nice? Do you like your office? Did you meet Vice President Bush?" she asked, thirsty for every detail.

"Yes, yes, and no," I said. "I haven't met Bush yet, but I met a lot of the staff."

"Well, meet him as soon as you can, baby," Mother said. "He needs to know how blessed he is to have a gem like you on his staff—black, beautiful, and smart. He needs to be shown what he's got."

It was vintage Mother; in her eyes, Bush was the luckier of us two.

· · · · ·

I MET THE VICE PRESIDENT several days later, in his office in the Old Executive Office Building. Steve Hart and I lingered in the outer suite, waiting to be ushered in to his inner sanctum. He was about to leave for his weekly Oval Office lunch with President Reagan.

Tim McBride stuck his head out from the inner suite, giving us the signal that the Veep was ready to see us. I felt as if I were about to be granted a private audience with the Pope himself, or at least Mother Teresa. As we entered, Bush was sitting at his desk, flipping through some index cards. Fleetingly, I thought he might be rehearsing his lunchtime conversation with Reagan. If that were true, then I was definitely in the wrong job. I'd heard of orchestration, but this was ridiculous.

Steve and I lingered uncomfortably a few feet away from his desk, still waiting for him to finish writing. Why had McBride ushered us into the office if the man wasn't ready to see us yet? I felt slightly irritated at McBride, and a little embarrassed. I didn't realize at the time, although McBride obviously did from years of close interaction, that this was simply Bush's way. As I was soon to find out through personal experience, he did it all the time. Even after he became President, there were many times when I'd walk into the Oval Office and see Bush sitting at his desk, head bent, intently finishing up a note or jotting down a last-minute thought. The other aides in the office would wait silently for Bush to finish. If I was the last to arrive, I'd drag a chair from the side of the wall to join the semicircle of white men surrounding his desk. Sometimes, particularly if Bush was ready to begin our meeting just as we were arriving, or when I reached the latter stages of my pregnancy, he'd get up and, ever the gentleman, bring an orange leather and rattan chair from against the wall so that I could join the group.

After what felt like forever, the Vice President completed his writing and placed the cap back on his pen. He rose from his chair, arm warmly extended. I was surprised at Bush's six-foot-two-inch frame. He looked much shorter on television.

"Sorry for the wait," Bush apologized. "I was just finishing up some notes for a meeting that I'm having later today. I like to jot my ideas down immediately, while they're still fresh in my mind." Saving grace and praise the Lord, I thought: He wasn't using crib notes for his lunch with Reagan after all. What I had believed about him all along was actually true: The man was unchoreographed, spontaneous, and not at all afraid to act on his own sharp political instincts. By contrast, Ronald Reagan was cut from much different cloth. He was deliberate in his actions, rehearsed with his gestures. Even during my first few days in the White House, I'd already heard stories about how Reagan's public events were carefully, painstakingly choreographed by his staff, with no detail left to chance. I'd heard from more than one staffer that an aide usually followed him everywhere, discreetly whispering into his ear the names of many of the people he was about to greet so warmly. Reagan was the ultimate actor who delivered his lines flawlessly, but who rarely departed from his planned text.

"Mr. Vice President, I'd like you to meet your new assistant press secretary, Kristin Clark Taylor," Steve said ceremoniously, suddenly adopting a more serious voice. I waited for some trumpets to blare from the wings.

"I'm honored to work for you, Mr. Vice President," I

said, gushing like a geyser. What an amateur. It sounded corny, but I really meant it.

"Well, I don't know how honored you'll feel after you've had a chance to get to know me," Bush joked. "Steve here can tell you—if he hasn't already—that I'm a real pain in the . . . Well, anyway," Bush continued, rushing on past the profanity and tickled by his own humor, "Fuller has said wonderful things about you, and I'm glad you're on our team and ready to work."

Fleetingly, I wondered what Craig had said. How had he described me to Bush? As a woman? A young woman? A young black woman? A young, attractive, smart black woman? The mother of a six-month-old child? I wondered if the color of my skin had ever been discussed between them. I decided it probably hadn't; surely they had more important things to talk about than that. But I somehow still knew that my race, gender, and age probably played a role, however minor, in bringing me into the fold. I don't think hiring me was a consciously manipulative, politically strategic PR move on anyone's part. It was probably just some tacit, intangible voice softly whispering, "Yes, this combination is good. Hiring an articulate, young, black, female Republican is good."

"Everybody treatin' you all right?" Bush asked, sounding genuinely concerned. "You findin' your way around this place?"

"Just fine," I answered. "Thank you, sir." I pictured Vickers sitting in her office. She surely must have developed some heavy-duty super-strength ultra-new-and-improved version of a yellow highlighting marker for The Man Himself, George Bush.

I wondered if, before I walked into his office, Bush even knew I existed. I wondered if Fuller had actually told him anything specific about me. It was as if Bush was reading my mind.

"How's that newspaper of yours doin', *USA Today?*" he asked. Well, either Fuller had briefed him or he really was turning out to be quite a kick. I glanced over his shoulder to see if my resume was anywhere on his desk. "They makin' any money yet?" Bush inquired.

I would soon come to discover that Bush was always asking how much money people made, or if they were doing well in their business. It was not quite an obsession, but always seemed foremost in his mind. Perhaps it hearkened back to his days as a Texas oilman. Business was in his blood; he genuinely admired people with entrepreneurial drive and spirit.

"Actually, the paper's doing pretty well," I answered. "We—I mean they—had predicted from the beginning that they'd put themselves into the black by year-end '87, after five years of publishing, and the figures look pretty good." I wondered whether I was delving into too much detail when all he really asked me was a casual, offhand question.

"Al Neuharth was an absolute genius to have conceived the idea," I added. I wanted to put in a good word for old Al. And I really did think he was pretty ingenious to have conceived the idea. Part of me waited for Bush to inquire about Neuharth's relative net worth or about the details of his executive compensation package, but he didn't, so I continued.

"They lost gobs of money those first few years, but they're up and running now," I said. Why didn't I just recite the Gettysburg Address while I was at it? And I kicked myself for using such an imprecise word as "gob" to communicate with the Vice President of the United States. Finally, his thirst had been quenched. No more questions.

"Well, glad you're on our team," Bush said. "You and Steve have quite a job on your hands, working with the press and all. I wouldn't trade places with you guys for all the money in the world," he said with a smile. Steve beamed with pride. It was clear he admired the Vice President tremendously.

"Now," Bush said, glancing at his watch, "I don't mean to be rude, but I do have a lunch I need to get to with the President of the United States. Wouldn't want to be late for that, now would we?"

He reached over and shook my hand again, clapping me warmly on the back and welcoming me to the White House staff. Then he did something I never thought I'd see from a man of his power and stature: He breezed out of the office and literally bounded down the stairs of the OEOB, taking two and three at a time, tie flapping in the wind. I somehow don't think he was worried about making his lunch on time. I think he ran because he enjoyed the rush. Because he approached everything he did with that same spontaneous, open-armed enthusiasm.

And because he enjoyed giving the flustered assistant trailing behind a real run for his money.

CHAPTER 5

. . . . .

Beware the
Dole Supporters
in Bush Clothing

. . . . .

PERHAPS THE MOST DISTURBING DYNAMIC that I could never quite reconcile during the '88 campaign was the fact that not everyone on the President's staff supported Bush for President. Supporters of Robert Dole, Jack Kemp, Pat Robertson, and even Alexander Haig slithered quietly along the halls of the White House, moving as inconspicuously as possible in the underbrush.

For those first few months on Vice President Bush's staff, I was the new kid on the block. And being a newcomer is not easy when you're playing by the rules of high-stake, cutthroat presidential politics. For the first few weeks, I felt as if I were being regarded with a wary, distrustful eye. As I was to learn later, it wasn't my imagination or paranoia, for I, too, found myself feeling slightly distrustful of those who came after me— at least until they proved they were one of us. We took no chances. Newcomers could be infiltrators. They could even be plants from the opponent's campaign.

I knew full well that it was irrational and naive to expect every Reagan staffer to support George Bush for President. Certainly we all had a choice in whom we supported. But a part of me was offended—appalled even—that not everyone in the White House was pulling for the man who'd faithfully stood by Reagan's side for eight long years. Everything we did on the Vice President's staff was done with an eye toward getting Bush elected President of the United States. We were all so submerged in achieving victory that we almost overlooked the fact that many of the people surrounding us were waging their own behind-the-scenes battles to keep George Bush out of the Oval Office. The Brooks Brothers suit sitting next to me during a planning meeting, or the smiling staffer looking over my shoulder as I edited a sensitive upcoming press release, may well have been supporting another candidate. Nobody wore "I support Bob Dole" buttons on his or her lapel; secrecy was the name of the game. Identifying those who opposed Bush was virtually impossible. They liked to hide in the underbrush, out of sight.

Marlin Fitzwater—Reagan's affable press secretary, and the former press secretary to Vice President Bush—would often ask for a rundown of the VP's upcoming long-term travel schedule during his morning meetings. Although I trusted Marlin unconditionally, I was always somewhat reluctant to go into the nitty-gritty detail in front of the group. You never knew where the information would turn up.

"Kristin," Marlin would say, sitting behind his curved desk, "What's the VP got cooking down the road that's interesting? Any long-term plans we might be able to help with or complement? How're we planning to do Dole in?"

"All I have is his short-term schedule, Marlin," I'd say, more to the rest of the people in the room than to him. "I'll certainly get my hands on his long-term look-ahead, though, and make sure you get it." I would, too. But you can never be too careful.

While it's probably safe to say that many of the Reagan staff did actively and visibly support Bush, the small percentage who didn't posed a significant threat. Quarters were too close within the White House complex for us to drop our guard. As a result, we all sharpened our information-sharing and intelligence-gathering skills. Over time, I came to learn the delicate art of sharing and disseminating information internally so as not to put George Bush's election at risk. Any proprietary campaign-related information—material which, if revealed or leaked to the opponent, could put our candidate at significant risk—was treated carefully. The handwritten notes taken during our strategic planning meetings, Bush's detailed, long-term block schedules, and plans for upcoming major speeches or appearances were treated, essentially, as close-hold information.

The VP's White House press office staff was quite small, probably less than a third the size of the campaign press office: Steve Hart and I were the only two press officers—the only staffers in Bush's White House press office who could officially go on the record with reporters. We divided most of our work with the campaign press operation by issue: Politically related media projects or press inquiries—those which centered around George Bush the candidate—were automatically handled by the campaign staff. Inquiries concerning Bush's official role as Vice President of the United States were handled by Steve and me. The campaign, for example, was only too glad to buck any and all questions concerning Bush's role in Iran-Contra directly —and quickly—to us.

Besides Steve and me, there were only two other full-time press staffers: a bright, gung-ho intern turned full-time press assistant named Sean Walsh, who helped coordinate press travel and plan media logistics for on-site VP events, and a staff assistant named Debbie McCune, who handled all the administrative and clerical work. Both worked hard at researching issues and providing critical background information for Steve and me. To supplement the staff, we'd always have one or two eager-beaver, fresh-faced college Republican interns, and at least one volunteer sent over from the Visitor's Office in the East Wing.

It was rewarding for me to witness the staff's personal growth during our time together; Sean, who grew to become my close friend, blossomed into a hard-driven, self-assured press officer. His political instincts sharpened; his thinking became strategic and purposeful. He came a long way from his college days at UCLA.

My daily responsibilities were varied and quite challenging, and our pace was incredibly fast. I wore the hat of senior staff writer in the press office, developed most of Bush's White House press releases, and produced most of his videotaped addresses. And as second in command, I wore Steve's hat when he was traveling on the road with the VP, which was often.

70

Using the secure lines on *Air Force Two,* I'd update Steve, Fuller, and on occasion (but not as often) the Vice President himself on the significant media developments occurring back at the White House.

The White House communications unit oversaw all ground-to-air transmissions aboard Air Force Two. Although the average outsider might liken such high-tech communications to a scene from a 007 movie, on reflection it wasn't always what it was cracked up to be: I sometimes felt more like Lily Tomlin playing her old role as the ditzy telephone operator in "Rowan & Martin's Laugh-In."

A typical conversation:

"Crown to Air Force Two. Crown to Air Force Two. Ms. Taylor, Mr. Craig Fuller is on the line. Stand by."

As I waited for Fuller to come onto the line, I imagined green olives sloshing around in martini glasses as the Vice President's staff bumped its way through some rough air, thirty-five thousand feet above Anywhere, USA.

Communicating with Air Force Two from my small second-floor office in the Old Executive Office Building always felt to me like something straight out of a Ken Follett or Tom Clancy novel. Any minute now, I'd take off my Magli pump, pull out an antenna from its toe, and start talking into the sole of my shoe. What a rush.

After a minute or two: "Kristin, this is Craig." Much static. The sound of someone crunching wax paper or dropping paper clips into the telephone. "Any news I need to be aware of? Over." The "over" part is what really killed me. Did we really need to say that?

"I need to give you a quick heads-up about a media opportunity we have," I said, resisting the urge to yell into the

71

phone. People in the White House were always using phrases like "heads-up," "wheels-up" (which simply refers to the departure time of Air Force Two), or "GBFP" (George Bush for President). It was an insider's club. You had to know the lingo.

I continued my update: "Just received an invitation for the VP to meet with *USA Today*'s editorial board. We can discuss it later, but it's one I think we should definitely accept. You might want to discuss it with him while you're on the road, so he can start thinking about it and we can get back to them sometime soon. Over."

More paper clips. The sound of a rusted hacksaw doing its level best to gnaw away at the invisible airwaves connecting us. Fuller hadn't heard a thing.

"U.S. News wants to endorse Bush?" he asked, his interest piqued. "I didn't know they did endorsements. And why do they have to do the interview while we're on the road? Why can't we just d—"

"Not *U.S. News,* Craig. *USA Today.* And they don't want t—"

I'd cut him off before he finished his sentence. Like two disc jockeys trying to speak at once, we were stepping all over each other's lines. It was at that moment that I came to recognize the importance of the word "over." Spontaneous give-and-take banter was impossible.

"Let's discuss it in more detail when I get back," Fuller said, to my relief. I was getting frustrated. "I won't mention it to Bush until we've had a chance to discuss it. But it sounds like a great opportunity. Anything else? Over."

"Well, yes." I suddenly remembered something. *"The New York Times* wants a—"

"You're breaking up, Kristin," Fuller said through thick

fuzz. I was losing him. More heavy static, then the line went dead. So much for the high-tech sophistication of the White House.

Our small group would meet every morning in Steve's office to begin our day. These morning meetings were hard-driven and full of energy, as was the work we performed. We reviewed the day's news clips from every major newspaper to see how the other candidates were being treated and to gauge what kind of ink Bush received on the events we'd helped coordinate the day before. Was there an extra spin we needed to try to put on an issue? Did we need to try to place a rebuttal op-ed or letter to the editor in *The New York Times* or the *Wall Street Journal* to keep our side of the story breathing?

Using the VP's detailed line-by-line schedule as our compass, Steve would guide us skillfully through a strategic look-ahead at each one of Bush's upcoming public activities. Should we list his meeting with black leaders as an open photo session with a writing pool? And should his meeting with the terminally ill children from the Make-A-Wish Foundation be closed to the press? Bush was a modest man and quite sensitive to the appearance of patting himself too heartily on the back. Particularly with sensitive, heart-wrenching events like these, striking the delicate balance—getting the public's attention without looking as if we're using dying kids as faceless props—was challenging at best. We'd usually err on the side of caution in situations such as these, bringing in a wire photographer for a two-minute shoot. No print reporters. No prepared on-the-record statements by the VP. The image itself was enough; we didn't need the words. Our job was to get the image out there and into the public domain.

On another morning, for example, we'd discuss the media

plan surrounding the Vice President's annual physical exam. For this we'd need to coordinate a good-sized travel pool: at least one major network, the AP, perhaps a local network affiliate, one or two stills, and a pool reporter who had a solid reputation for producing detailed, timely, and accurate pool reports. The pool reporter was charged with writing a detailed account of his or her assigned event to be used by all of the other publications. An issue such as Bush's health was critically important: Restricting media access to Bethesda Naval Hospital would have been sending a dangerous signal. The public needed to know that George Bush was in excellent condition. They needed to be assured that they could place their total trust and long-term confidence in a future with George Bush.

Working with Steve, I came to respect not only his judgment but his comfortable style with the press. All of the initial tension I felt during our first interview had dissipated. As it turned out, I came to count Steve among my closest and most trusted friends at the White House. I ended up learning more from him in the fifteen months we worked together than I did during any other job I've ever held, past or present. He taught me how not to overreact to a potential media crisis, how to respond to a false allegation without legitimizing it, how to interact confidently and effectively with Vice President Bush, and how to anticipate the VP's questions and concerns before he even had to verbalize them. Steve was a perfectionist, hot-tempered at times, who tolerated no mistakes. He was a good teacher, but very, very tough. And quite intense.

Steve's major fault was that he sometimes refused to allow himself to act on his own instincts, which were almost always right. The risks were high during the 1988 campaign, particularly during the weeks following the Democratic convention, which pushed Governor Michael Dukakis as much as 22 percentage points ahead of George Bush in the polls. Losing the election became a frightening but realistic possibility. There was absolutely no room for error. As a result, many of us picked up Steve's habit of thinking too much, strategizing too agonizingly long, when quick, rapid-fire decisions were needed. No one wanted to screw up. We preferred to hop along the road like scared jackrabbits rather than pole-vault like Olympic athletes. That was the safest way—and it was not as far to fall.

· · · · ·

WITH FULLER AS OUR CHIEF OF STAFF, we moved at a steady-as-she-goes clip.

The Reagan staff, naturally, saw the President as their sole client. Our function was to echo, support, and complement. We weren't there to set policy or to take center stage. We were the understudies waiting in the wings. We were the Supremes singing backup, while Reagan, in all his glitter and glory, was Diana herself. After only a short time on staff, I began to develop the gnawing feeling, like the beginnings of a stomach ulcer, that we were perceived by many on the Reagan staff as unwanted stepchildren, always underfoot. My interaction with the Reagan staff was not close or constant, but I was always left with the tacit feeling that, using Vickers' yellow highlighted check-off list as a gauge to measure political importance, most everyone on the President's staff—most assuredly in their own minds anyway—merited a yellow mark. The vice presidential staff—with the exception of Bush himself, and Fuller—was barely penciled in.

The most prominent exception—the one much needed

gust of fresh air during those Reagan years—was Marlin Fitz-water. Throughout the 1988 campaign, Marlin's political vision was twenty-twenty. His media strategies accommodated and encompassed both the President *and* the Vice President. Although Reagan was clearly his primary focus, Marlin's peripheral vision was acute and highly trained. He was too skilled to be myopic. In every public media event he planned for the President, he would also carefully evaluate the possible political repercussions for George Bush.

"The President's going to participate in a ceremony later this afternoon honoring war veterans," Marlin would say during one of his morning staff meetings, thumbing through Reagan's line-by-line schedule as he spoke. "Kristin, you all might want to consider having Bush attend. It's good color, and it ties in nicely with Bush's peace-through-strength campaign theme. You and Steve discuss it and let me know what you want to do."

If Steve and I wanted the VP in the photo op, Marlin would make sure Bush was strategically placed before the cameras. He was always looking out for the Vice President.

Marlin was unselfish in his allegiance. And fortunately for us, he was experienced enough to know how to strike a comfortable balance between the two highest (and sometimes competing) pinnacles of power in the White House.

Fitzwater reminded me of a baby doll I had as a child. Although most of my dolls were black, Wilhemina, like Marlin, was pink and pudgy, with chubby, kissable cheeks. Marlin had that same forehead, high and wide, with barely visible eyebrows and sensible-looking eyeglasses. But Marlin wasn't all cuddly and cute. If crossed, he was a razor: so sharp that the cut didn't smart until after the blood started flowing. He would become the only person in history to have held the job of press secretary for two consecutive presidents—Reagan and then Bush. His connections to both men were strong, his friendships deep. Life inside the White House did not easily lend itself to such competing loyalties. It was a rare and wonderful trait.

During the campaign days, Marlin considered his boss, President Reagan, the star. It was clear that Reagan regarded himself as a star as well. Perhaps he was right to do so. He was, after all, the President of the United States.

I met Reagan several times—all brief, formal introductions of less than, say, thirty seconds. Each time, I resisted the urge to ask for his autograph. I could have mailed his John Hancock to a girlfriend's daughter back home in Detroit who collected the autographs of stars. That's how it felt—as though I was meeting a movie star or Hollywood luminary, rather than a President.

At one point—and I believe it was just after we won the election—somebody made the decision to have President Reagan do what we used to call a "grip and grin" with Bush's entire vice presidential staff; it seemed placating, a bit contrived, and overly choreographed, but everyone was excited that afternoon as we crowded like cattle into the West Wing reception area, awaiting our turn to be plucked from the group and steered toward the Oval Office.

Reagan had just undergone minor surgery on his left hand to remove a noncancerous growth on one of his fingers. As I entered the Oval, my eyes were drawn first to the white bandage on his hand. Instinctively, I reached toward him, concerned about his mending hand.

"Are you all right, sir?" was the first thing I said. Perhaps it was inappropriate, but I was concerned. "Is your hand feeling okay?"

Reagan, ever the professional, turned my shoulders slightly toward the awaiting photographer without so much as responding to my inquiry. "Let's face the camera, this way," he said in almost a whisper. We froze and smiled. Bulbs flashed.

"That's the way," he said, turning away from me toward the next steer waiting to be branded. I got the feeling that he didn't want to be there, bogged down with inane photo ops, one after the other. He never once looked me in my eyes. And he never did answer my question about his hand.

The man was soft-spoken and appeared sincere, but something about him reminded me of an onion: No matter how many layers you peeled away, another one always remained. No matter how much heat he took, or how often he singed his fingertips on the flames of controversy or dissension—aid to the Contras, the invasion of Grenada, even John Hinckley's bullet, which lodged less than an inch from his heart and almost took his life—there was somehow always another layer exactly the same just under the surface. And like an onion, the man could bring tears to your eyes. He was graceful, classy, and eloquent, with a quiet "Everyman" sincerity. The speeches that were written for him actually brought a few tears to my eyes. But it was next to impossible to discover any layer different from the one that came before.

He faced the crises of his presidency with graceful, gentle nudges—more like waves lapping softly onto a beach. There were no tidal waves or political typhoons, no loud and violent storms. Bush staffers, on the other hand, wanted thunder and lightning. We wanted fireworks and excitement, bravado and bullishness. We wanted Bush's words and actions to light up the sky; we needed to get beyond his dull, "wimp" image, once and for all. And in January of 1988, we received just the jump start we needed.

CHAPTER 6

. . . . .

The Mouth That Roared

. . . . .

I T WAS MONDAY, January 25, 1988, our first major television
network appearance of the year—an interview with CBS
anchorman Dan Rather. After much haggling over the terms
and conditions with the producers at CBS, we had finally
agreed to the on-air interview. We clearly stipulated our terms:
The Vice President would participate in a "live" broadcast only
—no taping—which obviously precluded the possibility of the
network editing any part of Bush's comments or taking them
out of context. We didn't want his best comments left on the
cutting room floor or juxtaposed with other comments which
could distort or weaken his intended message. Initially, CBS
had proposed a live remote from the campaign trail, which we
rejected. Bush would conduct his interview on his home turf—
in his office on Capitol Hill.

Several Bush staffers had a hand in coordinating this interview; there was no single "action officer" involved. The written background material, however, emanated from the VP's White House press office; I wrote the briefing memo for the Vice President and sent it to him on the road before the interview, and both Steve Hart and I signed it. Days beforehand, Pete Teeley (Bush's longtime friend and senior media advisor during part of the 1988 campaign), Roger Ailes (Bush's media wizard), and Fuller all briefed Bush at length. The project was a coordinated effort among both the campaign and White House staffs, and—as it turned out—it was well worth the fireworks it would later ignite.

In the weeks before, as part of my standard preparation, I spoke several times with CBS producer Richard Cohen. We clarified the general direction of the interview and reviewed the specific ground rules. Each and every time we spoke, Cohen assured me (and assured several other people in the Bush campaign) that the interview would be a "general political profile" on the Vice President. When he was asked whether "hot button" issues such as Iran-Contra would figure prominently within the interview, his answer was always a resounding no, followed by a weak qualification: "But Rather might ask a question or two on the subject." This was precisely the information I included in my briefing memo to Bush: CBS was seeking a political profile, and while the issue of Iran-Contra might surface briefly, it was certainly not going to be a major feature of the interview.

The weekend before the interview, Teeley received several tips from reporter friends who warned him that they'd heard the Rather interview might well turn ugly. CBS began airing promos which indicated Iran-Contra might be more of an issue than what the network had previously indicated to us. We were about to be ambushed, Teeley concluded.

On the day of the interview, Bush returned to Washington from New Hampshire, arriving at Andrews Air Force Base at about four twenty-five in the afternoon. Teeley contacted Bush from the campaign headquarters to warn him that something was amiss; he reached the Vice President in his limo just as he was departing from Andrews. Both Craig Fuller and Roger Ailes were with Bush in the limo when Teeley's call came in; immediately, during the ride into Washington, the three men began developing an offensive strategy.

At some point during the limousine ride from Andrews Air Force Base to the Vice President's Capitol Hill office, the suggestion was made that if the on-air situation became truly untenable, Bush should remind the anchorman of his own embarrassing, childlike temper tantrum which occurred the year before—when Rather walked off of a live set for several minutes.

From the second the cameras started rolling, it was clear that we had been bilked. The network began what it had agreed would be a "live" interview with none other than a five-minute *prerecorded* segment on Bush's role in Iran-Contra. So much for the notion that live TV can be refreshing, spontaneous, and difficult to manipulate; the network had already found a way.

Seconds before going on camera, sitting in his Capitol Hill office, Bush was already fuming at what he believed was going to be a setup: "Iran-Contra affair?" he asked while listening to the taped segment. "I didn't know this was about the Iran-

Contra affair . . . They aren't going to ask me about Iran-Contra, are they?" A CBS technician in Bush's office, hearing the VP's remarks, reminded him, "Your mike is open, sir."

And then, before Bush even had a chance to collect his wits, the red on-air camera light flashed on, and the camera beamed his surprised face into millions of American households.

The Vice President issued an on-air objection to Rather immediately, saying, "This . . . is a misrepresentation on the part of CBS, who said you're doing political profiles on all of the candidates—and then you come up with something that has been exhaustively looked into." As I watched, I wondered whether Bush was angry at me for misrepresenting the nature of the interview in the written briefing material.

Dan Rather, abrasive and arrogant throughout the entire segment, interrupted Bush several times:

Rather: "You also said that you did not know—"

Bush: "May I answer that?"

Rather: "That wasn't a question, it was a statement."

Bush: "It was a statement and I'll answer it."

Rather: "Let me ask the question if I may, first."

This negative roundabout continued throughout the entire interview, with Bush getting angrier and Rather becoming more smug every second:

Rather: "I don't want to be argumentative, Mr. Vice President."

Bush (laughing): "Yes, you do, Dan . . . I don't think it's fair to judge a whole career by a rehash on Iran. How would you like it if I judged your career by those seven minutes when you walked off the set in New York? Would you like that?"

(Ouch. Yikes. Whammo! Bush was red-hot mad and willing to take the untouchable Dan Rather to the mat. Get it on, George-Man!)

Rather (momentarily flustered and embarrassed): "Mr. Vice President—"

Bush: "I have respect for you, but I don't have respect for what you're doing here tonight."

It was Rather who moved to lob the last salvo at the end of the interview, cutting Bush off prematurely before the VP could finish his sentence. Throughout the interview, the anchorman was embarrassingly unprofessional and disrespectful. But his final tag line, in my eyes, was the worst of all:

Rather (in closing): "Mr. Vice President, I appreciate you joining us tonight. I appreciate the straightforward way in which you've engaged in this exchange. There are clearly some unanswered questions. Are you willing to go to a news conference before the Iowa caucuses, answer questions from all—"

Bush: "I've been to eighty-six news conferences since March, eighty-six of 'em since March—"

Rather (cutting Bush off in midsentence and turning dramatically toward the viewing audience): "I gather that the answer is no. Thank you very much for being with us, Mr. Vice President. We'll be back with more news in a moment."

I watched from my White House office, shocked and angry. I had clearly been misled by CBS during the earlier planning stages. Within seconds, the phones in our press office began ringing. We were deluged. The first line I picked up was Sam Donaldson:

"What the hell just happened there?" he boomed into the phone. I couldn't tell from his question whether he was angry at Bush or at Rather. His next comment answered my question:

"Rather was more arrogant than I've ever seen him in my life! It was a disgrace!" He slammed the phone down. One after another, the calls came in from across the country. All were disgusted with Rather, supportive of Bush.

CBS and its affiliates were also receiving a torrent of calls. Their switchboards were lit up like Christmas trees. Final scorecard: Bush 1,000, Rather 0. The general perception was that Rather had been rude and disrespectful, but by expressing his indignation and outrage, Bush had positioned himself as a man under siege, unfairly treated by a bulldog of a journalist and disrespected as the Vice President of the United States. The exchange that evening put to rest the "wimp" image which had haunted us throughout the campaign. We emerged the victors; Rather, the insolent schoolyard bully.

It was clear that the network had had absolutely no interest in pursuing a political profile. The entire nine-minute on-air interview was Iran-Contra. As Roger Ailes said to me later, "We'd been snookered. They had changed it from a journalistic interview to a deliberate hit."

The result, as *Washington Post* television critic Tom Shales wrote the following day, was "repulsive journalism."

"Today," Shales wrote, "there are likely to be calls for impeachment. No, not George Bush's; Dan Rather's. Cries for his scalp may become deafening."

Post columnist Mary McGrory opined about the explosive interview, predicting correctly, "Rather has probably nominated the Republican candidate and may even have elected the next President."

Rather showed his true colors during that interview:

Black and blue were the colors he wanted to leave smeared all over Bush's face. Instead, the anchorman was left licking his own wounds.

Teeley told me, "Bush knew then what he was going to do. He didn't want to be briefed anymore, didn't even want anyone else around. He just wanted to do what he had to do. He was prepared to take Rather on. Let's face it: Rather really made a fool of himself."

The anchorman, for his part, limped back to CBS with his tail between his legs, not having uncovered one new angle, not one bit of new news. In the end, we had won the battle. And it was Rather who'd emerged with the black eye he had intended to give to Bush.

Ain't it just funny the way things sometimes work out? We had started the new year out with just the bang we needed.

· · · · ·

BUT THAT BANG, unfortunately, was reduced to a whimper during the following month. The Iowa caucus—our first real crisis during the presidential campaign—probably shook our morale more violently than any other single event during the course of the campaign.

It was February of 1988, a month after the explosive Bush-Rather confrontation. We'd gained a considerable amount of steam from that explosion, but unfortunately not enough to carry us into Iowa.

It was a crushing blow. George Bush finished a dismal third, behind Bob Dole and Pat Robertson—far worse than most of our projections. We knew it would be a struggle from the start, but we never imagined such a stunning loss. Second place would have been bad enough. But third place had tiny clusters of Bush staffers whispering desperately in the corridors of the Old Executive Office Building, sniffing back tears and wringing their hands with anxiety.

"If we can't even whip Pat Robertson," I overheard one frightened voice whisper, "then we might as well throw in the towel. Dole's gloves are off; he smells blood and he wants our asses. The sad part is that he'll probably succeed."

The final tally was glum: Dole received about 37 percent of the vote, Robertson 25 percent, and Bush 19 percent. To many, the presidential race was over.

The staggering loss shook our confidence more than we ever dared admit publicly. But to the outside world and to our political opponents, it was important that we maintain a polished veneer: We were still a well-oiled, well-funded political machine with enough brainpower, between the Veep's White House staff and his campaign operation, to pull forty-two of those John Deere tractors from one side of the state of Iowa to the other. I sought comfort in our strengths, but the Iowa loss dealt a blow to our morale which we did not need.

The Day After was bittersweet and confusing. The Dole supporters on Reagan's staff, who only weeks before were slithering along the West Wing baseboards, were now standing straight and tall—their faces filled with smarmy grins, eyes glinting with the prospect of a political overthrow, nostrils flared with the smell of victory. Something in the air had definitely changed. I was so disgusted I wanted to spit at somebody. Politics is indeed a fickle business—and it brings out the most fickle element in all of us.

But I held my head high—perhaps even higher than normal—and hovered close to my colleagues for comfort and support. I, too, had been jolted by the loss. But I never, ever let it show on my face. George Bush deserved better than that. And so did I.

The bittersweet part of the day came in the realization that most of my colleagues and I were saddened and upset not only because of the obvious—we didn't want to lose our jobs and have to bid farewell to the hallowed halls of the White House and all that it represented (power, prestige, and a surefire spot on the hottest cocktail party circuit in town)—but because we genuinely cared about George Bush and didn't want to see him wounded in battle.

Craig Fuller called the entire vice presidential staff together the moment he and the rest of the Bush entourage arrived home from Iowa. I like to remember it as our "prayer meeting." We came together, all of us, yearning to hear something that would reinvigorate our spirit and lead us back into the light. And that is just what we received. On that afternoon, Fuller showed his true colors as a motivational leader and a gentle, graceful lifter of spirits.

Everybody filed into the room: Vickers with her curly perm and ever present passel of invisible yellow marking pens; Steve Hart, eyebrows furrowed and face filled with that familiar intensity; Mrs. Bush's small staff of polite, well-dressed, intelligent women; kind, gentle David Bates (a longtime Bush staffer and close confidant), who was dark-haired, handsome, and man enough to reach out and try to comfort a few surrounding staffers with the squeeze of his hand or a warm pat on the back. Even the mysterious national security staffers emerged from behind their closed, combination-locked office doors. We all came, from clerical staff to commissioned officers, longing to hear the words which would put us back on the right course.

Fuller entered the room with a quiet smile and a few warm hellos to several people. I watched him make his way to the podium, and I hoped he wouldn't choose to stand behind it. We needed to be lifted, not lectured to. Indeed, what we got was vintage Fuller: He rested his left elbow on the side of the podium, his leg crossed casually in front of him. Fuller's instincts were always pretty much on target: Beyond being a pretty laid-back person normally, he knew that his entire staff was watching his every move that afternoon, waiting to be reassured that they were still in the game. His own relaxed manner and confident body language sent the signal he needed to send.

"The first thing I wanted to do when we landed at Andrews was get everybody together," he said softly. He picked at his thumbnail as he spoke, gazing out into the sea of faces.

"We suffered a loss in Iowa, yes," Fuller admitted. "And a significant one. I don't think anyone predicted we'd have quite as dismal a finish as we actually did," he said. But he wasn't apologizing or placing blame. He was only explaining, trying to bring us into the loop and make us feel a part of what he was feeling.

"But the Vice President is fine; his spirits remain high," he said with confidence. Yes! I thought to myself. Take us where we need to go, Brother Fuller. Talk the talk. Lead us to the light.

He continued, "This election is still ours to win, but we've got to continue to work as hard as we always have—even harder, in fact. We can't slow our momentum because of this setback.

"If anything," he said, warming up, "we need to jump back in with both feet. We all need to remain confident and realize that this race is far from over: It's only just beginning! Our next hurdle is New Hampshire, and that's right around the corner. And after we take New Hampshire, we'll face Super Tuesday head-on. We're ready to play! Let the games begin!"

Applause and more applause. The room had warmed. I suddenly felt comforted by the physical closeness of my friends and colleagues; I was relieved that we were all in that room sharing the same space. My concerns were their collective concerns. And we all felt better. I looked around the room: a smile here, a tear of relief there. Something in me wanted to begin humming one of my favorite gospel hymns, "I Don't Feel No Ways Tired."

Fuller thanked us, warmly and profusely, for all of our hard work and unwavering commitment, for keeping the home fires burning while he and Bush and his band of merry men crisscrossed the country, lurching through time zones and leaping over zip codes. He reminded us that we were still a vital, integral part of the overall political process, and that, perhaps most importantly, it was George Bush—our next President of the United States—who felt the most gratitude and pride in our individual and collective sacrifices and efforts.

We left that room just as we needed to leave: fired up, reinvigorated, and ready, at last, to take New Hampshire by storm.

· · · · ·

EIGHT DAYS AFTER the Iowa caucus, John Sununu proved to be worth his weight in gold. Sununu, then governor of New Hampshire, almost single-handedly helped Bush win his state's primary. For months on end, he organized statewide grass-roots support, worked the media relentlessly, crisscrossed the state from morning till dusk solidifying our already growing support base, and coordinated closely with the Bush camp in Washington. We took the state, receiving about 38 percent of the vote, compared with Dole's 28 percent. It was a victory that we sorely needed, and one which restored our momentum and set us back on track. Without it, we might well have lost the entire game.

Bush, perhaps more than anyone, recognized the significance of the New Hampshire victory—particularly in the face of the Iowa defeat. It had brought us back from the brink of political disaster. It was indeed what prompted him to appoint Sununu as his White House chief of staff: the ultimate thank-you for a job well done.

But the Iowa caucus and the New Hampshire primary made me realize, finally, that the process itself is slightly out of kilter. These two states, while important, carry far too much weight in the overall political scheme of things. It's a confusing, misleading media circus (I read somewhere that half of the nation's supply of satellite uplink trucks descended upon Des Moines for the February 8 caucus) and, perhaps most alarming, an inaccurate gauge of the country's overall political sentiments.

Perhaps I am a hypocrite: At the same time I denounce the inordinate importance of these two primaries, it was I who breathed one of the longest, loudest sighs of relief when we actually won New Hampshire. Sure, the state's primary might be misrepresentative and "out of touch with the American mainstream"; it may even be "insular" and "alien," as *News-*

week once said—but *damn* if it didn't feel good to be on the winning side again!

Steve had been urging me for weeks to get out on the road with the VP. He considered it an effective way for me to familiarize myself with Bush's tempo and tolerance—to watch him up close and witness him "mixing it up with the locals," as he used to like to say. With some reluctance, I signed onto a trip. Part of me grumbled at having to go. I had informed both Fuller and Hart, during my initial job interview, that travel wasn't for me; I'd much rather stay close to home, running the press office in Steve's absence (a process which was working out quite well) while still being close enough to tend to Lonnie Paul. I didn't want to start traveling regularly; once folks started seeing me on out-of-town trips, they might be more inclined to begin requiring Steve and me to rotate travel responsibilities, or they could pigeonhole me as Steve's on-the-road backup.

But Steve continued to gently insist, and I knew that the experience would be exciting and educational.

Traveling with the Vice President and his entourage was at once exhilarating and exhausting. There were no sardine-squeezed seating assignments or plastic cups (genuine glass only) on Air Force Two. There were complimentary booties for your feet if you wanted to kick back and get comfortable; you could have pocketsful of souvenir matches with the words "Air Force Two" emblazoned across one side and the vice presidential seal on the other. The back of the biggest plane comprised the working area: typewriters, a bank of telephones, a fax machine, a copier. We were a traveling city, an entity unto ourselves.

The morning we left, Steve and I simply left our bags in

the hallway outside of our second-floor press office, and somehow those crazy bags made their way into the belly of Air Force Two long before we even left the White House. Miracle of miracles.

As we flew through the sky, with a bevy of polite stewards hovering close around us to make sure we were comfortable, I flashed back to one of the first flights I took without my parents, as a young woman traveling solo, finally coming into her own. I was on a flight from Detroit to Washington, D.C. for the job interview at *USA Today*. I remember struggling to remember whether I was supposed to pay for the turkey sandwich the stewardess placed in front of me. Fishing in my wallet, I confidently pulled out a ten-spot. Big-city money. But the stewardess waved the money away, explaining politely that all meals were complimentary. Who would have ever guessed that only six years later I'd be flying aboard Air Force Two wearing vice presidential booties and chatting it up with my White House colleagues? It was indeed a heady experience.

In the air, Steve sat next to me nursing a drink as he opened his thick briefing file with a groan. Bush's advance team produced detailed briefing binders in preparation for every trip—binders of encyclopedic scope and excruciating detail about the geographic area the Vice President and his staff were about to visit. They included information on the state's grassroots political operations, population demographics, and weather forecasts, not to mention recommended attire for each event, local colloquialisms, and general biographical information on each state politician who would be meeting with Bush.

As I did six years ago when I tried to pay the poor stewardess for my turkey sandwich, I made a strong attempt to act coolheaded and unfazed by all the fancy-schmancy hoopla. Yeah, right. As though I traveled in such high style all the time. I tried to look without staring at the husky, handsome Secret Service agents filling up the aisle of the airplane, laughing together at some secret joke. They removed their jackets, guns visible in their leather holsters, and got more comfortable—as sure as they'd ever be, for the moment anyway, that their boss was out of direct danger.

I peeked into the private forward cabin where the Vice President, Mrs. Bush, and their inner circle convened. A part of me was disappointed that Bush didn't make his way back toward our section to at least say hello. As a relative newcomer, I wasn't yet part of his inner circle. But I felt more relieved than anxious by that fact, momentarily anyway. I didn't want to worry about Bush summoning me to the forward cabin, as he so often did with Steve, to answer some obscure question about the state's local newspaper (in this case *The Union Leader*) or about whom the paper endorsed in the 1944 presidential election. (Folks always seemed to simply assume that press secretaries were supposed to know everything about everything!)

Once we landed, Bush moved fast, and anyone who couldn't keep up with him would surely and unapologetically be left behind. He was clearly the star of our show. I lunged forward across the tarmac, my toes crunched toward the tips of my shoes, cursing myself for wearing such high heels and trying to keep up with his fast-moving entourage. The cold wind whipped at my face and bit my ears. Immediately Bush moved toward a group of waiting press and began what we called a "ropeline press availability"—an impromptu appearance for local media awaiting his arrival. Bruce Zanca, a campaign press aide with puppy-dog eyes and a wily sense of humor, kept the press behind the ropes while Bush talked and talked, promising to lower the deficit, pledging to keep alive Reagan's War on Drugs, and correctly refusing to hypothesize about who his Democratic opponent would be. Steve and I took careful notes as he spoke, until suddenly, as I was finishing writing a sentence, I happened to look up and see Bush bound toward the waiting line of cars. Within seconds, he was gone; he'd already disappeared into the lead limousine. I ran to the press van to keep up; the motorcade had already begun to slowly move out. Those same handsome Secret Service agents who only minutes before were laughing and slapping each other on the back on Air Force Two were now bulldog mean, staring stonily from the wide-open windows of their Blazers, their Uzis and submachine guns clearly visible and obviously loaded. I realized—after just ten minutes in the frigid air—that traveling with this man wasn't for me: His pace was too fast. And besides, it was just too damned cold.

On our first official stop, the audience and setting were quite informal. Most of the people were rural farmers wearing dungarees and red flannel shirts, sitting on bales of hay inside of a barn, sipping at their Styrofoam cups and waiting for Bush to begin.

I had planned to record the Vice President's remarks and the Q&A session, but in the rush to keep up with Bush, I'd forgotten my cassette recorder aboard Air Force Two. Digging through my purse, I fished out a piece of paper and again began taking notes as Bush spoke, just as I had on the tarmac minutes earlier.

A red flannel shirt leaned in close and spoke.

"You with Bush's group, missy?" he asked.

Missy? I thought to myself. Had I died suddenly and been transported into the middle of a "Petticoat Junction" rerun? I thought I heard a pig grunt somewhere in the background.

Naturally, I was just about the only woman and most definitely the only black person in that old, gray barn. Talk about feeling alienated. I grew weary of people always singling me out in a crowd, zeroing in on me because I was black and female. I was sick and damned tired of being alone and different, sick of being judged and evaluated. I actually felt a little angry at having been approached first.

"Yes, I am," I answered shortly, trying not to offend a potential supporter but wanting to get back to my work.

"What you doin' with that pad and pencil?" he asked.

"I'm trying to take some notes," I answered. "We like to keep fairly close track of exchanges like these." I sneezed. The hay was bothering my allergies. I hoped my asthma wouldn't kick in; I'd left my inhaler on the plane, too.

"You trying to catch a cold there, girlie?" my new friend asked.

I hadn't been called "girlie" since the days when my grandfather would send me sprinting across the street to the Dairy Queen. "Girlie" coming from Grandpa was one thing. The same word coming from a complete stranger in a musty old gray barn was quite another. I didn't like the sound of it at all.

I was on the verge of getting angry at what I considered borderline sexist behavior, but I certainly didn't want to cause a scene or do anything to jeopardize the political success of the trip.

"Just my allergies acting up," I responded. He looked puzzled. Either he was unfamiliar with the word or he was surprised that black folks had to battle with allergies at all.

He changed the subject and moved closer toward me.

"Boy, you sure do write fast," he said, leaning over to see my notes. "That shorthand? You're Bush's secretary, aren't you? You know him personally?"

My new friend continued his line of questioning.

"You Bush's secretary?" he asked again. "You got to take notes on everything he says, whenever he says it?" he asked.

My mind was mixing metaphors left and right: Jed Clampett was calling Scarecrow, Lion, and Tin Man in for supper. And Auntie Em was hitting Jethro in the head with a broom for eating all of her possum pudding.

"I'm not his secretary, no," I answered. I looked down at my black leather Bruno Magli pumps. A mixture of mud and cow manure covered both of my two-inch heels. Damn.

"I'm one of his press officers," I explained politely, all the while thinking hotly to myself, Now why must the only black woman in this damned, stinking, hay-infested barn be a secretary? Will we never, ever get beyond our own nasty stereotypes and banal preconceptions?

"And yes," I answered aloud, nodding my head. "I know the Vice President. He's a wonderful man and a skillful politician. Why don't we listen to what he has to say?"

"A press officer," he repeated slowly, listening to the sound of the title. He probably thought I was the officer in charge of making sure the Vice President's trousers and suits were pressed to crisp perfection every morning before he walked out the door.

I moved away from him, trying to continue my work. But

still he looked, regarding me carefully from the other corner of the barn. He wasn't flirting, I don't think, but I could sense that he was trying to figure out my role. By now, he'd probably made me into Bush's butler, cook, secretary, and seamstress all rolled into one. He probably visualized me wearing an apron or a maid's uniform under my Burberry trench. I swear: The human race will never get beyond its own limitations and archaic stereotypes. But people like him—middle American, flannel-shirt-wearing, tobacco-chewing potential supporters— were the very ones we were trying to reach. When we sat tucked away in our insulated offices in the White House, banging out press releases, middle America was our intended audience.

My experience in the barn that afternoon reaffirmed that prejudice can cut both ways. During an encounter which probably lasted less than two minutes, I was reminded of a universal lesson: that our own ignorance is what ultimately keeps us apart.

In the same way that I felt angry at the farmer for his sexist remarks and for automatically assuming I was Bush's secretary, I myself was equally guilty for assuming he was an uneducated, unrefined social misfit. I, too, was guilty of judging without benefit of prior knowledge—of falling down that same slippery slope of blind, prejudicial misconception. My grandmother would have probably even accused me of "looking down my nose" at him and regarding myself as somehow better than him because I wore expensive Bruno Magli shoes and rode on Air Force Two while he sipped coffee out of Styrofoam cups and had calluses on his hands the size of my wedding ring. We were both guilty of blinding ignorance. And worse yet, I did *nothing* to counter the negative free-association images which were floating around in my mind—images of Jethro and Auntie Em and cowbells. For all I knew, the man could have been a world-famous neurosurgeon or, worse yet, George Bush's second cousin, once removed.

But I rather seriously doubt it.

· · · · ·

WE FLEW ON TO FLORIDA that same day. In Miami, while Bush was giving a speech to a group of Hispanic supporters at a downtown hotel, I waited with a group of White House colleagues in the holding room which doubled as a staff office. Two young girls, perhaps in their early teens, peeked in.

"Are you actually with Bush's staff?" they asked, incredulous. Tom Collamore, a young White House colleague who often functioned as the VP's chief of staff during on-the-road trips when Fuller was absent, stepped forward. He was not one to mince words. Collamore was a straight shooter. Although he was a nice person, he wasn't demonstrative. I was surprised the young ladies even approached Collamore first; nothing about his demeanor indicated approachability. But Collamore stepped forward, and even had the nerve to put the slightest hint of a nice smile on his face. He was not given to social interaction, especially with strangers. He was the kind who'd rather mull over campaign statistics with the Vice President while sitting in the *front* cabin of Air Force Two.

He answered their question: "Yes, we sure are, ladies. We're on the Vice President's staff, yes." He looked around the room, blinking. They oohed and aahed.

"Can we have your autograph?" they asked Collamore, shoving a dog-eared piece of paper in his direction. Several of us stifled laughter. Signing autographs and being warm and fuzzy definitely weren't Collamore's style. He didn't miss a beat, but he waved the paper away.

"You don't need my autograph," he said with modesty. "Besides, my handwriting looks like chicken scratch." Steve Hart piped up from the back of the room, "Yeah, and nobody would know who Tom Collamore was, anyway. It wouldn't be worth the paper it's printed on." We laughed, happy at the momentary diversion.

But Collamore was undaunted; he rifled through a cardboard box, finally pulling out two vice presidential trinkets.

"Here, take these instead," he said. "They'll certainly be of more use." The girls opened the boxes. More oohs and aahs. Profuse thanks. The room erupted into applause after the two girls turned and left.

Collamore waved us away, turning to leave. "Go to hell, all of you," he said to us, trying to stifle a laugh himself while adjusting his glasses. "If any of you want my autograph for your mothers, I'll be in the hotel lobby signing cocktail napkins until happy hour." And he turned on his heel to leave.

It was a minor incident, but it showed a warmer, human dimension to Collamore that I never knew existed. I've liked him ever since.

During that Presidential campaign, we were a family. Like Fuller had done for us after the Iowa caucus, we buoyed each other's spirits when the going got rough. And, like Teeley and Ailes had demonstrated just before the Dan Rather explosion, we knew exactly what to do to protect our leader from mouths that roared and tried to bite. And, like Collamore, we demonstrated human warmth and kindness toward others as a matter of respect.

CHAPTER 7

· · · · ·

A Family Affair

· · · · ·

A S THE CAMPAIGN PROGRESSED, I came to learn some of Bush's quirks and idiosyncrasies, particularly as they related to his interaction with the media. He hates wearing both pancake and powder makeup but will grudgingly concede if the intended audience is large enough. When he's feeling under the weather, he generally prefers sipping freshly squeezed orange juice or hot tea; and any other time, especially on hot summer days, sparkling mineral water—with plenty of ice, of course—suits him just fine.

Clearly, Bush's family relaxed him. He relished having them close. His daughter Doro, who was about my age, would sometimes accompany him to interviews, lingering on the periphery while Bush was being primped and prepared. On one summer afternoon, Doro accompanied her father to a television interview that focused on baseball. I remember her standing several feet away, lifting her arm momentarily to wipe the perspiration from her face, waiting patiently for the interview to conclude so she could walk away with her father, arm in arm. I'd always say a quick hello to her, but I was usually too preoccupied with the Vice President's needs to delve into further discussion. Although we never knew each other, she seemed quite nice—the kind of person with whom you wish you could be friends.

George Bush was clearly a family man. This, more than anything, represented one of the most dramatic differences between Bush and Reagan. The Reagan White House just didn't generate strong family warmth.

Every morning during his staff meetings, Marlin would go around the room to see how each office would play a role in President Reagan's daily activities. Eventually, he'd come to Elaine Crispen, press secretary to First Lady Nancy Reagan, and the best-coiffed, best-dressed woman in the entire East Wing. In addition to the First Lady's schedule, Elaine's office coordinated most of the First Family activities.

"Elaine, the President is scheduled to attend an in-town event this weekend," Marlin said, flipping through his line-by-line schedule. "Are there plans for any of the children to attend? Looks like they'll be in town. And it would make nice color; Lord knows we could use a family shot," he said.

Elaine looked at Marlin as though he was a two-headed martian from outer space. The very thought of a full family outing seemed as remote a possibility to her as the White House janitor going along.

She pursed her lips, suppressing a cynical smile. Sitting on the arm of the couch in Marlin's office, nails freshly manicured,

104

she crossed her legs (correctly of course: calf to calf) and answered.

"I don't think so, Marlin," she said. "They're all busy this weekend. Besides, as you well know, it's not a good time for them in terms of family gatherings."

And that was that. On that issue, we seemed worlds apart.

But Bush was fortified and strengthened by the close, intimate gatherings he'd have with friends and family. He and Mrs. Bush entertained often; they didn't do it because they felt they had to, but because they genuinely, thoroughly enjoyed it. And so did we, the staff. Within his vice presidential office, it created a sense of closeness and family spirit.

Visiting the Vice Presidential residence felt a little like my childhood visits to Mama Lilly's house: You had to be ever mindful of your p's and q's, but you could still have fun while you were doing it. Bush's spontaneity was infectious.

During a staff Christmas party at the Residence in 1987, Bush took me aside.

"I thought I knew just about everyone on the staff," he whispered. "Weren't you just about the last one to join us?" he asked, genuinely curious. "If so, who *is* that woman in the hat?" he asked, gesturing wildly, arms raised high above his head, referring to one of the older volunteers who kept her tall, white fur hat on during the entire party.

"She just told me she works on staff. What's she got hibernating under there?" he asked, smirking playfully. But I had watched closely as he was introduced. Gracious and respectful as ever, he even feigned familiarity, which tickled her to no end.

He was in a jovial holiday mood that evening. He was on his own turf, in his own home, far removed from the protocol and formality of the White House. Roger Ailes lingered near the dining room table, stacking a growing pile of finger sandwiches, egg rolls, and Christmas cookies onto his plate. Bush, who spied Roger from clear across the room, joked aloud about his ever widening girth:

"Keep away from that gingerbread house, Roger," he warned, encircling the candy house protectively with his arms. "Bar and I had that especially made for this party. It's for decoration, not for consumption." Laughter filled the room.

I could hear the soft tinkle of a champagne toast in the sitting room. The banisters in the grand foyer were heavy with garland and large red velvet ribbons. Tuxedoed waiters offered holiday hors d'oeuvres and champagne from heavy silver serving trays. Lonnie stood at my side, as solid as a redwood and the most handsome man in the room. The Military Service Carolers—singers from the U.S. Air Force, Army, and Navy— had arrived and were preparing to serenade our group with Christmas carols and a holiday sing-along. I remember feeling so blessed at that moment, so much a part of something special and magical.

I needed a private place to give thanks, and I didn't want to wait until after the party was over. I wanted to do it right then, so I excused myself and found the bathroom. Inside, I closed my eyes and whispered my message of thanks, of profound gratitude to Him for placing me in this house, with these people. I felt smiled upon.

When I returned to the festivities, Bush had gotten caught up in his own humor, and he was primed to make people laugh now, louder and longer. He snapped his fingers as if remembering something important. "Have I got something to show you!" he said excitedly to no one in particular. He bent down to rummage through a drawerful of videotapes. After several minutes, he found what he was looking for, triumphantly pulled one videotape from the drawer, and held it up for all to see. Small groups of people began trickling in from the sitting room, the dining room, and the study. We stood patiently, watching as the Vice President fidgeted for several minutes with the VCR, trying to get it to work.

"Shouldn't you help him?" Lonnie leaned over and whispered in my ear. "You *are* a media person, and he's obviously having trouble." Just as I was about to move forward to offer assistance, the tape slid in. Bush banged the television loudly with the palm of his hand, triumphant. Silence for several seconds. "Watch this," Bush said. He was like a child in a toy store.

It was a tape of a recent "Saturday Night Live" skit, a takeoff on the presidential debates. There sat actors playing George Bush, Robert Dole, Pat Robertson, and Jack Kemp, lighting into each other and generally making fools of themselves. Dole spits some nasty comment out at Bush, something like, "Why, I ought to slap you with this one good hand of mine." Bush was cast as a buffoon, speaking in incomplete, whiny sentences, using wildly exaggerated hand gestures. Hilarious.

What was interesting was Bush's reaction as he watched this spoof of himself in his own home. He reared back and laughed again and again, wiping his eyes. The rest of us didn't know quite how hard to laugh. After all, he was our boss, and they were making a complete spectacle of him—"a shamefaced fool," as Mama Lilly used to say. It *was* hilarious, and some staffers laughed politely, watching Bush's reaction out of the corner of their eye. But Lonnie, bless his soul, leaned back and laughed loudest of all—great, gulping laughs, even louder than Bush. I tried to nudge him gently with my elbow. "Cool it," I wanted to say. "Let's not go overboard, buddy." But he had moved from within elbow range. There he stood in the hallway, he, too, wiping away tears. The whole scene was funny, but quite strange.

I've thought about that evening many times since. The warmth of the rooms. The beautifully decorated Christmas tree standing tall in the corner of the sitting room by the window. The frosted gingerbread house. The tall white hat. The infectious laughter of both Lonnie and Bush. And the prayer of thanks I whispered to my Lord God for allowing me to be a part of that magical Christmas scene.

· · · · ·

PART OF THE INTIMACY and close interaction we enjoyed on the Vice President's staff overlapped into our personal lives. Bush was always happy to meet another person's child, spouse, parent, distant cousin, or significant other. People came away feeling that he was as genuinely honored and enthusiastic about meeting them as they were about meeting him.

His meeting the various members of my family was an experience in and of itself. I often wondered if he'd ever come in contact with a black family like this.

Bush met my firstborn son, Lonnie Paul, at a picnic at the Residence in the early fall of 1988. The event had been on our schedule for weeks, and weeks were what it took for us to help Lonnie Paul master the art of a firm handshake.

We would practice in the evening, just before bedtime. Lonnie Paul was about one and a half years old, but I took great maternal pride in the fact that his grip was already becoming purposeful and steady. Still, something inside me wondered, even as we practiced, whether we were beginning the "yuppiefying" process too prematurely—whether we were submerging our baby boy into the waters of upper-middle-class mentality before he was ready to swim. Was it too early to inculcate him with protocol and proper salutations and all of the preening and appropriate social graces that come with growing up in a successful, ambitious family? Lonnie and I finally agreed that we were simply beginning the process of fitting our young son into his social matrix.

Besides, I was brought up to believe that the way you greeted someone upon introduction spoke of your character and your self-confidence. There's nothing worse than seeing children and teenagers—particularly black children—look down at the ground when being introduced, kicking their feet, mumbling under their breath, keeping their gaze averted and downcast. My mother would never have allowed such behavior from her offspring. There is no pride or dignity in that. It smacks of subservience. Any child of mine was going to learn to meet people head-on, eye to eye, man to man, with self-confidence and energy. Anything less was unacceptable.

So we practiced with Lonnie Paul: His first successful handshake would be with the Vice President of the United States.

Lonnie would get down on his knees and look at our son in surprise. "Well hello there, young man," Lonnie would say in an exaggerated, booming voice. "And what is your name?" Lonnie Paul would pause momentarily, going over it in his mind. "Wonnie Pa," he'd answer softly, amused by but accustomed to his father's playacting. "Well, it's certainly a pleasure to meet you, Mr. Paul," Lonnie would continue, extending his arm for a handshake. Lonnie Paul knew that the extended hand was his cue, and he knew, from practice, how to act on it. After hesitating slightly, he reached out and placed his tiny hand around his father's huge fingers. He even pumped it up and down, like the tiny piston in a miniature engine. Handshake complete. My baby was learning the ways of the world. Hugs and kisses all around.

When the day finally arrived, Lonnie Paul arrived at the Residence with his father, spit-shine clean, with new black and white saddle shoes and madras shorts with yellow suspenders. He took one look at the tree swing—the swing that Bush's grandchildren loved to use—and toddled toward it, falling in with a small group of children already forming under the tree. He romped and played all afternoon. He ate the first hot dog of his life. He consumed more potato chips than I thought physically possible for a child his size. And then, the moment of truth.

Bush spied Lonnie Paul playing near the porch and knew immediately he was my child. I wondered, momentarily, how he knew. But a quick survey of the crowd revealed the obvious: My baby was the only black child in the group.

Bush walked toward Lonnie Paul, who was just bending down to pull a flower from its soil. "Well, Kristin, who have we here?" he asked, leaning down to examine my son.

It was showtime.

I hoped that all the hot dogs and afternoon excitement hadn't blurred Lonnie Paul's memories of our hours of practice. I rested my hand on his small shoulder. "Sir, this is my son. Sweetie, can you tell the Vice President your name and maybe shake his hand?"

In my mind's eye, I saw Bush's hand disengage from his body, hanging like a severed limb, waiting for something with which to connect. Hours seemed to pass. "Sweetie, can you say hello?" I asked, with more urgency in my voice than I'd anticipated. The hand still lingered, gruesome and disconnected.

"What's your name, son?" Bush asked, leaning into his face. Then my fine firstborn son did his mother proud. He looked up directly into Bush's face, extended his arm, and murmured his answer: "Wonnie Pa," he said, pushing his little brown hand out into the air. The two shook together proudly, boy to man. I beamed from the sidelines, proud mama with tears in my eyes. I never wanted to forget the scene.

Bush picked him up, pleased by the reaction. "Well, it looks like we have quite a gentleman on our hands," he said, swinging Lonnie Paul high up onto his shoulders. "How about a nice shoulder ride, Lonnie Paul?"

The Vice President bounced up and down in place, pretending to gallop like a horse. He looked silly. Lonnie Paul held on to Bush's head with delight and surprise. And then, to my horror, I looked up and read something in my son's face.

"Sir, I think we better let him down," I said. "He doesn't look like he's feeling too w—" But Bush was completely oblivious. He assumed Lonnie Paul was enjoying it. "Sir," I interrupted again, trying to avoid certain doom.

"Ever ride a horsie?" Bush continued, still cavorting around like a crazy circus clown. I looked up again at Lonnie Paul's face, now ashen with sickness and nausea, his cheeks inflating. All I could do was ready the cloth diaper I held in my hands. I was watching a geyser about to blow.

And then it happened. My baby had mastered the art of shaking hands with the Vice President of the United States, but he couldn't keep himself from spitting up all over Bush's head. He had eaten one hot dog too many, had one slurp too many of Hawaiian tropical fruit punch surprise. He just couldn't contain himself. There had been too much excitement for one day.

I reached to wipe Bush's hair with the cloth diaper, dabbing at his forehead as gingerly as I could. Bush lowered Lonnie Paul to the ground, patting him gently on the behind. "Remind me not to hold that kid again, Kristin," Bush joked, taking the diaper out of my hands to finish wiping himself off. "I didn't realize I had such a profound effect on people."

Never mind that he had spit up on the Vice President's head. My baby had learned his first interactive social skill.

· · · · ·

QUITE BY SURPRISE one afternoon, Bush also met my sixteen-year-old nephew, Brant. I'd invited Brant to the White House to witness the arrival ceremony of Soviet President Mikhail Gorbachev on the South Lawn. It was a historic event—the first time in history the Soviet leader had visited the United States. President Reagan hosted the visit in all its regal splendor. The icicles of the Cold War were finally beginning to melt.

Brant arrived in my OEOB office shimmering with nervous adolescence, looking as handsome as ever—and wearing a tie, no less.

We walked over to the South Lawn and watched as Reagan and Gorbachev shook hands and exchanged pleasantries.

After the ceremony, I took Brant for an impromptu tour of the West Wing. Now that both leaders had been safely tucked away, staffers were free to move within the complex.

We headed to Bush's West Wing office. I wanted him to meet Linda Casey, a kind, sweet woman who was Bush's secretary in the West Wing.

The presence of the Secret Service agents standing in the reception area told me that Bush was in. I could hear his voice inside, moving toward the door.

"I'll bring you back later," I told Brant as we turned to leave. "Oh yeah, sure," he whispered, half smiling, poking his finger into my shoulder playfully. "Like I'm really going to meet the Vice President of the United States or something. What do you think I am, a complete trapezoid?" he asked incredulously, not realizing the door behind him was opening.

Bush spied us before I could shepherd Brant out of the reception area. "Whoa there, Kristin," he said. "Who's this handsome young man you're sneaking around with?"

Brant turned to look, incredulous, mouth gaping.

"Mr. Vice President, I'd like you to meet my nephew, Brant Anderson," I said. "Brant, this is Vice President George Bush." I looked at Brant, willing him to respond appropriately and courteously.

The Lord was with us. Mother would have been proud. Brant kicked into high gear—polite, confident, a trapezoid no longer.

"Pleasure to meet you, sir," he responded, arm extended.

I was pleased and mildly shocked. I didn't even know he *knew* words like "pleasure" and "sir." Still, I wanted to lean over and whisper into his adolescent ear, "More eye contact, boy. Look him directly in his face. Stand up straight. Be a proud young black man and face him head-on, with confidence." But this was a surprise encounter, completely unplanned. I took what I could get.

"Well, young man, what did you think of Mr. Gorbachev today?" Bush asked.

"Well, I didn't talk to him, but we're studying him in school," Brant answered, eyes holding Bush's gaze. Good, I thought to myself. Look him straight between the eyes. Don't you dare let your gaze drop to the floor. Brant continued his assessment of Gorbachev: "Pretty cool, I guess."

"What school ya go to?" Bush asked casually. Tim McBride stood by, trying not to show his impatience at the unexpected delay, which would alter Bush's schedule by several minutes at least. Tim checked his watch, smiling at me with tired eyes.

"Walter Johnson High School, sir, in Bethesda," Brant responded.

"Thought of which college you want to attend?" Bush asked.

"Probably Brown," Brant answered.

"Brown's a good school," Bush admitted, hands in his pockets, nibbling on his lower lip. "But a little too liberal for me. Ever thought about Yale?"

"Not really. I guess Yale's pretty good, though."

Bush turned to me in surprise, saying, "Kristin, I somehow never imagined you as someone's aunt."

What a strange thing to say. What does "someone's aunt" look like, anyway? A dowdy, elderly woman with bifocals and blue hair? A middle-aged spinster wearing thick support hose, Hush Puppies and a natty powder blue cardigan? Bush had seen me play my role as vice presidential aide, as wife, even as mother, but never as aunt, and I supposed it surprised him. My guess—my hope—is that he had more important things to think about than that.

114

He clapped Brant broadly on the back, moving to leave. "Good to meet you, fella," he said, sounding like my father. And then, over his shoulder, "You've got a pretty great aunt there."

"Yeah, I guess," Brant answered, as Bush disappeared through the door.

"You *guess?*" I asked Brant with mock indignation. "Boy, you better get yourself out of here so I can get back to work," I said. "I've been fussing over you for too long already today." I lead him to the Southwest Gate of the White House by his ear.

Outside the gates, he turned and smiled, giving me a triumphant thumbs-up sign. I stood inside the White House gates, smiling and waving back, realizing that he was slowly turning toward manhood. I felt happy and thankful that he was so healthy, so well adjusted and handsome. And as I waved, I also felt the slightest twinge of anxiety about the battles that were lingering just around his corner: the challenges of adulthood, of having to not only survive but (certainly as his family would expect of him) thrive and excel in a rough-and-tumble, competitive world.

· · · · ·

EXPOSING THE YOUNG PEOPLE in my family, particularly my own children, to life inside the White House was an intentional effort. When I made speeches to students or visited youth groups, I always used myself as the vehicle to send this optimistic message: Bumping into the Vice President of the United States in the corridors of the White House is not an implausible notion; spitting up on his head, although slightly embarrassing, is completely within the realm of possibility; working in a place that puts you smack-dab at the center of the highest levels of American power is both attainable and realistic. I wanted them to know that George Bush is not some vague, distant vision on a television screen but a living, breathing human being who cracks corny jokes and gives shoulder rides to children.

Black children need to be shown that women and men of color do hold respectable, powerful jobs at the highest level of government (although such people are unfortunately few in number), and that this country is not just driven by white males. They need to be reminded, in very deliberate, positive terms, that there is—or can be, with hard work and perseverance—a place for them in the overall scheme of things. They need to see that success is attainable, not a vague abstraction. We are obligated to keep them from losing hope.

One of the most vibrant role models this world has to offer is Colin Powell, the first black man in history to be named chairman of the Joint Chiefs of Staff, who directed the Persian Gulf War and emerged a national hero. He, too, shines his light into the dark corners of hopelessness and despair, trying to inspire young black children to work hard and do well. Sitting at a table in the Sheraton Carlton one afternoon, we discussed the dilemma of today's youths. He looked at me through dark eyes and said, "Too many black kids are trapped in poverty and see no way of penetrating upwards. They begin to lose hope and take the quick way."

He remembered his own childhood. "When I was coming up—when you were coming up was much, much later than when I was coming up, Kristin—but you always believed in upward mobility, that you could improve your lot. It didn't

116

mean you became rich or became a general. It meant you could make a living."

We have lost almost an entire generation of our black youth to drugs, hopelessness, despair. I do not believe that government is totally or even mostly responsible for this tragedy. I believe that, somewhere along the way, we have lost our moral bearings.

Too many parents have somehow let slip the strong grip they once had on the lives of their children. Where is that fierce, protective compassion and guidance we once used to shower all over our babies? Integrity, respect, and healthy spirituality do not lend themselves to partisan politics. Who we are, and what we're willing to sacrifice to help our children, are issues that transcend White House politics. Our children are our sheep, and we have not been attentive shepherds, for they are sadly astray. We are failing in our jobs as their protective shepherds. The things we do inside the home, the values and beliefs we create in our children's lives and hearts, will be what turns the tide.

A young African-American woman once approached me just after I'd made a speech outlining this same message: "What can I do to make sure I bring my small son up correctly?" she asked.

My answer: Help your child know God. Praise His holy name together, as a family unit—but encourage solitary prayer as well. Nurture and monitor his spirituality; when it lags, lift him up. Constantly reinforce the unconditional love and pride which you feel for him. Make clear your expectations, and never apologize for pushing him more than he wants to be pushed. Read to him often. Hold him close. Teach him to communicate effectively, without fear of reprehension. Encourage him to express himself not only with his childhood friends, but with the adults in his life. Remind him through your actions that his presence makes a valuable, substantial difference in your life, that his opinion matters, and that he can effect change. Teach him that power, influence, and financial success are not reserved for people with white skin. Black children need to know that; they need their inner strength and confidence reinforced early and often. We are obligated to instill these ideas directly into their lives, for *those* are the messages which will help them maneuver more effectively in the world later in their lives.

For this reason, I worked hard to make the White House a normal part of my children's lives. I recognize that most parents do not have the luxury of utilizing the White House as a backdrop, and I never once took the opportunities I had for granted. But as often as I could, I would take Lonnie Paul and, when she was born a few years later, my daughter, Mary Elizabeth, for walks through the Rose Garden. (The Uniformed Division guards frowned on staffers taking long, casual strolls through the garden, but I took my babies anyway, under the guise that we were "on our way" to another location within the complex.) My children used to love running down the long halls of the OEOB, floors as slippery as ice. They were blessed to have romped on the White House grounds together—hunting for Easter eggs in the spring, or falling asleep on the South Lawn on hazy summer nights as they watched the dazzling display of Fourth of July fireworks. Mary Elizabeth has heard her screams reverberate off the Oval Office walls. Lonnie Paul has rubbed his sticky, fruit-punch-stained hands through Bush's thinning hair. Lonnie has taken them for long, leisurely walks through the U.S. Capitol; he has squired them around like the proud, doting father that he is through the halls of the Hart Senate Building, introducing them to U.S. senators and Members of Congress.

We wanted our children to have fun, but we *knew* that it had to be more. It had to be a strong but subtle attempt to focus their vision, to help them see that events like these were well within their grasp. They needed to know that shaking hands with the President was as normal as shaking hands with Santa Claus at the mall. They needed to see their mommy's face in, say, *Ebony* magazine, standing in between the two other most highly visible women of color in the Bush White House at that time—Condoleezza Rice, director of Soviet and European affairs, and Anna Perez, press secretary to the First Lady. They needed to hear how the article characterized us: "Three Trailblazers Making History at the Highest Level of American Power." Rather than be embarrassed by the media attention, I used it as a vehicle with which to sharpen the vision of our black youth—for I was representing not only myself, but all of those African-American women who were to follow.

I am trying to teach my babies precisely what my own parents spent their lifetime trying to teach me: that going above and beyond the norm—reaching for the heaven and the stars— is commendable but should be considered par for the course, a part of our everything we do. It should be as natural as the truckload of my sister's Ph.D.'s.

There is no room in a black child's life for modesty or self-effacing behavior. Too many other negative, destructive images already crowd the field. My babies—and all of our children collectively—need to know that their potential and their horizons are boundless, as high as the sky and as wide as the

119

universe itself. My children need to know that their mother was the first black woman in history to have this particular job —that I was the first, but I certainly won't be the last. They need to know that their daddy worked twelve-hour days while he was in law school, working on Capitol Hill during the day and going to law school at night. Certainly our professional and personal accomplishments help bolster our own pride and self-esteem. But they also strengthen and more sharply define the legacy that Lonnie and I will leave for our children—and the legacy that my parents, and Lonnie's parents, so lovingly left for us.

We, as black parents, should feel responsible for providing our children with the moral compasses and cultural anchors they need to maneuver in today's rough-and-tumble world—a world where they will always be looked upon as somehow "different" because of the color of their skin or their ethnic origin. We have to help them strike a happy medium. It will not just "happen" if parents don't make a concerted effort to make it happen. The balance is elusive, mercurial.

Children of color, of any nonwhite nationality—particularly those who move in predominantly white environments—desperately need these cultural anchors in their lives. They need constant, tangible reminders of their family origin and ancestral history—particularly if they perceive themselves as isolated and alone. They cannot fully know themselves without knowing their own history.

There are historic compasses we can rely on—the black church, regular contact with members of the extended family, stories and traditions handed down over the generations—to guide our children through the dizzying, disorienting process we call racial "assimilation." The term "assimilation" itself is something of a misnomer because it is so one-sided: Whites don't want or need to make as much of an effort to adapt. Blacks *must,* if they want to survive. It is our own children who must struggle to strike the balance, who must make all of the appropriate emotional and social adjustments. And as they do, they need to be reminded that their tree of life can indeed blossom and bear beautiful fruit to be enjoyed and appreciated by people of all cultures, all races. They must be intimately familiar with the roots which are responsible for holding their lives securely in place; they must be knowledgeable about their ancestors from bygone generations who worked so hard to cultivate the soil that they now enjoy—and they must work to keep that soil rich and fertile.

Black children face the world with an entirely different set of circumstances from those of whites. In everything they do, they will *first* be judged and evaluated by the color of their skin, rather than by their character, their innate skills, or their intelligence. Not solely, necessarily—but initially. They need a leg up, an outstretched hand that will help them begin their long journey. Let me save my modesty and self-effacing behavior for my friends and neighbors.

I owe my children much more than that.

CHAPTER 8

· · · · · ·

In Search
of the
Sensitivity Factor

· · · · · ·

T HE VICE PRESIDENT was quite comfortable with the media, which was good, because even the best spin doctors
and handlers in the world cannot "manage" a candidate's genuine comfort level. Comfort and confidence are not things that
can be produced, directed, or choreographed. Either they're
there or they're not. And with Bush, they were generally there.
His years of on-the-road politicking—as congressman, U.S.
envoy to China, CIA director, Vice President, presidential candidate, and finally President—had taught him the critical importance of the media.

Unlike many politicians, Bush didn't regard the media

warily, as a swarming, seething mass. He saw them individually, and his penchant for fairness and accessibility made him a favorite among the White House press corps. (The most common complaint I received from reporters was that Bush's pace was too fast and too sporadic. But with Bush, that was simply par for the course.)

The invitation we'd received for Bush to visit *USA Today*'s editorial board was one I had strongly recommended—not just because it was my old stomping ground, but because I knew the board would be fair (although tough), and because *USA Today*'s reach and influence had increased dramatically. I was proud of what the paper had become, and I was proud to have played a tiny role in its birth.

We decided to accept the invitation. The date was set: July 27, 1988—almost three months before the election.

For me, it was a proud homecoming. As our entourage moved through the *USA Today* building, I saw many familiar faces and old colleagues. As we rode up in the elevator, I said a silent prayer of thanks to the Lord for bringing me full circle—for making it possible for me to have seen such rich, rapid progress in my life in such a relatively short period of time. Only several years earlier, I had ridden in that very same elevator as a twenty-three-year-old, teary-eyed, homesick young journalist trying to adjust to the working world. Now I stood proudly, as a mother, a wife, and a more mature woman, with the Vice President of the United States at my side no less, bending his tall frame closer toward me to listen to my last-minute advice. The irony of life's repetitive, circular patterns was showing itself again. It felt like déjà vu.

The prebrief for this event had not been easy. Just before we departed for *USA Today*'s headquarters in Arlington, Virginia, I sat with Bush in his West Wing office. Sheila Tate, the campaign press secretary, was also in the room. Bush looked to her to begin the briefing, but she responded generously: *"USA Today* is Kristin's old stompin' ground, as you know, Mr. Vice President," she said. "We should let her run this show today. Kristin?"

It was true. This event was tailor-made for me. From years of lengthy daily editorial meetings, I had come to learn the beliefs and styles of each board member. The board was composed of a group of mostly liberal, progressive thinkers, passionate about their beliefs and completely uninhibited about vocalizing those beliefs (they themselves sometimes called it "pontificating" every morning during our spirited editorial board meetings). After Gibson left, I (along with a colleague named Jerome Becker, who also eventually left the Board to join the Reagan White House) carried the Republican torch.

I did not then, nor do I today, consider myself a "conservative" in the absolute, purest sense of the word—but many, if not most, of my personal beliefs align themselves quite comfortably with those of my Republican colleagues: I am a strong advocate of affirmative action policies and programs, but I reject the notion of outright quotas. Quotas are too often arbitrary, not deliberately tailored to rectify past injustices, and they are ultimately discriminatory against others. I also reject the notion of "Big Government" and bristle at the thought of our government growing exponentially—the less government intrusion into people's lives, the better; and while there are certainly some social programs of intrinsic value to those who are deserving, far too many create cycles of dependency and are prone to waste and mismanagement.

I believe that free-market forces and the unbridled spirit of free enterprise create the underpinnings for a strong, viable economy. And I raised my hands with relief and happiness as Communism fell throughout Eastern Europe and, indeed, much of the world. And yes, like many in the Republican party, I do not believe that abortion should be used as a form of birth control; rather, greater emphasis must be placed on counseling and education—both at home and in the schools. Nevertheless, and on this I obviously depart from the conservative mainstream, I believe the ultimate decision must rest with the woman, based on her moral compass and religious dictates.

I knew this board well; I was familiar with their political leanings. Almost without exception, the board publicly and vehemently cried out against any infringements of First Amendment protections. Most stood in opposition to tuition tax credits, issues involving U.S. military force (like the U.S. invasion of Grenada), prayer in school, Reagan's aggressive military stance against the Soviets, and his Strategic Defense Initiative. They were a tough, stimulating group—willing to listen to opposing views, and quite engaging. It would be a tough forum.

But Bush was in a sour mood as we sat in his West Wing office during the prebrief. He was weary and irritable; the wear and tear of the campaign was upon him, and he was not at all excited about the prospect of going before the editorial board. It was one of the rare moments when I saw him actually look weary and run-down.

I launched into my briefing.

"Why are we doing this?" he interrupted, taking off his glasses to rub his tired eyes.

From the sound of his tired, irritated voice, I almost believed he was referring to the campaign itself. Surely I knew better.

"Because, sir, *USA Today* is the third largest newspaper in the country, with a daily circulation of over 1.3 million. I strongly beli—"

"No, you missed my point," Bush shot back without looking up. "I know all I need to know about *USA Today*. I also know that the current plan does not include my sitting down with absolutely every editorial board in the country. Why are we sitting down with *USA Today?* What I'm trying to ask, Kristin, is what, specifically, do we stand to get out of this actual meeting?"

What a crabber. I switched gears and played it straight. He was in no mood for flowery talk. "At a minimum," I said, "we can probably count on a front-page, above-the-fold news story and the text of your interview being published in its entirety on their op-ed page, which they call the 'Inquiry' page." He was still rubbing his eyes, but I could tell he was listening. I continued: "You know that *USA Today* is a splashy, sunshiny, feel-good paper. This will be a good opportunity for you to convey your personal side: to talk about your values, your family—the issues that *USA Today* likes to cover. You should also pl—"

"Just tell me how many people will be there," he interrupted. I'd never seen him this way. The immediacy of the campaign was upon him. "How many people are on the board?" He was really fed up.

At moments like these, I thought of my friend Cookie. If she'd been sitting in my place, she surely would have gone back at him head to head with something spicy like "Now wait a ham-sandwich minute. You don't want to go, you don't have to go. Don't catch an attitude with me. Just let me know what it's going to be."

"About twenty-five people will be in attendance, sir," I said quietly. I knew my answer wasn't going to go over well.

"Twenty-five people?" Bush repeated, almost yelling. "Why so many? What are we doing here?"

I had covered all of this in my briefing package, but I launched into it anyway, explaining that there were going to be news editors present, one or two political writers, the editorial board, and several executives. He was not a happy camper.

"Let's get out of here and get this thing over with," he grumbled, rising from his chair to leave. McBride, Valdez, and all of the other usual suspects fell into place as we walked out of his office, following behind him like a gaggle of ducklings.

Somehow, his mood lifted during the ride over into Virginia. By the time we got to the bank of elevators in the *USA Today* building, he was even smiling. He was a hard man to figure out sometimes: rarely moody (from what I saw myself), but given to minor irritability when tired or under stress—like anyone else.

We arrived on the seventeenth floor of the *USA Today* building several minutes late. Everyone was already seated. The tables were arranged in a large square shape rather than theater-style (my guess was to facilitate more uninhibited dialogue). I was happy to see so many of my old friends seated around the tables.

Bush opened the meeting graciously, and even made a warm statement about me. (My guess is that his generosity stemmed from his guilt; he probably felt bad about how he had acted minutes before.) He said something like "I know this is Kristin's old territory, but I must tell you I'm awfully glad to have stolen her away from you." All of my former colleagues in the room turned to look at me and smile. I beamed from the back of the room. The man could be nice when he wanted to be.

During the interview, Bush talked about himself and his family. He might have been tired and frustrated in the West Wing only minutes earlier, but he had listened to what I said. The next day's headline in *USA Today* read: BUSH: "I HAVE TO OPEN UP" PERSONAL SIDE. He talked about his affinity for pork rinds and country music, the love he felt for his children and grandchildren, and the fact that he needed to show the public more of his true self—more of the real George Bush.

"There's a tendency to have you fit in a mold," he said to the board philosophically, "and the mold for me is kind of Ivy League elitist, and I resist it . . . I know I have to open up a little," he admitted. He closed the session by urging people like Jesse Jackson to stay away from armchair diplomacy. Characterizing him as a "loose cannon" (which also made the front page), he charged that the good Reverend shouldn't be acting as a Mideast envoy in an effort to free the hostages. Bush has said that about Jackson before, publicly and privately.

Overall, it was an extremely productive visit. On the way out, he clapped me on the back. "Good job, Taylor. We need to do more of this kind of thing. When's our next one of these?"

Go figure.

. . . . .

Bᴜꜱʜ'ꜱ ʀᴇʟᴀxᴇᴅ, ᴄᴏɴɢᴇɴɪᴀʟ ᴍᴀɴɴᴇʀ with the media stood in direct contrast to the style of the newly announced Democratic nominee, Michael Dukakis. It was an advantage that we worked to our favor.

Dukakis, in my eyes, seemed a vaguely handsome but essentially lifeless automaton, responding on cue, rarely smiling, his stooped shoulders wallowing in rumpled, off-the-rack suits from Filene's Basement. His comfort level with the media seemed forced and contrived.

Basic Public Relations 101 dictates that a candidate must look good, stand tall, and never, *ever* wear oversized Army helmets. "The Duke" gloriously violated the last rule in September, about a month and a half after our *USA Today* visit: In an attempt to convey to the world that he would, indeed, be strong on military defense, the governor visited a defense plant in Sterling Heights, Michigan. Someone invited him to take a spin in one of the M-1 tanks, and to his detriment (where were his spin doctors, for goodness' sake?), he accepted. What America saw that evening was a droll-faced Dukakis—sporting an oversized Army helmet—bouncing around the field in an M-1 Army tank looking half scared, half dismayed at being silly enough to have ever agreed to such nonsense in the first place. The image was ludicrous. But it was too late. The networks had already picked it up.

My father, who called me every time Bush or Dukakis visited Michigan so he could provide his own personal feedback, was on the phone when I walked in the door that evening. It was funny, but throughout the campaign Daddy would refer to Bush, when speaking to me, as "your man," and to Dukakis as "this man." And I always knew whom he was talking about.

130

"Sweetheart," Daddy said, "they've got this man up here riding around in a tank with an Army helmet on his head looking like Beetle Bailey."

He sounded so disgusted. I stifled the urge to laugh. Daddy would have thought it cruel.

"I saw it, Daddy," I said. "What'd you think?"

"I think it's one of the silliest things I've ever seen in my born days," he answered. "Your man has already won this election. Tell him congratulations for me."

Try as he might, Dukakis kept stumbling. Even his campaign manager, Susan Estrich, admitted the campaign was over when, during the second presidential debate, she heard Dukakis' response to CNN correspondent Bernie Shaw's now infamous, shocking hypothetical: "If Kitty Dukakis were raped and murdered, would you favor the death penalty for the killer?"

Dukakis, taken aback by the ferocity of the question, stumbled and never quite recovered. The millions of viewers never saw so much as a flicker of emotion pass over his face. He managed to spout off a few prepackaged statistics on the crime rate, but never once did he display the required visceral rage and anger that naturally should have come—to both his face and his mind—at the very thought of his wife being raped and murdered.

I, too, knew that he'd just sustained a major blow which would most probably prove fatal to his campaign efforts. Lonnie and I watched the debate in bed, pillows propped in all directions and Lonnie Paul burrowing his way back and forth under our thick down comforter, making imaginary holes between our sheets like a busy little gopher.

"It's all over," Lonnie said quietly the moment he heard

Dukakis' response. "Your boss is going to be the next President of the United States. Hallelujah!"

In Steve's meeting the next morning, we discussed the dismal job Dukakis had done. We were all gleeful.

"Dukakis dropped the ball right on his wife Kitty's foot," Steve said. "The man has about as much personality and feeling as my big left toe. Thank you, Bernie Shaw!"

We rifled through each of the morning newspapers, reading aloud with smug satisfaction the negative feedback Dukakis was receiving for his performance in the debate.

Sean Walsh agreed, resting his copy of *The New York Times* on his knees. "Let's face it," he said with a smirk. "The man is a moron."

And then, turning in my direction and calling me by the nickname he himself had created for me (a phonetic combination of the first two initials in my name, K.C., which he'd shortened to simply "Case"), he said half jokingly, "Come on, Case. If somebody asked Lonnie what he'd do if you were murdered and raped and he responded like Dukakis, you'd chew him out, wouldn't you? You'd put him out of the house."

"Doggone right," I said, keeping the humor going, feeling buoyed and a little cocky by Bush's solid performance the night before. The smell of victory was indeed in the air. The mood was optimistic. We were glad that Dukakis had stumbled and fallen. Something about it felt a little meanspirited, but my hesitancy was overpowered by the collective excitement about the prospect of our own victory.

It was an important lesson: Always consider the personal reaction of your audience before you speak. It is crucial to weigh how a particular choice of words will make the voters *feel*. This was an issue we ourselves faced during the campaign. We had recently almost misspoken and alienated an important audience.

Vice President Bush was to address a group of about three hundred black supporters, and as I reviewed the speech I was appalled to stumble over the word "nigger" buried within the text.

His speech was written to reaffirm the importance of the black vote and to send the signal that minorities do, indeed, have a place within the Republican party. The speech was designed to make black people feel good about themselves, secure about their economic and political futures, and confident that they were indeed an integral component of the party of Lincoln. The address touched on the politics of inclusion, economic empowerment, and the need to put an end to racial intolerance and bigotry—all noble enough themes, but the Vice President's message, to my thinking, would be seriously diluted by the use of that one raw word. It was vile.

I scribbled my editing remarks in the margin, strongly suggesting that the word be deleted. ("Word 'nigger' doesn't work in any context; we shouldn't have VP utter the word at all. It's vile.") For Bush to utter the word "nigger" to a roomful of black folks would send cold chills down many a sequined spine. People probably wouldn't get up and walk out, but that word—no matter what the context—would most assuredly cause a bitter bile to form at the backs of many throats. The last thing we needed to do was alienate our modest support base among black Americans; it was already shaky at best.

An office intern took my edited draft directly to the man

who wrote the speech, Reid Detchon. He was one of Bush's most talented writers—a quiet, intense man whom I considered my friend.

Reid walked into my office minutes later, flopping down in my armchair. He looked me dead in my face. He was tired. Everyone was tired. The campaign had taken its physical and emotional toll.

"So you really have a problem with this one word?" he asked, fingering his Republican-looking tie. "Can we talk about it?"

"You know we can," I answered. "Reid, I have a serious problem with the VP making a direct reference to the word at all. You aren't experiencing the same visceral reaction that I am right now, but I can tell you that the word sends shivers down my sp—"

"Are you carefully considering the context in which it's being used?" he interrupted. Reid always spoke like a high school English teacher. I found myself watching my diction when he was around. "You mean it doesn't come across that he's saying he strongly *objects* to the use of words such as these?" Reid continued, almost pleading. "That he opposes with every fiber of his being such racist, ignorant thinking? What he's saying, Kristin, is that he, too, regards racial bigotry as intolerable."

Reid was right. Bush wasn't condoning the use of the word at all, but the fact that it even appeared in the speech would surely, in my mind, spell bad news. Reid didn't have a clue that he was about to take our boss down the wrong road. And that I even had to bring it up at all told me that we—"we" meaning African-Americans and the Republican party—hadn't come as far as I thought, and hoped, that we had.

I looked at Reid sitting in my chair, and for some reason I thought about Lonnie Paul, about the struggles my son would face throughout his young life—about the inevitable moment when he would catch the full force and fury of that hideous word being hurled at him by a white friend. How would I react? What would I say? How would I comfort him? My boy was fine, for now. It was his mother who was going through all the changes.

No matter how much I tried to explain, Reid would never completely empathize with the personal, bitter ugliness of the word and all that the word represents. Nor would he know the frustration of having to explain his loathing. Hearing a white man utter the word—any white man—seemed an improper invasion of the past. Surely we'd come further than that.

"Isn't there an important distinction to be made here having to do with context and character?" Reid the intellectual asked.

"Doesn't matter," I answered shortly. I didn't want to lose my temper. I didn't want the conversation to become personal, because then I might lose my civility. Reid and I were friends. We were having dinner with his family at their home in a few weeks. I took a deep breath.

"The context in which he's using the word is irrelevant, Reid," I said. "Black folks feel like they've gotten past all of that bullshit. We feel like that battle's already been fought. Like we've progressed far past the point of ever having to hear that word surface in intelligent, mature conversation." I regarded Reid, who was looking increasingly thoughtful in my armchair. I had his attention.

"These folks who are coming to hear Bush speak are paying *much* money to sit down, eat some rubber chicken, and hear him thank them for believing in him and in the Republican party," I continued. "The last thing they want to do is listen to some inane, primitive word like 'nigger' come out of his mouth—any more than a Jewish audience of supporters would want to hear the word "kike," an Italian group the word "dago," or a Hispanic group the word "spic." It raises hackles —no matter what the context. Why even take the risk?"

Reid looked at me, then looked down at the edited speech he was holding.

"The rest of your speech is fine," I said matter-of-factly. It was, too. "You just need to remove all references to that one blasted word before it blows us all to pieces. Take it from me on this one, Reid. This runs deeper than what you understand."

"I don't know if I'll have a chance to get with the VP on this before we leave for the speech," he said, looking slightly worried now. Perhaps he realized that I just might be right. He got up to leave. "I'll see what I can do."

On his way out he stopped and turned. "Thanks for the feedback, Kristin. It helps to hear a personal perspective."

And then he was gone.

Steve Hart and I had lengthy discussions about the event in the weeks before. David Bates, Bush's longtime senior aide whose office was just across the hall, helped us strategize ways to garner attention to the speech from the black groups who would be listening carefully and from the media. We were debating whether to make the speech open to the press or bill it as a closed, private event. The audience members were supporters. The environment would not be combative. The press could cover Bush's remarks, but they wouldn't be able to participate in an active, on-the-record Q&A. We decided to leave it open.

On the evening of the event, Bush was moving fast, allowing no time to read his facial expression and giving no cues to interpret. He spied me and clapped me on my back. "Everything okay in there, Sergeant Taylor?" he asked.

But he seemed distracted. No smiles. A slightly furrowed brow. The lip biting worried me.

After several "grip and grin" photo ops with the VIP guests in the hotel's private holding room, Bush followed his advance man through the back hallways toward the stage. We were always moving through cordoned-off corridors in the bowels of buildings. After a while, all the hallways and corridors and makeshift blue velvet backdrops (for backstage photo ops) seemed to blend together. As I moved with the entourage, butterflies danced a jig in the pit of my stomach as I wondered if Reid had relayed my editing suggestions.

It was showtime. I stood in the offstage wings, in a section reserved for Bush's White House staff, as the Vice President approached the podium. I peeked around the curtain to survey the crowd.

Everyone was dressed to the nines: the men in their fine, expensive, custom-made suits; the women in their sequins and silks and three-hundred-dollar shoes.

At the sight of the Vice President, the room opened up with warm, hearty applause. Everyone rose to their feet for a standing ovation. The warm welcome buoyed Bush and strengthened his performance that evening. The speech turned out to be a resounding success.

I listened closely as he spoke. Somewhere between my conversation with Reid and the editing of the final draft, someone had listened. The "n-word" had disappeared completely. In fact, every one of my editing suggestions had been incorporated into his remarks. I don't remember whether the dreaded word found its way into any of Bush's addresses after that. But the flag of sensitivity had at least been raised.

In this particular case, we had had the benefit of foresight. But later the Vice President was slapped almost as hard as Dukakis had been—by the media and by just about every minority group in the country—for referring to his own grandchildren, three of whom are of Mexican descent, as "the little brown ones." I watched from our press office as the evening news report showed Bush warmly embracing his grandchildren as they ran to greet him on the airport tarmac. Tousling their hair and obviously happy to see them, he called his grandbabies "the little brown ones." *Ouch,* I thought the second I heard it. There'll be hell to pay for that comment, sir. What you consider a casual, offhand remark—even a gesture of love and affection—might well end up burning our collective butt.

Immediately, the media started in. They claimed, and I agree, that his characterization showed a lack of cultural sensitivity, a gap in his reality. Bush loves his grandchildren probably more than he loves himself—his remarks just showed that he hadn't been properly schooled or sensitized to the potential "tender spots" among cultures different from his own.

We remained on the offensive throughout the campaign, painting Dukakis with broad brushstrokes as soft on crime— denouncing him for opposing the death penalty for drug kingpins, and strongly criticizing him for his role as master architect of one of the most lenient prison furlough programs in the nation. The Bush camp, with hard, heavy, repetitive strokes, kept hammering the message to the voters: Dukakis was more interested in protecting the criminals than he was in protecting the victims—the precise concept which eventually gave rise to the infamous Willie Horton ad.

Willie Horton insinuated himself into my life in a very direct way—perhaps most frequently through many of my black friends in social settings.

"If you're so concerned about heightening racial sensitivity within the Republican party," a friend of a friend asked me at a dinner party one evening toward the end of the campaign, "then why don't I hear you condemning this racist Willie Horton ad campaign?" She took another of many deep swallows of white wine and ran a manicured hand through her freshly permed "do."

"How could you have ever let yourself become involved in such blatant, race-baiting prejudice and self-hatred?" she continued. "I'd heard you had so much on the ball. Where's your soul, girl? Where's your sense of propriety and dignity?"

A whole fish looked up at me from a black and gray marble platter. He was covered with thinly sliced cucumbers and surrounded by parsley. They could have at least cut his damned head off before they laid his body out on the table like that, I thought to myself. The crazy-looking eye was making me sick. And it was too damned hot in that room. The woman wanted to debate. I could see her temples throbbing. And her right foot was going to town—wiggling and wagging as fast and furious as if it were motorized.

Willie Horton had somehow single-handedly changed the nature of so many of my personal friendships. He had diminished my ability to have comfortable, congenial fellowship with many of my black friends. I had grown frustrated with the fissures he had created in my relationships, and I was slightly embittered at having to constantly defend a principle in which I strongly believed.

I'd had to defend George Bush's right to paint Dukakis as soft on crime a thousand times before. Tonight was no different. But tonight a crazy fish eye gazed up at me, wild-looking and askance, and the temperature in the room was making me bristle. Tempers were about to flare.

With the Willie Horton issue, I was always struggling against the current, always taking exception, constantly and staunchly defending what I knew many of my black friends regarded as racist. Along with their accusations, of course, came the implicit suggestion that, because of my association with George Bush, I, too, harbored an element of "self-hatred," as my interlocutor had characterized it earlier.

Constantly having to defend myself and the Vice President on an issue so volatile—especially in social settings, among people who were normally my friends—was emotionally and physically exhausting. But my spirit was buoyed by a single fact which unburdened my heart and completely unbridled my conscience: I would have resigned from George Bush's staff if I'd actually believed he was a racist. I did not believe it. Not with one fiber of my being.

Bush was a good man with a kind, gentle heart and a strong desire to be fair and judicious. I reject completely the ugly, wild charges of racism which were lobbed against him during the 1988 campaign.

I watched as the hostess got up to refill my wine glass. She then moved into the kitchen, looked around momentarily, and returned to her seat at the table. I knew her well. She was normally what I would describe as the sedentary sort during dinner; she enjoyed long, languid, free-flowing conversations with her dinner guests. She always spoke carefully and listened attentively, usually with her legs tucked underneath her at the head of the table. But on this night, she was moving about more than ever, full of nervous energy, which told me more about her general discomfort with the subject than about her role as hostess. She was not the type to get up and pour wine for her guests. In her comfortable home, everyone always got whatever they needed for themselves. But I finally spoke when the last drop had been poured.

"Willie Horton was a convicted murderer and a vicious rapist," I answered slowly, enunciating every word. "He was first convicted for robbing and killing a teenage boy. The young boy's friend found him stuffed into a garbage can with his feet jammed up near his chin. He'd been stabbed nineteen times."

A thousand times, I had imagined the boy's mother being told by the police how her son had been found, and a thousand times I had thought of Lonnie Paul—of the sweet brown toes I used to kiss during his infancy.

I continued, undaunted and not at all intimidated—only very weary.

"Then, while Mr. Horton is out galavanting around on a weekend party pass, compliments of Michael Dukakis, he decides to travel to Maryland, break into somebody's home, rape an innocent woman, and beat the shit out of her fiancé." The profanity sent the hostess scurrying into the kitchen again, this time to make sure the oven timer was indeed working correctly. "He raped her twice and slashed her fiancé twenty-two times across his stomach."

Momentary silence. *"That* is what I see when I see Willie Horton," I said. "I don't see the color of his skin. I don't see the texture of his hair. I don't see the whites of his eyes. I see a cold-blooded killer and a violent, vicious rapist," I finished.

It was her turn for rebuttal: "Then you have a vision problem, sister—if that's all you see," she shot back. "Inciting that kind of racial fear in the hearts of the voters is a cheap, manipulative shot," she spit out. "Picking Willie Horton as an example of Dukakis' failed furlough program—and showing the face of a mean-looking black man to a nation full of scared white folks—is the cheapest kind of dirty trick. And I think you know it."

It was no longer a conversation. It was a frontal assault. The hostess got up nervously again to open another bottle of wine. The fish sat uneaten on the platter, his crazy eye frozen in its horrible, crooked position. The rest of the guests at the table tried splintering off into private clusters of conversation.

We were both taking the issue very personally, and the sparring continued. I tried to point out her error: that not *one* of our Bush campaign ads ever showed Horton's face; that we took deliberate steps in every one of our political ads to avoid ever alluding to the color of his skin or his ethnic background. The ads which did show his face were produced by an independent outfit. They did it on their own. Neither the White House nor the Bush campaign condoned their use.

She rolled her eyes, unimpressed. If I saw one more eye rolling around in that room—hers or that damned fish's—I was going to get up and leave. But I wanted to get everything off my chest. I needed to say a few more things.

"Are you objecting, then, to the very act of using Willie Horton—a black man—as an example?" I wanted to know. "It would have been okay if Horton had been white?"

"It would have been better," she shot back. "Putting a

black face out there in the public domain is certainly not fostering better race relations in this country, if that's what you mean," she answered, sarcasm stinging her every word.

"Do you realize we're sitting here in this dining room, drinking wine and hypothesizing on the color of the man's skin while we ignore completely the atrocity of his crimes?" I asked.

"And just out of curiosity," I asked, "how did you feel when a local Massachusetts newspaper, the *Lawrence Eagle-Tribune,* published a Pulitzer Prize–winning, in-depth series on the Horton crime?" I asked. "Why don't I hear you screaming about that?

"Were they race-baiting their subscribers or simply enlightening their readers? Why weren't all those ugly charges of racism being hurled at them with the same velocity? I know the audience is different, but the principle remains exactly the same," I said.

"And why didn't I hear the same charges being hurled at Al Gore," I continued, "the candidate from your very own political party, when he first brought up this entire issue of Dukakis' furlough program? Your man Gore was the first on the scene; he was the first one to uncover this entire issue. Don't you remember when he first brought it up—right to Dukakis' face during a candidate debate—a week before the New York primary? Why wasn't he conveniently labeled a race-baiting, fear-inciting white man, too—for even bringing the issue to light at all?"

"Gore never mentioned Horton's name or color, and you know it," she hissed. "Now you're mixing apples and oranges."

I shrugged. "By simplifying this issue as much as we are, and by isolating this to a racial matter, we're conveniently losing sight of the pain and misery Willie Horton inflicted upon so many people. We're overlooking the heinous crimes he committed—crimes which could have been avoided if it hadn't been for the state's lenient prison furlough program." I was getting tired. I didn't want to be there. But I needed to finish. My emotions were speaking more than my intellect.

She interrupted, "Aren't you even the slightest bit remorseful that a black man had to be the center of this debate?"

"I will never apologize for Horton being a no-good murderer," I finished. "If it had been your son he killed—or mine —and your mother he raped—or mine—you can bet we wouldn't be sitting around analyzing and reanalyzing the color of the man's skin. No, I don't think so. We'd want the bastard put in the deepest, darkest prison in the world. And the fact that he was allowed to perpetrate these crimes on a funky weekend pass would have made our loss all the more bitter."

"We're on different wavelengths, sister," she said. "I see no reason for us to continue this conv—"

"I don't see a reason, either. It's unfortunate that we can't communicate."

"Oh, we've communicated, all right," she said. "I hear you loud and clear. It's just that I don't agree with where you're coming from," she finished, getting up to leave. "I'm a lifelong Democrat and proud of it. And I've got to get home. We've got an election to win." And with that, she smiled, bent to kiss the hostess, grabbed her wrap, and walked out of the door.

I sighed, propped my stocking feet up on an empty chair, and nursed myself through a cup of strong, hot coffee.

Twenty minutes later, I left, too.

What disturbed me more than anything about the entire

Horton ad campaign was that people lost sight of the real issue; so many conveniently jumped onto the "racial prejudice" bandwagon, and they didn't take the time to realize that they themselves were equally guilty of the same sort of prejudice. Willie Horton doesn't represent the entire African-American race. What's unjust, in my mind, is to automatically assume that Willie Horton is all of black America. He is not. He is black, but he is certainly not a symbol of everything black. He is not my brother. He is a vicious killer. I think more highly of myself and my people than to open my embrace wide enough to include him—and only him—as the sole representative of our race. It saddens me that some of my friendships suffered as a result of this man. I regret that the issue exploded into a mean, divisive, tangled mess. But my heart knows no guilt.

· · · · ·

By the time the campaign was just about ready to come to a close, wild charges were flying everywhere—charges not only of racism, but of marital infidelity. With only a few weeks left, things were getting down and dirty.

About two weeks before the election, Donna Brazile, a twenty-eight-year-old African-American woman who worked as a deputy field director for Michael Dukakis, publicly raised questions about George Bush's marital fidelity. Apparently hoping to fan the flames of a rumor that *The Washington Post* was preparing to publish a damaging story about Bush and his alleged extramarital affairs, Brazile remarked to the reporters accompanying Dukakis on a campaign trip that "the American people have every right to know if Barbara Bush will share that bed with him in the White House," and that the Vice President "owes it to the American people to fess up" about the ugly rumor.

Brazile's remarks, combined with the rumor of the impending *Post* piece (which turned out to be false—it never ran), helped trigger a near disaster on Wall Street: a precipitous forty-three-point drop in the Dow Jones average, with the market falling about twenty points in fifteen minutes, all in direct reaction to the rumors of the Vice President's infidelity. The *Post* even took the unusual step of denying that it had been working on such a story, putting Robert Kaiser, then the assistant managing editor for national news, on the record for a rare public comment. "There is no such story," Kaiser claimed in a statement to the Associated Press.

Although Brazile resigned only hours after making the remarks, the damage, of course, had already been done. Although she slipped into quiet oblivion, she'd doused the rumor with gasoline, effectively—and strategically—leaving everything ablaze. And both the campaign and White House staffs were left scurrying to extinguish the flames.

In this case, as I was to learn from Steve, no comment was the best comment. Responding to a story like this would only breathe new life into the accusations. Steve called me at home that weekend with this admonition: "If you get any press calls on this, don't say a word. Any official White House response— even if it's only a denial of the accusations—will breathe new life into the story." "Don't let them drag you into a discourse on Bush's marital life. Both you and I know we're dealing with a pack of unfounded lies. But we don't want anything on the record. Any statement, from you or from me, will give them a fresh new headline. Keep quiet."

It was an important lesson, and one I've always remem-

1966-City and Country School of Bloomfield Hills-1967

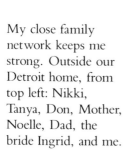

As a child, I traversed a delicate path between a secure home life (here I'm with my father) and the uncertain world of a posh private school.

My close family network keeps me strong. Outside our Detroit home, from top left: Nikki, Tanya, Don, Mother, Noelle, Dad, the bride Ingrid, and me.

The confusion I felt about my racial
identity came to a standstill when I found this
1938 article about my mother, the Brown Venus.

Mother's strength and determination drove us
all. After almost seven years of juggling classes
with motherhood, my mother graduates
from college, a feat with which even the
Detroit News was impressed.

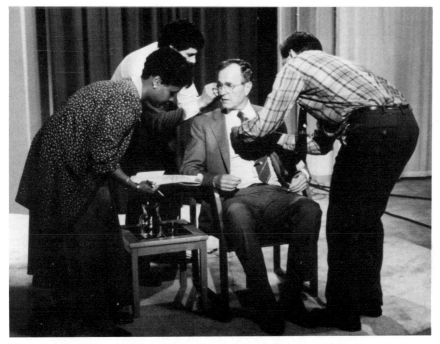

Once in the White House, I learned that having Bush's children and dog Millie around always seemed to make satellite interviews even more effective. *(White House)*

To: Kristin Taylor —
It's great having you at my side — Sincerly
Geo Bush

The fateful horsie ride of my son, Lonnie Paul. *(White House)*

Lonnie Paul was a staunch Bush supporter.

Pregnancy highlighted the complexities of a working mother's life: How do you check last-minute details when the President of the United States is telling you to sit down? *(White House)*

Minutes before an interview with Black Entertainment Network. *(David Valdez/White House)*

Testosterone levels were high that day! Arnold Schwarzenegger, chairman of the President's council on physical fitness and sports, visited the Oval Office. (From left) Press Secretary Marlin Fitzwater (on couch), Deputy Assistant for Domestic Policy Jim Pinkerton, Domestic Policy Advisor Roger Porter, and I joined the muscle-flexing.

The President's men (and woman). From Bush's right: national security staffer Robert Gates, Marlin Fitzwater, Roger Porter, National Security Advisor Brent Scowcroft, me, Communications Director David Demarest, and Andy Card, deputy chief of staff. *(Susan Biddle/White House)*

We were never sure *what* questions were going to be asked at press conferences, but during one session I arranged, we were worried about *who* would be asking the questions. *(Carol Powers/White House)*

The highlight of my years with Bush was the day my parents—James and Mary Clark—came to visit. *(White House)*

James & Mary Clark.
With Warm Regards and Great Pride
in Kristin
Geo Bush

The question: "How much do you think he's worth?" Bush is interviewed by John Johnson, chairman and CEO of Johnson Publications; seated with me are Simeon Booker, Washington bureau chief of *Jet* magazine; Chriss Winston, White House staffer; and Robert Johnson, *Jet's* executive editor, face away from the camera.

Lonnie, Lonnie Paul, and Mary Elizabeth joined me to say goodbye on my last day in the White House. *(White House)*

Lonnie Jr   Good Luck —   Geo Bush

bered. In just about every follow-up story, every one of us—
Steve, campaign press secretary Sheila Tate, me, and any other
of the campaign press officers—responded with a universal "no
comment." James Baker III, then campaign chairman for the
Bush campaign, also followed suit, responding that he wasn't
"going to dignify the comments" of Brazile by reacting to
them.

Dukakis apologized to Bush prior to a joint appearance
the two candidates were to make at a charity fundraising dinner
in New York City. But, as we feared, even the news of the
mere apology—supposedly genuine and heartfelt—gave birth
to a spate of fresh headlines, which again kept the story alive. I
don't doubt that the primary reason for Dukakis' apology was
to keep the story alive. For about a day, his strategy worked.
The headline in the *Los Angeles Times* the day after the apology
read, AIDE'S REMARKS PROMPT DUKAKIS APOLOGY TO BUSH. *The
Washington Post* ran the headline FALLOUT FROM REMARKS ON
BUSH: AIDE QUITS, DUKAKIS APOLOGIZES.

Eventually, the Dukakis-Brazile offensive against Bush
backfired: While the Dukakis camp was still dallying in rumors,
Bush picked himself up and moved with dignity beyond the
bickering and empty, unfounded accusations. He spent the
days immediately after the firestorm highlighting his foreign
policy experience by mapping out a plan to abolish chemical
weapons. The image of Bush as the political statesman was
what eventually stuck in the minds of the public.

I was personally offended by the cheap, amateurish attacks
on Bush's character. George Bush is decent and caring, with an
unwavering sense of propriety and family strength. We were
powerless to stop the media from covering the story, but we
weathered the storm.

But for me, there were other storms looming on the horizon—vicious, violent storms which whipped and swirled through my personal life and offset my emotional momentum as the campaign steamrolled into its final days.

Something was wrong with Mother.

CHAPTER 9

. . . . .

A Mother's Love

. . . . .

M Y MOTHER WAS PROUD that her baby girl worked in the
White House, though she carried her pride in her
seven children quietly. She was much too dignified a woman to
brag and boast, but at the slightest urging she'd relish the
chance to update friends and church parishioners on her children's latest accomplishments. I am blessed that she lived long
enough to watch me take my rightful place in the long succes-
sion of refined, remarkable women from which she herself
came. And I know I was blessed with the common sense to tell
her I loved her as often as I did.

As Mother's strength began to ebb over the years, I tried
to prepare myself for the arrival of my parents' "golden years."
Our entire family gradually began making adjustments to accommodate Mother's declining health. We discussed moving
my parents' bed downstairs into the television room to avoid
Mother's daily battle with the stairs. Portable oxygen tanks

were delivered to the house each month for her daily inhalations. We created meticulous timetables and charts (and recreated them countless times) for her medication schedule. My sisters and I held bicoastal conference calls to discuss our parents' lives and livelihoods.

Only now can I fully appreciate—even empathize with—that unconditional, unwavering source of spiritual strength and inner power which black women carry within them. Only now can I fully understand the fierce, protective power of a mother's love; the burning need to teach our children to love to learn; the overwhelming desire to teach our babies to embrace life's challenges as passionately as a long-awaited lover; the stubborn determination to help them realize, with clarity and confidence, that they are the next link in our living legacy.

Mother left me all that. And only recently have I finally reached the point where I can seek solace and joy in my memories of her—of her and me together.

One memory that still shines brightly is Christmas 1987. Mother and Daddy flew in from Detroit to spend the holidays in Washington and to meet their daughter's boss, Vice President George Bush, in his office at the White House.

Even then, Mother's pace had slowed considerably, but she still moved about with elegance and grace, her head held high. Fortunately, our meeting with Bush was scheduled to take place in his office in the Old Executive Office Building (rather than his West Wing office, which was a longer walk), but I was still concerned about how Mother was going to handle the incredibly long, marble halls.

On the morning of the meeting, before my parents arrived, I called Tim McBride and explained, "If it's all right with you, Tim, I'll need to bring my parents downstairs about a half hour early in preparation for their meeting with the VP. My mother will need a few extra minutes to rest up after tackling these long halls. Can they hang out in the outer office?" I asked.

"Don't say another word," Tim answered. "Bring them down whenever you'd like. We'll make them comfortable. By the way, the VP is really looking forward to meeting them."

My parents arrived at my second-floor press office right on schedule. They had landed in Washington the day before and had spent the day fawning over their oldest daughter, Joann.

Today was my turn.

After warm hugs, I studied Mother carefully to see if she was unusually winded. I had learned to gauge how she was feeling by her posture: If she sat straight up on the edge of her chair with her hands on her knees and her lips slightly pursed, she was having trouble breathing. I could tell by her conversation: If she was unusually quiet or her answers succinct, she was struggling. I could measure her physical progress by searching Daddy's face: Furrowed lines between his brow meant trouble; a hard, clenched jaw usually meant they had bickered about her taking her medicine.

In preparation for her visit, we'd had two portable oxygen tanks delivered to our house. Mother stayed on her oxygen for most of the morning in eager anticipation of her White House visit. I could feel her trying to conserve her energy. But both Mother and Daddy were animated and talkative. A part of me uncoiled with relief. The Lord was with us.

As I finished a media interview on the phone, they circled each other in my small office, picking up photos, peering out the window. As I watched them moving about, I was suddenly overwhelmed with having both of them there with me, close enough to embrace. Mother ran her index finger along the windowsill, lifting it to the light to inspect it closely. Finding it gray with dust, she feigned a sneeze.

"You'd think they'd keep this place spotless, wouldn't you?" she asked, incredulous and disappointed. She may as well have found a dandelion in the Rose Garden, a paper plate among the White House china, or a fat, shiny, brown roach scurrying for cover in the First Family's kitchen. She peeked under my computer keyboard for more evidence of malfeasance and found it immediately; the wood of my desk was ringed with a dark Diet Coke stain from a morning spill.

I nodded at her without really listening, smiling at her diminutive beauty and at the handsome, rugged lines of my father's face. I wanted to preserve forever the memory of the three of us in my White House office, preparing to walk downstairs to meet the Vice President.

I turned to finish up a media advisory on Bush's upcoming family vacation to Kennebunkport when Mother leaned down close, squeezed my shoulders, and whispered, "My Krissy baby. You give me more pride than you'll ever know."

After a few minutes, we descended carefully down the winding, marble stairs toward the VP's first-floor office. I held her hand protectively, in the same way she used to hold mine years ago when we would descend the winding staircase at the Detroit Institute of Arts during our frequent Saturday afternoon outings. I marveled at the beauty of life's cyclical patterns overlapping with the passage of time: Almost twenty-five years later, we again found ourselves moving in that same cautious way down the winding staircase, hand in hand. But this time it was Mother's hand who sought mine for strength and reassurance.

Once downstairs, our threesome moved carefully down the corridor, a stark, almost comical contrast to the serious White House staffers scurrying past us on their way to meetings and briefings and more meetings.

By the time we arrived at the VP's outer office, Mother was tired and slightly winded. Tim McBride came out and greeted us warmly. Fuller's secretaries hovered around us like well-meaning flight attendants, pampering my parents and clucking quietly. They excused themselves after a shorter-than-usual introduction, making quick, courteous retreats back to their desks. (My guess, although I never asked him, is that good, gentle McBride had already made them aware of Mother's delicate health. McBride was one of the last of the world's true gentlemen.)

Feeling slightly off-center, I waited with my parents in the outer office. Their nervousness was disorienting. For a lifetime I had seen them calm and always in complete control. But on that afternoon, they were different.

After a few minutes of waiting, Daddy stood up and adjusted his tie, throwing the knot even more off-center. Then he sifted through his change, making muffled jingling noises inside his pocket. One of the receptionists looked up from her work with a polite, questioning expression on her face, as if Daddy's jingling change were a request of some kind. People didn't jingle their pocket change much at the White House. It was a hard noise to interpret.

After a minute or two, he sat back down and leaned over toward me, whispering, "How should I address this fella after you've introduced us?" In my eyes, Daddy had always been as brave as a warrior, completely unflappable. Daddy was a hero's hero, larger than life. His every movement was strong and sure (why, I'd seen him slice the head off a red snapper taller and heavier than I was as a child). Suddenly, he was slightly unsure of himself and trying not to show it. There he sat, leaning over to seek advice from his baby girl on the proper way to address the Vice President of the United States. You couldn't help but love him.

"I think 'Mr. Vice President' is fine, Daddy," I answered in my most casual voice. And then to both of them: "He's very laid-back. You'll see. You'll be very comfortable."

Mother rustled softly beside me in her new peach-colored suit. I could tell by the way she held her small, brown hands in her lap that her breathing had stabilized. McBride appeared again, this time to tell us that the VP was running on schedule and would receive us in about two or three more minutes. The countdown began.

I turned to adjust Mother's necklace, then to straighten Daddy's tie after he'd knocked it askew. After years of my parents' fussing and fretting over their youngest child, it was my turn to return the favor. They waited patiently while I tweaked and fiddled with them. I hoped that this was one of the high-lights of their lives. I knew that it was one of mine.

McBride appeared a minute later, still as warm as ever but freshly changed into his "it's showtime, folks" air of crisp au-thority. I could always tell when Bush was anywhere in the vicinity by observing the behavior of the people who sur-rounded him: McBride's posture changed. His gait became more purposeful. His facial expression remained pleasant, but it became slightly shadowed by a new no-nonsense, no-mistakes pallor. Throughout the White House, whenever Bush was anywhere within direct line of vision, body movements—even speech patterns—suddenly became more efficient. It was a place where everyone cued off of each other, as with a finely tuned orchestra or a perfectly choreographed dance troupe. A quick nod of the head by photographer David Valdez meant Bush was following only feet behind. An almost imperceptible narrowing (or rolling) of McBride's eyes as he moved into a room, with Bush a half step behind, warned me that something was amiss, or that the VP was in a quirky or sour mood. The staff—or at least those of us who surrounded Bush with any regularity—had learned how to read each other well.

"The Vice President is ready and eager to meet you now," McBride said to Mother and Daddy, ushering them graciously into the inner office, trying hard to resist the urge to shove these two elderly people through the door in an effort to stay on schedule.

As we approached, I could already see Bush moving toward the door, his long legs taking great strides toward my parents, his hand already outstretched in greeting.

I launched into it. "Mr. Vice President, I'd like you to meet my parents, James and Mary Elizabeth Clark," I said proudly. Hot air swam around my head. Time seemed to have stopped. My father moved to connect with Bush's outstretched arm, but the Vice President changed his mind and withdrew his hand as suddenly as if he'd been burned. Instead, he grabbed Daddy in a full embrace, slapping him heartily on the back. Daddy blinked rapidly several times, mildly surprised at Bush's unanticipated warmth.

And then, turning toward my mother with the deference of a man who's been taught to respect his elders, Bush half-bowed, bending down to envelop her small body in a gentle hug. For an instant, Mother disappeared within his six-foot two-inch frame. All I could hear was the rustling of her new peach gabardine against his worsted wool, and photographer David Valdez clicking and whirring beside me.

"I am honored to meet the two of you," he said warmly. "I am proud to know Kristin. Proud to have her on my staff. She's a shining star." He was dazzling. Daddy blinked again. Mother beamed like a proud peacock, finding her voice: "She's our shining star, too. She's our baby girl."

The air was getting thick. Though embarrassed at suddenly being made the center of attention, I felt almost intoxicated, standing in the White House being complimented by two of the most important people in my life and the Vice President of the United States to boot. But so much gushing had to go. I am uncomfortable with accepting profuse praise. (My sister Noelle, the clinical psychologist, would probably characterize that trait as a sign of insecurity and self-doubt.)

Bush and my parents immediately found a close, comfortable conversation piece, a common bond: their families and the love they felt for their children. 'Twas the season. All three were caught up in the warmth and excitement of spending the holidays with their children. They compared their broods: "You've got me beat by two," Bush joked of his five children. "Together, our kids make an even dozen," he said, smiling at me again.

"Krissy tells us you're about to leave for Kennebunkport for the holidays," Daddy said. I winced slightly. The use of my childhood nickname in the White House suddenly took on an irritating Barbie-doll ring to it. I wondered if Bush would nudge me about it later.

"Absolutely," he answered with a wide grin. "The whole clan will be there," he said. "I know you can relate to this when I say my children rejuvenate me. They keep me grounded and focused. Can't wait to get up there with them," he remarked, turning serious as he gazed at the collection of family photos behind his desk.

"Amen," Daddy said, reaching into his pocket for another jingle of change. "Our children keep us going, too. They mean the world to us," he said. This was unusual for Daddy, who rarely expressed deep emotion, especially with complete strangers.

The tension and the nervousness in the room disappeared.

What remained was a simple thing: three parents who deeply loved their children. The love and pride they felt toward their children created a level playing field which transcended power and political stature, reducing them, quite simply, to proud, loving parents. Although I, too, knew parenthood, having given birth to Lonnie Paul only nine months before, I felt slightly distanced from their bonding, set apart from their deep expressions of affection. My parents and Bush shared between them a lifetime of raising their own progeny. While I certainly knew enough about parenthood to recognize the uncomplicated, unconditional love any mother feels for her child, the entire sensation was still new to me. I was still testing the waters of new motherhood, still getting used to the sensation of being a giver of life. Frankly, I still felt a little wet behind the ears.

Daddy gestured toward the framed photographs clustered on a table slightly behind Bush's desk: the photo of the entire Bush family perched on the rocks at Kennebunkport, the ocean at their backs; the Bush grandchildren at play; Mrs. Bush with her brood.

"You've got a beautiful family, Mr. Vice President," Daddy said. He delivered the "Mr. Vice President" line as though he said it every day. What a smoothie.

"Thank you, sir," Bush answered, smiling. "They keep their old man pretty happy. Tell me about all of yours. What are they doing?"

It was Mother's time to rock and roll. Here was a woman who loved nothing more than fielding inquiries about her children.

In her gracious, casual way, she ticked off our accomplishments: six beautiful girls, one charming boy; the Ph.D.'s, the law and master's degrees, the beautiful grandchildren.

Bush let out a low whistle. I wondered if he'd ever met a black family like ours before, up close and personal. It would have been a sad and sorry shame if we were the first. I assumed (and hoped) that we were not the first, given that his list of friends spanned every corner of the world and his love of people and social interaction was clearly apparent.

Even if we weren't the first, Bush still needed to be reminded that families like mine were not atypical—that there were millions of other black families out there just like us, who had achieved as much and more. He needed to be shown the real thing rather than be briefed by his cadre of Anglo-Saxon academics. He needed to see firsthand that there are black families in every corner of the world who are not dysfunctional, who are closely and spiritually intertwined, who are not the products of broken homes, who are loving and literate, who are not pathological or abusive. My parents were living examples, and it showed in the progeny they produced. In the same way that Mother and Daddy were forming personal perceptions about George Bush as we sat in his office that afternoon, I hoped that he was forming similar perceptions about us—about the perseverance and strength of the black family unit, about the love and laughter we shared between us as naturally and effortlessly as breathing.

"How'd you do it?" Bush asked Mother. "What was your secret to raising a family like that?"

Mother shrugged her small shoulders slightly. She just as easily could have been talking to the mailman down the street. "We brought them up in a loving, intelligent environment," she answered matter-of-factly. "Even as I carried them, before they were even born, we let them know that their potential was limitless." She considered whether to say more, then continued, smiling softly. "We never allowed our expectations to become stumbling blocks for them. From the beginning, excellence and the ability to achieve were all they ever knew. It was the norm rather than the exception."

Boy, was she good. I was moved to hear her speak like that about her children. Hot tears threatened to sting my eyes.

"Well, it worked," Bush answered. "You've got a lot to be proud of."

While we were on the topic of family, I halfway expected Bush to ask some broad question about political affiliation: Were we a family of lifelong Republicans? Did the Clark children (and their parents) have a political lifeline which dated back to the original party of Lincoln? The answer: yes and no. While I often discuss issues and political philosophy with my siblings, we rarely identify ourselves with one party or another. It is assumed, of course—and correctly—that I am a devoted Republican, but party preference is not (and never really has been) a burning issue between us. We respect each other's right to privacy. Thankfully, we are not a family of aggressive political animals.

Stretching his arm out in my direction, Bush continued the sugar-sweet overload: "I guess you don't need me to tell you how special Kristin is." His long arm fell around my shoulders, and he squeezed. "We're very proud of her."

It was too much. "Okay, Mr. Vice President," I said, venturing humor to cut through my embarrassment. "Your check is in the mail." Laughter all around. Out of the corner of my eye, I could see Mother's shoulders stiffen slightly. Her posture told me that she considered my check line inappropriate to have uttered to the second most important political figure in the country. She was the princess of propriety.

Bush opened a desk drawer and removed two small boxes. He handed them to my parents. A vice presidential tie clip for Daddy. A beautiful vice presidential stickpin for Mother. They cooed quietly. McBride appeared at the door with pleading eyes—eyes that told me our boss was about to fall behind in his schedule. As usual, I took my cue and moved to conclude the meeting.

The visit ended with hugs rather than handshakes. Bush promised my parents that he'd "watch over" me after they returned to Detroit. They wished each other a merry Christmas, and I ushered my parents out of the office.

Outside in the hallway, Daddy became the father again. He leaned toward me and said, "Real nice fella. Very genuine, down-to-earth. We're awfully proud of you, sweetheart. Now go upstairs and get your mother's coat. We'll wait for you here."

I smiled to myself that the meeting went so well.

At twenty-eight years old, I had been blessed to give Mother the gift of a lifetime.

It was her last Christmas.

. . . . .

OVER THE NEXT NINE MONTHS, Mother's health continued to deteriorate. I made more frequent trips home to Detroit. I became irritable, listless. I was losing sleep, and my concentration level dropped dramatically. Our small press office staff, bless their souls, rallied behind me to redistribute my workload during my frequent absences. Never once did they complain or gripe. Their support made the entire difficult process a little more bearable.

As Mother became even worse, I felt I needed to share the news with Bush. As much else as he had happening in his life, and with the election then only weeks away, he still would want to know.

The two of us sat in his OEOB office one afternoon in August of 1988, the day he left for the Republican convention. The mood in the White House was reasonably upbeat; the general sentiment was that Bush's acceptance speech would put him over the top and position him as the clear victor—or at least the confident, commanding standard-bearer of the Republican party. Everyone recognized and appreciated the magnitude of this trip, especially Bush.

Steve and I had arranged a series of preconvention media interviews, and Bush was just finishing up with a media session in his OEOB office. It would be the last time I saw him before he left for the convention, and I wanted to wish him luck, to assure him of the pride we felt in him—to remind him again of our confidence and our support. Daddy, too, had asked that I pass along their best wishes for a successful convention.

Bush smiled a tired smile and thanked me, genuinely, for my words of support. As I passed along Daddy's message, he looked at me for a minute or two from behind his desk. Perhaps he sensed my uneasiness.

"How are your parents doing?" he asked, studying my face.

He had made the way for me to share my burden.

"Dad's good," I answered in a whisper, suddenly fighting tears. "My mother's pretty sick," I said simply. "Not doing well at all." I was beginning to sound like Bush, who had a habit of speaking in incomplete sentence fragments and uttering ideas in short, staccato bursts.

I shook my head, afraid to continue speaking.

"Oh my Lord," Bush said, leaning forward in his chair. "I am so sorry to hear it. Is she in the hospital?" he asked.

"In and out" was all I could manage.

"Is there anything I can do?" he asked. The question was heartfelt, but it seemed strange. Like *what?* I thought to myself. Can you use your influence and convene a conference call of the world's most knowledgeable and experienced medical experts to make everything all right again? Can you use your political power to put things back into place? Can you call her doctor, or maybe the chairman of the hospital's board of directors, and demand that she not be forgotten or neglected like so many other sick, elderly people at the end of their lives? (I always had the gnawing sense that older people were often given less than adequate medical care, either consciously or subconsciously, simply because they had reached the end of their lives.)

I looked at the Vice President: What is it *you* or *anyone* can really do? I thought.

Bush still leaned forward, waiting for an answer, biting the inside of his lower lip. Lip biting was his habit when he fretted or concentrated very hard. "You holding up okay?"

I could only shake my head. My chin trembled slightly.

Realizing I was on the verge of tears and unable to continue speaking, Bush uttered quiet words of encouragement and support. He asked me to thank Mother and Daddy for the kind, supportive send-off.

The reporter sat through our entire conversation, not knowing exactly what to do. She shifted slightly in her chair, pretending to study her notes. Under normal circumstances, I wouldn't have broached a personal, emotional matter like this with Bush in the presence of a reporter. But these weren't normal circumstances. Mother was seriously ill. Bush was about to leave on the most important trip of his political career. And this was my last chance to speak with him before he left. I felt too sad to be made uncomfortable by the reporter's presence.

After our conversation, I shepherded the reporter out of the White House and retreated upstairs to my office. I felt relieved to have shared the burden, but hot, heavy tears still stung my face. I sat at my desk, crying for Mother, struggling to compose myself, fighting to find the emotional energy to make it through the rest of a busy day. About twenty minutes later, Tim McBride stepped quietly into my office.

"The Vice President wanted you to see this before he

departed for New Orleans," McBride said to me with sad, sympathetic eyes, holding out an envelope. "It's only just gone out."

Inside, a photocopy of a note card with Bush's southpaw scrawl, addressed to my mother, noting that while he was about to leave for the biggest event of his political career, he wanted to send his best wishes for a speedy recovery and to express his pride and gratitude for having me on his team. On top of that photocopied note, another handwritten message to me, from Bush: "Keep your chin up and stay strong for your mother. We're all here if you need us."

. . . . .

MOTHER WAS HEARTENED by the note, and very proud to receive it. She placed it proudly in a small, gold easel and displayed it in our living room on Woodland Street. Over the next several weeks, I spent a lot of time traveling back and forth to Detroit to visit Mother. Her condition deteriorated even more.

I got the call while I was in the shower.

"Krissy, you better come home, honey," Joann said gently over the phone from Detroit. "We had to bring Mother back to the hospital. She's going to need emergency surgery, and we all need to be here for her." I was still dripping wet, standing there naked in our bedroom, listening to the urgency in Jo's voice, fighting panic.

A little more than two hours later, Lonnie, Lonnie Paul, and I were in the hospital surgical waiting room in Detroit with the rest of my family. Mother did make it through the surgery, but the journey had only just begun.

The waiting was the worst. The pain of sitting there in

that waiting room for hours on end, visualizing Mother only a few feet down the hall, still dazed from the surgery and tethered to lifelines and feeding tubes, was more than I could bear. I recoiled to somewhere deep within myself. The television mounted from the ceiling provided much needed distraction for everyone in Sinai Hospital's cardiac intensive care waiting room.

I was sitting in that same waiting room on September 7, 1988, when Bush's infamous Pearl Harbor gaffe occurred—when he identified incorrectly the anniversary date of that historic event. Departing from his prepared text to the American Legion (one of many campaign speeches on "peace through strength"), Bush remarked to the crowd, many of them World War II veterans themselves, "I wonder how many Americans remember, today is Pearl Harbor Day? Forty-seven years ago to this very day," Bush continued, "we were hit and hit hard at Pearl Harbor and we were not ready."

I watched the television monitor closely and imagined my White House friends and colleagues wincing in pained embarrassment as the Vice President spoke. The people sitting around me in the waiting room sat forward in anticipation, excited about the prospect of discovering his mistake, eager to be diverted from their own personal traumas. Bush's error that afternoon proved a much needed distraction to their worries.

"In a Bush administration, that lesson would not be forgotten," he continued, still not yet realizing his mistake. A legionnaire in the audience shook his head furiously at Bush, signaling the mistake. I watched as Bush's facial expression changed. Finally, he realized his error and moved immediately to recant.

He apologized, recovering from his stumble. "Did I say

165

September 7th?" he asked, embarrassed. "Sorry about that. *December* 7th, 1941. I'm glad I corrected that."

But it was too late. The gaffe immediately became the lead story on every major network that evening, and the national media refused to let it die for the rest of the campaign. George Bush, decorated war hero running hard on a platform of patriotism and military strength, had forgotten the date of the attack on Pearl Harbor. It was spoon-fed ammunition for the Democrats. And it was the talk of the waiting room that afternoon.

"And he's supposed to be a war hero?" the woman sitting next to me snorted, addressing no one in particular. "He flew combat missions during World War II and can't even remember the anniversary date of Pearl Harbor?" she asked with a nasty grunt. How could she have ever guessed that the quiet, teary-eyed young black woman sitting in the corner was one of Bush's staffers?

"What an idiot," she said with clear disgust.

"Idiot" was more than I could handle.

"The man made a *mistake,* dammit," I answered back in a hot whisper, my head in my hands. I even surprised myself.

"All of us in this room have loved ones lying five feet down this hall, struggling to stay alive, and all you can do is bitch and moan about a simple *mistake?"* I asked. "He's human like everybody else. Get off of his ass."

Stunned silence.

"Get off his *ass,"* I said again for effect, letting the s sound escape through my lips in an evil hiss. It felt good.

I was white-hot angry, but certainly not at Bush for making the mistake. I was angry at that stupid woman. I was angry

166

that Mother was so deathly ill. Compared with life-and-death problems, Bush's gaffe seemed insignificant and irrelevant at best. I had had it up to my red, tear-filled eyeballs with political armchair quarterbacks. I took it personally. And I was dismayed that Bush's mistake would even be a concern to her. Certainly there were other, more urgent matters on her mind!

I would probably have even said more, but poor Daddy was coming toward my chair, his eyes imploring my sisters to help calm me down. I saw the slightest hint of a surprised smile on Noelle's face. Joann winked her eye at me so quickly it was almost imperceptible. For two weeks, I had been withdrawn, sullen, and almost completely silent. But I had finally spoken.

My outburst that afternoon was the first time I admitted that Mother might actually be "struggling" to stay alive. But I somehow still refused to accept her death as a realistic possibility. I had tricked myself into believing that no matter how sick she became, she'd be fine once we got her home where she belonged. All we had to do was get her back onto Woodland Street, in her own, comfortable home, among her own family —close and reconnected to everything she knew and loved.

A breathing tube inserted down Mother's throat prevented her from speaking. But her eyes told me that she was petrified. Although she was glad to see her children gathered around her bedside, our presence, and the beeping, pulsating life-support equipment surrounding her bed, told her that something was irrevocably, horrifyingly wrong. Her eyes told me that she was appalled and paralyzed with fear at her sudden and total inability to communicate.

"Please, God," I prayed. "Smile onto my mother. Let her be stronger. Let there be some sign of improvement."

Soon, her eyes no longer connected with mine. They were clouded over. But she could immediately feel my presence at her bedside. She would turn her head slightly in my direction, but she could no longer focus.

I inhaled slowly, deeply, trying to maintain control and hide the shock and disappointment at her weakened condition. It was the first time in my life that God had not answered my prayers. Taking her hand and leaning close in, I whispered, "I love you, Ma. I'll always love you."

I didn't want to cry; she would sense my tears even before they started flowing. I tried breathing slow and easy to maintain calm.

"Whatever happens," I continued, "every one of your children will be okay. Daddy will be okay. Lonnie Paul will be okay." I rubbed her hand, unable to continue. I didn't want her to worry about having to let go; she needed to be assured that it was all right to leave us where we were. I wanted to hold her warm hands in mine forever.

"You are beautiful," I whispered into her ear. Mother's looks were always important to her. She needed to be told that her physical beauty and her dignity remained intact. But my time was running out, and the nurses were strict about enforcing the fifteen-minute intervals.

"I know you can hear me, so listen carefully," I instructed, leaning in closer.

I couldn't believe I was actually where I was, saying the things I was saying. I didn't know whether my words would be the last she'd hear—whether this would be the last time I would see her alive. It felt surreal. But there was no time left for hesitation or reflection. I didn't want my words to sound like a final goodbye, but I knew I had to speak quickly and clearly. It was imperative that she comprehend. It was the hardest thing I've ever done.

"I am your baby girl—the last of your legacy," I said in a proud whisper. I was inches away from her left ear. "And I promise you that I will continue the family. I'll have more children." I paused, struggling to remain composed. "You have five beautiful grandchildren who have already carried us over into the next generation," I said, referring to Joann's two children, Paige and Brant; Nikki's daughter, Kianna; Ingrid's son, Kevin; and my own Lonnie Paul. "All that we are—and all that you have helped us become—will last forever. We will live forever, Ma."

She squeezed my hand and turned her head ever so slightly.

"I love you more than you know," I said, hugging her small frame as delicately as I could. I felt the nurse's presence behind me. My time with Mother was up. I touched her warm, wonderful hands goodbye—those healing hands that calmed my nerves and soothed my soul.

· · · · ·

To everyone's surprise, Mother improved marginally the next day. The doctors even told us to go back to our homes and return to work. Death was not imminent, they believed, and they were even realistically hoping for improvement. She'd made it through surgery, they said—through the toughest part of the journey. Now they needed to focus on rebuilding her strength.

Joann and I flew back to Washington together. It was a blessing that I ended up living in the same city with my oldest sister. She was so strong and wise, just like Mother. She was a good woman to linger close to; her strength emanated toward me like warm rays of sun.

I edged back into life at work and at home. I could breathe a little easier. My concentration level began to improve. I allowed myself to believe, again, that the worst was now behind us.

God had answered my prayers after all.

CHAPTER 10

. . . . . .

*A Time
for Grief*

. . . . .

"Now is your time for grief."
—JOHN 16:22

ABOUT A WEEK after I returned from Detroit, God changed
His mind again. I had just returned to my office from a
West Wing meeting with Marlin Fitzwater's staff when I
looked up from my desk to see Lonnie standing in front of me.
He filled the room. Three thoughts surfaced simultaneously:
Who had cleared him into the complex without telling me?
Why on earth was he suddenly standing in my office in the
middle of the afternoon? What was that strange expression on
his face that I'd never seen before? My heart stopped. I felt as
though I was going to lose control of my bladder.

Lonnie moved quickly toward me, bringing me close inside his arms. For once, I couldn't hear his heartbeat as I rested
my face against his chest. Before he'd even uttered a word, I

171

was already going into shock. Everything sounded muffled. Out of the corner of my eye I saw Steve Hart reach in quietly to close my office door. He already knew something. My sphincter muscle tingled.

"We need to get on a plane to Detroit," he said softly, stroking my hair. "Your mother's had a cardiac arrest. Joann is going to pick up Lonnie Paul from home, and we'll all meet at the airport."

Something snapped inside of me. What kind of cruel game was God playing with me? I thought He'd allowed me to believe that Mother was out of danger. I suddenly lost the strength to keep standing. Lonnie must have called for help, because Sean Walsh came in immediately. Lonnie and Sean guided me gently into Steve's office and sat with me on the couch. Sean ran to get my car, and I heard Steve's muffled voice talking on the phone to someone in his serious voice. A White House physician appeared seconds later, bringing me sedatives from the medical unit. I must have really been pretty bad off.

We moved slowly toward the office door, Lonnie on my one side, Steve on the other. I was moving underwater, unable to catch my breath, stuck in a slow-motion nightmare. Even so, I remember being cognizant of the staffers who watched from their doors as we moved down the hall. Word had traveled fast. But no matter how hard it got, I wouldn't lose face in front of everyone. I held my head high as we walked, and I gently shook away Steve's hand at my elbow. I looked straight ahead, unwavering. I wouldn't lose face. I came from stronger, prouder stock than that.

When we arrived at Detroit Metropolitan Airport, Joann was paged on the house phone. Minutes later, she returned, her eyes pink. "It was Daddy," she said. "He told us to go straight home rather than to the hospital." I tingled again, disconnecting from some part of myself. Lonnie Paul banged at my knees with his red plastic fire engine. I picked him up and patted his soft hair absently, nuzzling my face into his neck. His warm, soapy smell comforted me.

A distant relative picked us up at the airport. I stared at the back of his head as we made our way down the highway and into the early evening traffic, uninterested in trying to interpret his body movements or his demeanor. Did he know whether Mother was still alive? Had he heard the news? Why hadn't one of my sisters come to pick us up? The drive was quiet, devoid of small talk. The sun was setting; purple streaks marked the sky.

As we rounded the corner to our house, the first thing I noticed was a cluster of people standing outside on our lawn. The neighbors were standing in their driveways. I opened the door and leapt out of the car while it was still moving, running up the porch steps and into the kitchen, looking for Mother.

Inside, a strange scene. Aunt Bunny, Mother's sister, was standing in our kitchen, frying chicken. In all her life, Aunt Bunny never fried so much as one piece of anything in our house. She refused to turn around when she heard me come in. Daddy stood at the kitchen counter, looking lost, alone, and suddenly much smaller than I'd ever seen him before. Aunt Bunny remained at our stove, wearing Mother's apron with the grapefruit pattern on the front, standing in the place where only Mother used to stand.

"Where's Mother?" I demanded. They were my first words. There was no time for greetings or salutations. I was on the verge of hysteria. Daddy turned toward me, his eyes ripping into that part of me I had fought so hard to protect for so many months. He stepped toward me.

"Where's Mother?" I asked again, screaming this time, angered by all the blank, stupid-looking faces in my house. At the sound of my scream all activity stopped, except for Aunt Bunny, who kept turning the chicken. No one spoke.

I was losing control. I disconnected from myself, observing the scene from somewhere high above. By this time Lonnie had made his way into the house, pushing his way through the crowd, calling my name. As he moved toward the kitchen he barked an order for someone to take Lonnie Paul upstairs, away from the commotion.

Daddy's voice broke. He looked so very, very sad.

"She's gone," he answered. "She couldn't go on."

"Where's Mother?" I screamed again. I turned to my sister Noelle, ignoring Daddy. I didn't want to hear his words. He didn't know what he was saying. He had obviously been under too much pressure and had lost his grip on reality. He was delirious, nonsensical. I was sliding downhill fast, a breath away from complete hysteria.

Noelle, sweet Noelle, tried to embrace me, tears streaking her pretty brown face. "She just died about two hours ago, honey. She's gone." My sisters immediately moved in around me like the Secret Service, closing ranks, trying hard to rally strength and preserve that last ounce of fierce family pride.

Something in me died along with Mother right then. I prayed that I would die, too. I prayed that the news would shock me, literally, to death. I couldn't keep living without her. I felt an immediate, deep, visceral anger at Mother for leaving me, for giving up on life, and for not being strong enough or willing enough to fight the good fight. Of course it was completely irrational; only days before, I had all but told her to let go. But still, I heard myself asking, Aren't we a family of strong black women? Weren't we raised to endure, excel, achieve, surmount all challenges? How could she have given up when she spent her entire lifetime teaching us not to?

She had succumbed to the challenge, leaving me there to fend for myself in a world without her. Leaving Daddy a widower and all seven of her children motherless. Abandoning her baby girl forever. It felt as if someone had taken a pair of rusty garden shears and snipped through the umbilical cord that had so closely and inextricably tied us together. For the first time, Mother had suddenly let my hand slip from within her strong, protective grasp, and I went plunging headlong into a dark, endless, horrifying abyss. I knew I wouldn't be able to bear the pain, to withstand the trauma. My sisters pressed against me, showering me with their support, rocking me in a collective embrace.

Lonnie reached me through the throng of people at the precise moment that I began to crumble. I must have been waiting to feel his presence. The moment he touched my arm, everything washed away. For once, there was no more pride.

"Mommieeeeee!" I was a child again, screaming ferociously. My back slid down along the wall and I pitched forward, collapsing onto the kitchen floor. Lonnie lunged for me.

It took Lonnie and four of my relatives—all large grown men well over six feet tall—to hold me down on the kitchen floor. I looked up into Lonnie's face as I lay on the floor; tears were streaming down his face, too. Daddy knelt over me, but he did not try to subdue me with the others. He whispered comforting things down into my face, looking lost and confused. A kitchen chair crashed to the floor, toppled from the

175

force of my kicks. My clenched fist connected hard with flesh and muscle; I had punched someone powerfully, probably in the chest. Someone's eyeglasses fell to the kitchen floor. A water glass fell from the table, shattering and cutting my leg as I thrashed.

Inside our house on Woodland Street, pandemonium. Outside, Cookie was trying to reach me through the crowd. She could hear my hysterical screams and wanted desperately to be close. I heard murmuring. Someone was calling for help.

Minutes later, Tony Porter, a lifelong family friend and physician, pushed his way into our crowded kitchen.

"Okay, baby girl, you've had enough," he said, deftly assembling the hypodermic needle which he'd pulled from his bag, studying me as I lay sprawled on the kitchen floor.

"Goddamn it," he yelled at the crowd over his shoulder as he knelt over me, trying to find a vein, "let's give this child some air, people."

I fainted before he even had a chance to inject me.

· · · · ·

IN MANY WAYS, the day after Mother's death was even more painful than the moment I actually received the news. My body felt physically sore, as if I'd undergone major surgery. My legs and arms were dark with bruises; I was in deep shock. My vision wasn't exactly blurred, but colors seemed muted, watered down. Even Lonnie Paul's bright red fire engine looked rusty brown.

I temporarily lost my ability to read; it came in fits and starts. I could identify individual words on a printed page, but comprehending those words was beyond my grasp. Ironically, I could still write fairly well, and my sisters urged me to write Mother's eulogy, hoping that the exercise would rejuvenate my darkened spirit.

Writing Mother's eulogy did seem to help guide me back on track, but I still had no words for speaking. My family was worried. My beautiful sisters rallied around me, patting my forehead with cool cloths, hugging me quietly, showering sad affection on Lonnie Paul, all the while draped in their own dark, thick grief. But they had already begun the process of picking up the pieces and moving forward—preparing the funeral arrangements, hovering close to Daddy, receiving guests, talking quietly together at the kitchen table. Lonnie was my haven; he never once left my side. He was my firewall, my Rock of Gibraltar. The Lord had sent me this man to stand watch over me.

All of our extended family filled the house with food and warmth. Cookie came to the house every day, studying me carefully, holding my hands in hers. She'd cock her head ever so slightly in measured concentration, listening to more than the few words I spoke, trying to sense whether I was out of danger.

Flowers, cards, and messages of condolence flowed into our house in a steady stream. I was still unable to read the ones which were addressed to me.

"Here's another one, a telegram," my uncle said to me as we all sat in the den the day after Mother's death.

"You read it, please," I said to my uncle, turning my head away.

He opened the envelope and read aloud to the group. It was a telegram from the Vice President and Mrs. Bush, urging us to be strong and expressing their heartfelt sympathy.

"Well, I'll just be damned," my uncle said. "A message of sympathy from the Vice President of the United States. If that don't beat all," he said. He reread it again to himself, his lips moving silently, as if to make sure he'd read it correctly. My distant relatives knew I worked in the White House, but I don't think they ever visualized me working closely or directly with Bush, or even knowing him, for that matter. They were surprised that Bush would even have known that Mother was gone, much less that he would have responded directly to her passing.

My uncle rose from his chair in the den and began moving slowly through the house, reading and rereading the telegram to clusters of people in the living room, to people out on the front porch, to the young people sitting on the stairs. Each time, he read with more flourish, pausing for dramatic effect before coming to the final two words, the name of the sender: "George Bush," he said, smiling.

In his unique way, and without even realizing it, Bush had not only comforted me and everyone in my house, but also reinforced the pride in all of us. Mother was a glorious, dignified woman; her life and her death were worthy of a personal message from the White House. For people who didn't know him outside of his White House image, that message humanized George Bush. He had reached straight into our living room, into our own white house on Woodland Street on the north End of Detroit, to show that he cared and that he, too, wanted to pay final respects to this wonderful, remarkable woman.

Through it all, messages and telegrams kept pouring in from the White House, from Bush's vice presidential staff.

Phone calls, flowers, and letters trickled in from a wide range of staff people—from the highest-level staffers to my friends in the mailroom and on the housekeeping staff. The friendships I had created since I'd joined the White House staff felt like a family. Just like my sisters, my colleagues, too, rallied around me, showering me with encouragement and support. It made the grieving process easier.

The family decided to establish a foundation in Mother's memory, with the donated proceeds going toward a college scholarship for some deserving African-American student. As important as higher education was to Mother, she would have wanted it. It helps to have friends in the media; the *Detroit Free Press* ran a mention of the foundation in its obituary, and even *USA Today* ran an obituary and mentioned the foundation, giving it national exposure.

A day after the news of the foundation became public, we received our first official donation. We were sitting at the kitchen table when Daddy walked in, carrying an envelope. Inside, a single check for $250. Signed: George Bush. Written in his own, familiar hand, it was drawn from his personal checking account.

"God*damn,*" the same uncle said again. "Is he flying in for the funeral, too? This man is serious about his condolences, isn't he?" he said. "How could I *not* respect a man, black or white, Republican or Democrat, who gives my sister's memory that kind of respect?" he asked, looking across the table at me with tired, smiling eyes.

The impression Bush's generosity left upon the people in my kitchen and in my close-knit community was personal and lasting. Daddy said later that there was quite a pleasant commotion when he walked to our neighborhood bank to deposit the check into the foundation account. Ours was a tiny inner-city branch whose standard transaction usually involved the processing of Social Security and welfare checks. The bank tellers, mostly young black women, smiled and giggled in excitement. They, too, had known and loved Mother. They, too, were moved and touched by Bush's direct outreach.

Bush's reaction to Mother's death acted as a catalyst to form our friendship; it added a new dimension to my perception of him. In my eyes, our friendship grew out of that conflict: He had evolved from a boss and the second most powerful man in the free world to a father-figure-friend who cared enough to reach out to ease the pain.

. . . . .

WITH THE PRESIDENTIAL ELECTION now only weeks away, I began to feel the need to get back to work. I had worked too long and too hard on this campaign to sit the election out. I could finish licking my wounds when I got back to Washington.

I eased myself back to the White House, working quietly behind an office door that was always closed. In the media business, where the written and spoken word are so critically important, my cognitive weaknesses must have certainly put a damper on my performance. But if they did, no one mentioned it.

I saw Bush several days after I returned from Mother's funeral. I was going to accompany him to a speech. He was standing at the elevator outside of his OEOB office, reviewing his note cards, when he looked up and saw me. Without a word or a greeting, he opened his arms wide for an embrace, then looked closely into my face.

"What are you doing back here?" he asked. "How are you feeling?"

"I felt like I needed to come back, sir. Like I was missing out."

"Missing *out?*" Bush asked incredulously. Tim McBride stood at his side, looking down at the second hand on his watch. A cluster of other aides stood nearby, waiting for the entourage to begin movement.

"I don't want to hurt your feelings," Bush replied quietly in what was almost a whisper, "but if you're not ready to come back, then you should be at home, with your family." He sounded stern.

An agent shifted his weight from one foot to another. Bush was biting the inside of his lip again. I couldn't tell whether it was because he was displeased with the speech or displeased to see me. I bristled slightly.

"You're good at what you do," Bush assured me, not wanting to hurt my feelings, "but we can win this election without you," he finished. "Go home and be with your family."

Here I had planned on thanking him for all he'd done, for all the compassion he'd shown, and here he was standing there telling me, in effect, to get out and go home, that my services were not necessary to win the election. "Shouldn't you be home with your family?" he asked again, this time more gently.

"I'm fine, sir," I answered with more of a clip in my voice than I'd intended. "A little tired, but fine."

I was in this thing for the long haul, and I didn't need him or anybody else telling me what was best for me. If I'd needed more time to recuperate at home, I wouldn't have been standing there, dammit. I was made of stronger stuff than that. I felt slightly angry that Bush had questioned my judgment about returning to work, however subtly. In hindsight, I realize that he might simply have been uncomfortable with the subject. The topic of death and dying—and having to respond to someone who is deeply grieving—is difficult at best.

Wanting to end my conversation with Bush, I turned and began talking with McBride.

With a slightly raised eyebrow, an exaggerated sweeping motion of his long arm, and without another word, Bush held open the doors of the elevator and allowed me to enter. Taking Bush's outstretched arm as a cue, the rest of the entourage also moved fluidly into motion behind us.

· · · · ·

BUSH'S REACTION helped spur me into action. His reservations about my returning to work so soon made me want to prove, perhaps to myself as much as to others, that I could weather the storm. After a long hiatus, my pride finally began to stir. I had to demonstrate that I could keep on keepin' on. Perhaps it was the generations of strong black women who came before me, whispering into my ear:

"Okay, girl. It's time to wipe your weeping eyes. Always remember that in everything you do, in every move you make, you are being silently observed, judged, and evaluated by your superiors, your peers, and your subordinates—perhaps more closely and more critically because you are the one black in a sea of white faces. How well you handle this crisis is an indication of the strength (or weakness) of your character; it is a measure of your resilience and tenacity. Pick yourself up and get yourself together."

In my eyes, maintaining my professionalism was almost a test; I knew I would be judged and graded. I felt a commitment to stand tall, not only for myself but for all women, and for all African-Americans. I didn't want to do anything to perpetuate the age-old, cobweb-wearing stereotype that women under pressure were a sniveling, whining bunch of uncontrollable tear ducts—or, in search of a less cruel characterization, that we buckled under the slightest pressure and simply couldn't hang when the situation got rough.

It was also imperative that "the black woman" on Bush's vice presidential staff, whom these blue-blooded, fairly high-brow white men saw every day, remain strong, proud, and sure of herself—no matter what. I represented a race, a culture, an entire world which these white males would never know intimately or personally; I was fully aware that their perceptions of black folks could subtly, in some indecipherable way, be influenced by their interaction with me. In many cases, I was their primary connection to all things ethnic, or at least all things black. I owed it to my black female sisters everywhere— be they Republican, Democrat, Independent, or, hell, even unregistered—to convey a positive image. Throughout my tenure in the White House, I felt as though I was, in a sense, representing black women everywhere. My responsibility was universal.

With few exceptions, my colleagues on Bush's staff were smart, engaging, and fun. But I knew I could never "hang" with them in the same way that I hung with my homegirls during trips home to Detroit. Inside the White House, I could never allow myself to express the full scope of my grief. No matter how cozy things became, a part of my guard was always up. The White House was a place that did not easily lend itself to open expressions of grief or emotional suffering. Everyone watched, and everyone judged. All eyes could see everything.

Seven months later, on the day that the White House made public Bush's 1987 tax returns, the issue of Mother's death surfaced publicly—in the form of an inquiry from a press corps reporter during Fitzwater's daily briefing. Her death could know no solitude.

I was slowly recuperating, immersing myself in my work and wrapping myself closely around my family and my Lord for emotional reassurance and spiritual strength. Bush's tax returns were made available to the press on the same day that Bush, by then President, was to address the American Society of Newspaper Editors, an influential group of the nation's leading newspaper editors who had appealed to me months earlier to request his participation. I had strongly proposed Bush's participation months before the meeting, and the approval had finally come back from the White House scheduling staff, then from Sununu, and finally from the President himself. The group was convening its annual meeting at the J. W. Marriott Hotel a few blocks away from the White House. I, along with Domestic Policy Advisor Roger Porter and Director of Speechwriting Chriss Winston, briefed the President in the Oval Office about an hour before the speech. Immediately after the briefing, I left ahead of the President's entourage to make sure everything was running smoothly at the Marriott.

Arriving early gave me time to organize the ASNE leadership in the hotel holding room for a quick introduction and meeting with Bush upon his arrival. The Secret Service and the White House advance team had determined days beforehand which entrances and corridors would be used—even which exits were available for an emergency.

I looked at my watch. The agent in the outside hallway poked his head inside the room to give me a quick nod. Translated: The President's motorcade had just pulled into the hotel complex. "Timberwolf" was on the premises.

With calm precision, I arranged the ASNE leadership into a short receiving line, "blocking" the shot of where the group would stand with the President during the quick photo session. One of the ASNE executives had his young daughter with him —a sweet, demure girl, but I instinctively knew that her presence would slow Bush down by at least a minute or two. Young people were endearing, yes, but—much like elderly groups wanting to spend time with him—they always delayed his schedule. (The age of the audience Bush was scheduled to meet with at any given time was always an important detail to consider when we were planning the precise timing of his schedule. We automatically lobbed on several extra minutes when planning events with the elderly and with youth.)

I glanced around the room one final time, making mental checknotes of everything Bush might need during his few minutes in the room; a pitcher of ice water rested on a table in the corner, covered with plastic wrap.

I moved to the outside hall and waited with the agent, watching as all of my cues fell comfortably, predictably into place. First to appear in the entourage was silver-haired, smiling David Valdez, moving fast as he adjusted the flash on his camera. The smile translated: Bush was in a good, relaxed mood. McBride came next, head down, adjusting his shirt cuffs as he walked, seconds away from handing the President his file cards which held the text of his speech. Next came one or two agents talking into their wrists. And then, finally, Bush and his men: Marlin Fitzwater; National Security Advisor Brent Scowcroft, white-haired and drowsy-looking; Attorney General Richard Thornburgh (the topic of the address was ethics in government, and for this reason Thornburgh had been invited); weeble-wobble John Sununu; and finally the President, standing taller than all of the men surrounding him.

Bush spied me immediately at the other end of the hall.

"Okay, Ms. Taylor. What have you gotten me into now?" he joked. Valdez's cue had been on the mark: Bush was indeed in a comfortable, relaxed mood. "These editors gonna burn me at the stake?" he asked. Fortunately he was far enough down the hall so that the newspaper executives lined up inside the holding room couldn't hear his comments. I could see the headline now: BUSH PREDICTS SURE DOOM: "NEWSPAPER EDITORS WILL BURN ME AT STAKE," HE SCREAMS. Sensational journalism at its best.

I met Bush halfway down the hall and briefed him again quickly as we walked, reviewing the names of the people who were waiting inside the holding room, and zipping off three or four possible issues which might surface during the on-the-record question and answer session following his speech. I re-capped quickly as we walked, offering suggested language:

- Oliver North's trial: "You obviously cannot comment on anything to do with Oliver North's trial while it is in progress."

186

- Government involvement in the *Exxon Valdez* oil spill: "You won't settle for anything less than a complete restoration of the environment, which is why last week you announced new federal efforts to help in the cleanup."

- Drug czar Bill Bennett's newly unveiled aggressive antidrug, anticrime plan for Washington, D.C.: "You stand fully behind Bill Bennett's ambitious plan, and you're hopeful that Mayor Barry will work closely with us as we work to drive the scourge of drugs from this city."

"Gotcha," Bush said, cocking his head slightly to the side and concentrating as I spoke.

As we entered the holding room, I introduced Bush to each ASNE executive. One of the editors, John Seigenthaler, was my old boss and mentor at *USA Today*. It was a pleasing, proud moment for me to make the introduction. When Bush reached the end of the receiving line, he turned to me quietly, his back momentarily facing the ASNE executives, and extended his arm for a handshake. "And who might you be?" he whispered, bending low in a gentle bow. The ASNE people strained their necks, trying to hear what Bush was whispering to me. "I don't believe we've met," he continued. He was in a silly mood. I rolled my eyes toward the ceiling, deciding to go along with his joke. "Oh, I'm sorry, sir. Franklin," I whispered. "As in Aretha," I continued, taking his hand and pumping it furiously. "Hail from the big Motor City," I said. After several minutes of discussion and a quick photo op, the group began to move.

"Love your music," Bush said quietly over his shoulder as he moved. We weaved through the back hallways of the Marriott Hotel toward the stage. Not having heard the quiet exchange between us earlier, no one in the entourage really knew what Bush meant by his "love your music" comment anyway.

As we made our way down the back halls, Marlin leaned his head in my direction and whispered, "We released Bush's tax returns to the media this morning. I got some media questions about the President donating money to your mother's foundation."

The light, jovial mood Bush had established in the holding room immediately dissipated. I caught my breath at the very mention of Mother. Several of my emotional stitches popped rudely from their wound. Marlin must have read it on my face.

"Nothing serious," he continued, his arm resting lightly at my back as we negotiated through the back hallways. "A couple of reporters just wanted to know what, precisely, the foundation was, and why Bush had donated money to it."

"What'd you tell them?" I asked, trying to remain calm. It had taken me seven months to quietly tuck away at least some of the painful memories. Now the memories were flooding back—as a result of a White House press briefing in the lower West Wing press office, no less.

"I said that Bush had donated $250 to a memorial fund which had been established in memory of the mother of one of his staffers," Marlin answered. "They wanted to know which staffer it was, and I told them it was you. I explained that he made the donation when he was Vice President, that it was unsolicited, and that he simply wanted to make a contribution to the foundation." Marlin looked at my face as we walked, continuing, "I wanted you to be aware of it . . . I'll probably buck any further detailed media inquiries about the foundation to you, if there are any," he said gently. "You know more about all the details than I do, kiddo. You okay?" I was touched that he was trying to be so gentle.

But I wasn't okay. I sat through Bush's entire address distracted and in pain. I longed for Lonnie's closeness, to hear his voice. After seven months, I still wasn't handling her death effectively.

. . . . .

Bush's speech was well received, as was the Q&A session. It was comforting to look out into the audience and recognize so many old friends and faces from my journalism days. They nodded and smiled. Sure enough, just as I had predicted earlier, Bush did receive a question about the North trial—from none other than a good friend of mine and former colleague at *USA Today,* Dan Martin.

I leaned over and whispered to Sununu, "Bingo. We figured someone would ask about North."

"Who *is* that guy?" Sununu shot back. "What an asshole."

"He's actually a friend of mine," I answered, slightly offended. And then I said, in Martin's defense, "The question is legitimate, and we knew it was coming. It didn't take the President by surprise," I whispered. "I think we're okay."

"Well, just *fuck* 'em," Sununu whispered. I swear. Sununu was always ready to fuck somebody. "Some asshole journalist is always trying to start some shit," he hissed.

Because of either sheer luck or divine intervention (I prefer to believe it was divine intervention), my direct contact with Sununu was infrequent. But I was amazed at how often he

189

uttered the "f-word" during the few conversations we did have. Perhaps it made him feel invincible. Or macho. Or virile. Or wild and bestial.

Sununu seemed to be in a constant state of simmering, red-hot anger, always threatened by what he perceived as unwarranted advances against him or the President, always poised like a plump python ready to strike, ready to exact revenge on anyone he regarded as an enemy. He had a tendency to alienate people and, put simply, to hurt their feelings. Rich Bond, a lifelong friend of the Bush family who left the White House in February of 1992 to become chairman of the Republican National Committee, told me that Sununu "was an overzealous gatekeeper who didn't permit those who once had a very positive relationship with George Bush in the past to continue that relationship." Something sparked in Bond's eyes as he spoke. I couldn't tell whether it was sadness or anger. Perhaps it was both. "Those of us who loved George Bush," Bond said of Sununu, "suddenly found ourselves with the ax between our eyes, or in our back, or chopping off our arm or our tongue. It was totally unnecessary."

Sununu wielded his access to the Oval Office like a weapon—one that proved lethal to his political popularity and viability inside the White House. He made folks feel sad and angry. Unfortunately for him, and perhaps for George Bush, his mean streak undercut his true brilliance. What was originally conceived to be the perfect political balance—the good cop/bad cop dynamic duo of George Bush and John Sununu—actually turned out to be much too much bad, not quite enough of the good. Unfortunately, it also worked to diminish the President's own true, kind qualities.

The editors' speech was over—and it was a great success. I

sighed with relief as we moved toward the awaiting White House motor pool for departure.

. . . . .

As we rode back to the White House in the presidential motorcade, sirens screaming, the usual crowd of onlookers gathered along the street to wave hello. Tourists snapped pictures. Through my darkened window I looked as one face leapt out at me. I sat up straight and peered at her. It was Joann! This was Jo's stomping grounds, a familiar walking route. The Department of Commerce, where she worked, was a block away from the hotel. I resisted the urge to quickly roll down the window and scream, "Hello, ol' Jo!" People in presidential motorcades didn't roll down their windows and scream greetings.

But something about the moment—about seeing Jo's face as we sped down the crowded street—eased the knot of pain which still rested deep in my stomach from Marlin's mention of Mother. Seeing my sister's face—even though she never even saw mine behind the darkened windows—was tremendously powerful and spiritually comforting.

I know that the Lord works in strange ways, and that He helps us all through periods of difficulty in different, sometimes indecipherable ways. A part of me believes that He guided Joann to that place at that precise moment, and that He helped me locate her face in the midst of the crowd as we sped past. A part of me believes that she was put there for a purpose: so that I could feel comforted, assured. I smiled inwardly as we returned to the White House, the line of cars pulling quietly up to the south entrance.

As I moved through the Rose Garden and through the press briefing room toward the OEOB, I could sense that even though I was in pain, the wound was not quite as deep as I thought it was. I had begun the recovery process.

Losing Mother showed me a grief and pain I never knew. But with the passage of time, it also helped me grow. I have come to recognize the critical importance of having role models like her, of passing excellence down through the generations, of developing our children's minds and nourishing their identity and sense of self-worth. Mother left all of her children with that real, tangible, transferable asset, which I will now pass on to my own children with happiness and the utmost care. All of my siblings and I, and all of our children and our children's children, are the custodians of Mother's legacy. I am proud and eager to carry on the torch to preserve her memory.

Although the next few months would prove to be, in some ways, even more difficult, I knew that a bright, burning torch had been lit within me. I had been fortified by my own inner strength.

The Lord is indeed good. I understand Mother's words now when she used to always say, "He never gives us more than we can handle."

Because of His goodness, I made it through Mother's death and through the presidential election—both within weeks of each other.

CHAPTER 11

· · · · ·

Never More Than You Can Handle

· · · · ·

A s we drew closer to Election Day, it was quietly assumed that victory would be ours. But nothing in this
life comes with absolute, unconditional guarantees, and no human on this earth—not Craig Fuller, not Lee Atwater, not
George Bush, not even my own mother—could have guaran-
teed a win with 100 percent certainty.

November 8 loomed large on every calendar in the White
House. We had all worked tirelessly, compassionately, toward
the single goal of getting Vice President Bush elected President
of the United States, and one day—one twelve-hour time
frame—would determine our success or failure. Our individual
efforts had propelled the collective unit forward, as with the
Georgetown crew team I used to see gliding through the waters
of the Potomac.

The pressure came from having to survive—and thrive—in an environment where there was no room for error. It was an altruistic time: We were completely unselfish in our motivation and commitment, willing to sacrifice whatever was necessary to grab hold of that brass ring.

For me, the highest pressure took its toll during the last several weeks of the 1988 campaign and the weeks just after our victory. I had to face not only the transition of power and the loss of Mother, but the news of my unexpected second pregnancy. Although Lonnie and I were happy (yet shocked) to get the news, part of me felt embittered and frustrated, primarily toward men. They would never know (nor, actually, would most of them ever care about) the emotional and physical roller coaster that comes from being with child: The all-male kingdom within the White House didn't concern itself directly with matters of motherhood and maternity. These men—even those who were fathers—knew nothing of the added pressures and professional constraints it created. Simply put: There were no pregnant women in the White House. It didn't fit.

I was in a bad way. My heart was still heavy with grief, I was worried about finding a job in the new Bush Administration, and I knew that a bulging stomach and swollen ankles—or soon-to-be bulging stomach and swollen ankles—were definitely not strong job attributes. Charles Darwin would definitely have marked "being with child" in the "weak" column: A pregnant gazelle cannot run as fast as the strong buck if pursued by a hungry tiger. I assumed that there were probably quite a few sympathizers of Darwinian evolutionary philosophy on the White House staff, so I decided to keep my mouth shut about the news for the time being. Word of my pregnancy could have lessened my chances of getting a prime position. I'm not saying unequivocally that it would have, but I certainly didn't want to take the chance during this critical selection process. I was already batting zero—I hadn't secured even one lead on a job—and I didn't want to exacerbate the situation.

I continued working hard, though my emotional and physical strength was ebbing. I felt nauseated and weak in the mornings and throughout most of the day, drained and disconnected in the evenings. I kept a box of plastic sandwich bags in my briefcase for when my nausea came on suddenly and there wasn't time to make it to the bathroom. The strength and confidence I brought to the White House were beginning to weaken. The rigors of the political game were wearing me out.

But somehow, at the same time, I was determined to stay on in the new Bush White House, and no matter what else was going on in my life, I was not going to be forgotten.

Each morning, Lonnie would place a saucerful of saltines on the nightstand to help me fight the nausea. I'd struggle out of bed, throw up, shower, throw up again, pull on clothes, and finally seek refuge within his strong arms.

I learned, during that time, that the most wonderful thing about a strong, solid marriage is that burdens are shared. Unlike the disturbing uncertainty of politics, the love Lonnie and I share is predictable, absolute, and unconditional. We allow ourselves to grow—both as individuals and as a collective family—and from that growth emerges a coming together of body and soul. And even though I felt fortified by the relationship with my husband and firstborn son, I still felt worried, disoriented.

But although it was the most stressful time in my White House tenure, it was, with macabre intensity, the most exciting as well. The turmoil came with the inability to control my future. As is generally true, there is a certain amount of frustration and anxiety in having to stumble along in life not at all sure of what happens next. It *feels* better to know final results and bottom lines. In politics, there are no absolutes, and bottom lines are mercurial at best—at least until the voting booths close and the final results are tallied.

The anxiety followed me into my dreams. About a week before the general election, I dreamt that Michael Dukakis was in the Oval Office—*his* Oval Office—wearing an Army helmet and a rumpled suit from Filene's Basement. He and Kitty had just returned from his inauguration. They'd let me stay on in the White House as a maid. I was bending over polishing the brass doorplates in the Oval Office when I looked up and saw Dukakis untie his shoelace and pull it out of his shoe. He was trying to pick a piece of lettuce from between his teeth, using the plastic part on the end of his shoelace. Bush had managed to get a job as a street photographer, taking photos of tourists standing beside cardboard cutouts of the President and Miss Kitty—six dollars a pop, two for ten. They were stressful times indeed. Learning to cope was a must.

Pressure slipped into people, resurfacing in various forms and manifestations: a nervous eye tic in one friend, migraine headaches in another, stomach ulcers, frequent colds, occasional tears. It wasn't always destructive, but its presence could always be felt.

Before we knew it, Election Night was upon us. It was exciting, but bittersweet. A large group of Bush's White House staff reserved a suite at the Washington Hilton; the older lady in the tall, white hat was there (the same one who came to Bush's

Christmas party almost a year earlier), along with several of the women from David Bates' staff. Sean Walsh and several of our office volunteers and interns were also present. Each corner of the room was tuned to one of the major networks—ABC, NBC, CBS, CNN. We held our breath as the results were being tallied. Champagne bottles filled every bathtub and sink, waiting to be uncorked at the official call of victory. Every table scattered throughout the suite was filled with food: vegetable platters, chicken wings, and sweet desserts. A larger celebration was also taking place downstairs in the ballroom. Lonnie and I had booked a room in the hotel for the night—a well-deserved but brief break from Lonnie Paul for one night. We moved with excitement from the ballroom to the staff suite and finally to our room so that I could get out of my heels and get more comfortable.

Bush won in a landslide, carrying forty states. And although I wept with joy and relief when he was finally declared the official victor, I could also feel some new layer of pressure already weighing on me: The actual transition of power was immediately upon us.

· · · · ·

Bush's political future was now secure, but that of his staff was much less so. People weren't sure whether they'd be asked to stay, asked to leave, or simply overlooked. I was never an "in your face" personality. My profile in the White House was fairly low-key, which made me anxious about falling through the cracks. I didn't want to be forgotten or overlooked.

There was much jostling about after the election so that

everyone could remain in Bush's and Fuller's direct line of vision, lest they be forgotten. Folks were pulling out their old Rolodexes, trying to reestablish contact with any and all political contacts who might be able to help them secure a position in the Administration. ("Better make a list of everyone you know—inside and outside—who can help you find a position," Steve urged me immediately after the election. "Better approach this thing methodically.")

We weren't a crew team anymore. We were all paddling furiously in our own little boats, struggling mightily to stay afloat. Charles Darwin would have been pleased to see "survival of the fittest" put into such beautiful action: In this environment, only those staff members with the sharpest fangs or the fattest Rolodexes would survive.

Each time I approached a department head to express my desire to remain in the new Administration, I knew that twenty or thirty of my colleagues had come before me, also seeking jobs and political guidance. Staffers were protective of their own interests; there was not much talk between us of which jobs each of us were actually going after. Perhaps out of a sense of self-preservation, we kept those specifics close to our chest.

Jockeying for positions and having to sell ourselves and our capabilities all over again was a little degrading. It somehow felt like a beauty pageant; the judges were all looking closely, evaluating our every move.

Every eye watched, with keen, vested interest, the formation of Bush's senior White House staff. His selection of chief of staff would be crucial. Naturally, Bush's vice presidential staff was rooting—and lobbying strenuously—for Fuller. In him we had an ally and a loyal protector. Bush's choice of John Sununu for the post only increased my anxiety.

I didn't know Sununu "from Adam's dying house cat," as my mother used to say, but I was worried by the things I'd heard about his hot temper and acidic manner. For the White House, losing Fuller meant losing one of the sharpest political minds in the country. For me, it meant losing an important ally. It seemed as though suddenly he had vanished. I just looked up one day and he was gone. My worries mounted with each passing day.

As the formation of Bush's White House senior staff became complete, an impenetrable buffer zone was erected between the President-elect and the rest of his White House staff. It wasn't Bush who erected the barrier; it was his handlers—all white, middle-aged males who thought they were doing the right thing by trying to protect and insulate their new Leader of the Free World from people like me who were knocking on doors, not wanting to be forgotten.

Sununu brought in a lot of his own people. Andy Card, a longtime political operative in the state of Massachusetts, was appointed deputy chief of staff. I'd heard that Andy was a softer, more gentle version of Sununu: intense, intelligent, quick-witted—but fair. He had a kind (and handsome) face. Later, what I'd heard was proven true. I decided I liked him. I was also impressed with his undying loyalty to George Bush.

David Bates, who'd worked for Bush for years and with whom I had developed a warm friendship, snagged the highly coveted senior White House post of Assistant to the President and Secretary to the Cabinet. It was a crucial appointment, and one which held tremendous political importance—inside as well as outside the White House. I breathed a small sigh of relief: It was important to have at least one friend (besides the President-elect) in my corner at the top. Fitzwater's appointment as White House press secretary was not surprising, but it was certainly a wise move. Marlin could talk an alley cat down from an oak tree; he was the smoothest, smartest operator in the White House. In him, too, I had an ally. (Shortly thereafter, Marlin recruited Steve Hart as his deputy press secretary. Steve was thrilled—and I was thrilled for him.)

But still, nothing was popping for me. As much as the President-elect might have liked and respected me as a person, as a friend, and as a professional, he liked and respected thousands of others as well. The man had a country to run, an Administration to form, a national mood to set. My personal anxieties paled in comparison.

I began to feel the twinges of bitterness and humiliation setting in like gangrene. And it showed in my work. Steve Hart pulled me aside one afternoon and touched my arm.

"Your attitude is showing," he whispered. "I know you're anxious about your future. We all are. But don't let it get in the way of your job," he reminded me. "Keep your chin up and a smile on your face. People will think more of you for it."

Steve, as always, meant well. But it was at that point that I made the conscious decision to stop internalizing my anxiety, to stop hawking myself like a used-car salesman, and to place my heavy burdens at someone else's door. Doing otherwise was unproductive for me and unhealthy for the baby growing inside of me. The situation had slipped from beyond the grasp of my direct control.

One rainy afternoon I made my way through Lafayette Park, hopping over puddles and scurrying toward St. John's. Inside the chapel I shook the rain off and knelt in the empty church. I said a prayer I had whispered many times before:

"Help me renew my strength, Lord, for it is ebbing. Carry me

through each day, for walking has become a struggle. Lift me up above this rat race. Let me rise above all that is swirling around me and find a way to distinguish myself from the rest of the maddening, groping crowd. Ease the pain of losing Mother, Lord, for my burden is heavy and the weight of my grief is paralyzing. Nurture and protect this life within me, Jesus, and give me the strength to give it strength. Let me place my burdens at Your feet. For in You, I have all faith."

I went back to the White House, my wet feet squeaking like a nurse's shoes on hospital linoleum. David Bates, who was helping the President-elect complete his transition efforts, stopped me in the hallway.

"Got a minute?" he asked. "Can you come see me in my office?"

"Let me drop my coat and change my shoes and I'll be there in one second," I answered, trying to speak in even, measured tones.

We sat together on his couch. "Kristin," he drawled comfortably, one hand resting on his crossed leg, "something interesting has just happened."

"Really? What?" I asked, sounding more anxious and less conversational than I'd wanted.

"Patty Presock just sent over a note that Bush just wrote," David said.

Patty was one of Bush's closest, most trusted personal assistants. Nothing happened in the White House without her knowing about it beforehand. She was Bush's alter ego: discreet, professional, and thoroughly plugged into every move Bush made or was even thinking about making.

David continued. "The note is about you. I guess you could say Bush has issued a directive of sorts: He wants to make sure you're placed, and that you're happy where you are."

A warm glow began deep in the pit of my stomach.

"Never, ever underestimate the power of prayer," I heard the voice of my mother saying. I could feel her presence: "You know He never gives you more than you can handle." I could smell the lavender smell of her skin.

"I'm too wet and tired for jokes, David," I said with a smile, wanting with all my heart to believe he was serious. "What do you really want?" I asked, searching his face.

"Would you like to see it? I've got a copy right outside," Bates answered innocently, gesturing through the open door to a secretary, who breezed in efficiently, bringing with her a piece of paper which she handed to David.

I took it, and sure enough, there was Bush's familiar southpaw chicken scratch. He'd written over an earlier note that I'd sent to him, in which I thanked him for giving me a beautiful, intricately spun gold lapel pin adorned with the vice presidential seal. It wasn't like the thousands of standard-issue White House lapel pins which were stuffed in supply drawers throughout the complex for visitors and relatives of dignitaries. This pin was exquisite, heavy and handmade—a beautiful, thoughtful gift that I wore, and still wear, with great pride. His nine-word message was brief, but firm: "Discuss her future with me. She must be placed. GB." (The word "must" was underlined.)

And then, in the far left-hand corner, a typed note from Patty to Marlin Fitzwater. This one showed that Bush had followed up and inquired again about my future since writing his first note: "Marlin: The Vice President asked if anyone has talked to you re: Kristin Taylor. See attached."

"I guess that means you're a must-hire, doesn't it?" David

202

asked warmly. "Have you thought at all about what you'd like to do? Where you'd like to move?"

I had been lifted up above the din. A way had been made.

"I want to stay with Bush in the White House," I answered. I really did, too. Bush was a man of character—caring and compassionate. I felt guilty that I had underestimated his ability to get beyond the layers that insulate him—to reach out in his human way and touch people, making sure they're happy in what they're doing and justly rewarded for their hard work. Here he was, weeks away from being inaugurated the forty-first President of the United States, inquiring and even following up about my future, making sure I was "okay" in the same simple way my father calls from Detroit twice a week to check and see how I'm doing.

"I don't want to move to an agency, David," I said. "I haven't thought much beyond that. But I do know I want to stay with Bush."

"A word of advice," David said. He spoke slowly and had the unrushed manner of a man who was completely comfortable with himself. He was schoolboy handsome, with a quick smile and a next-door-neighbor aura. Everyone in the White House knew that Bush loved and respected him. The two had known each other for many years.

"This note will move around quite fast because of who wrote it. Go to every interview you get. Explore every avenue," he said. "Don't eliminate anything just yet. I'm always here if you need counsel or advice. Congratulations!"

As I stood to leave his office, I wanted to reach out and warmly embrace him, to thank him for the good news and his sound advice. Instead, I shook his hand and held it for several seconds, smiling into his dark brown eyes. Bates was a good, gentle man. And he had dropped a ray of sunshine into my life.

Bates, of course, and my sweet, gentle, good Lord God.

. . . . .

CONVERSATION WITH MY CREATOR was then, and remains still, my greatest source of strength and inspiration. The wondrous beauty of prayer is that you can do it anywhere, anytime.

I never let a day pass without giving thanks for all that is good and positive. I am teaching my children to do the same. I am teaching them to be actively grateful for all they have and all they are capable of being, to not take anything for granted, and to always, always stay in close contact with their spiritual center.

Throughout the transition of power, I continued with my prayer and positive visualization. Soon thereafter, as if by magic, my nausea began to subside. I began to feel stronger. The spring returned to my step. And, although much more laboriously, I continued to work through the grief and anger associated with my mother's leaving me. Bates' prediction had been correct: Several interviews did begin coming my way. During at least two, my eyes wandered across copies of Bush's note—one in a file left open on a desk, and another as the interviewer rifled through a stack of papers. It had made its way into the hands of the people who mattered. A way had indeed been made.

Having faith in something larger than myself is a wonderfully reassuring thing—infinitely more powerful and valuable than even my friendship with and respect for the Leader of the Free World.

My faith is active and self-propelled. It doesn't make me immune to pain, but it strengthens me and helps me withstand life's harsh blows. It doesn't make me a superwoman, but it does allow me to balance all of life's demands in a harmonious, comfortable manner. I am by no means worry-free, but I do have somewhere to turn when the road gets rough.

Isn't that a wonderful, glorious thing? For what can be more comforting than the knowledge that, for the rest of our living days, we'll never, ever have to walk this road alone?

CHAPTER 12

· · · · ·

*Stepchildren
No Longer*

· · · · ·

BUSH'S HANDWRITTEN NOTE on my behalf had classified me as what was quietly known as a "must-hire" within the White House. It was a directive from the President-elect, an edict from the Man himself.

Over the next several weeks, certain people faded out of vision. Fuller, for instance, took a key job in the private sector as a partner with the political consulting firm of Wexler, Reynolds.

Finally, I received an offer that sounded right on target: director of White House media relations. I'd have my own staff, a comfortable amount of access to the President, and a free hand to mold and shape our objectives the way I saw fit. My new boss would be David Demarest, whom the President-elect had just appointed as White House director of communications. I'd heard he had a reputation for being a team player—that he was fair, cautious, and intelligent. Steve Hart had actually cheered when he heard the news that Demarest had gotten the appointment. If Steve regarded him so highly, I thought, he must be okay.

After our first meeting, I decided that I liked him, too. He was not quite as aggressive and forceful as I had grown accustomed to during my tenure in the White House, but a nice, gentle sort nonetheless. I hoped he was strong enough to not let people walk all over him. It mattered to me that he'd already developed a friendship, of sorts, with Sununu. That meant our office of communications would have a leg up when it came to the allocation of resources and fairly unencumbered access to the President. Sununu's liking Demarest empowered all of us; we wouldn't be an insignificant, facile part of the White House process. This important strategic alliance with Bush's right-hand man was critically important, particularly since I'd had no former dealings with our soon-to-be chief of staff at all.

Demarest proceeded with the formation of his staff thoughtfully and carefully. In an effort to gain important historical knowledge of the jobs he would be filling, he had already had some preliminary discussions with Reagan staffers who still remained in the office of communications. He seemed to be doing things right. He was cut from different cloth; not as buttoned up and steeped in the rigid formality of so many of those on Reagan's staff. He admitted that he'd even been a bit of a "hippy" in his younger days. He rolled his sleeves up to his elbows when working on a big project. The man even smoked —absolutely taboo within the hallowed halls of the protocol-conscious White House, but an indicator, nonetheless, that he didn't mind bucking the rules and walking to the beat of his own drummer, thank you. He seemed quite comfortable with himself. Our working together is going to work out just fine, I thought to myself.

I wasn't shy about asking questions: "Will I have direct access to you?" I asked him. From an operational point of view, I felt I needed to know. Too many damned layers would hamper my job. "How much control will I have over the hiring—and firing, if necessary—of my own staff?" I needed to know the precise degree of my influence. "How will we interact with Marlin's staff?" I asked. It was critically important for the White House press office and the office of communications to work closely together. I was slightly worried that Demarest's less aggressive demeanor would be no match for a world-class veteran like Marlin—that is, if the going ever got tough between the two offices.

"Don't worry about Marlin," Demarest snapped, with the first hint of bitterness in his voice. "He has his staff and I'll have mine. My staff is larger than his; we'll be able to cover more ground. I'm not going to be pushed around by him or anybody else."

Well, *damn!* I thought to myself. All I asked was a simple question—one that I thought had more to do with procedure and operations than it did with turf fights and power plays. But I was wrong. Something already seemed to be brewing in Demarest's mind about Fitzwater; maybe he was covetous of Fitzwater's already close relationship with Bush. Maybe he was just plain intimidated by the man and his reputation. I decided to let it slide. But in my heart, I knew the truth: Given the choice of political allies, I'd rather have Fitzwater than Sununu any day. Sununu was mean—too damned mean for his own good. Fitzwater was a friend—tried and true and as loyal as they come.

But Demarest was still sending the right signals. He seemed a man of thorough preparation. He suggested the name of someone I could talk with in an effort to get a better idea of what my responsibilities would be. He was right.

I'd seen her off and on throughout my days in the White House. She rarely smiled and always seemed to wear black, as if in the throes of a perpetual state of mourning. We rarely spoke. She was a prime example of someone on Reagan's staff who had, in the earlier days, treated the Bush people like stepchildren; I always got the feeling that, when she saw me in a crowded room, she had to fight the urge to summon me to bring her a glass of ice tea or Chenin Blanc. Now that we were stepchildren no longer, it was clear that she was unhappy about having to relinquish her prestigious White House job and all that it represented—the power, the access, her direct connections to the President. She seemed angry that Reagan had been forced to relinquish his place in American history, and she was completely uninterested in assisting in the transition.

Reaching her was difficult. I was lucky if she returned my phone calls. Never once did she accept my invitations to sit down, nor was I ever invited into her office even for casual conversation. Every time I entered into her suite of offices, her door was closed. She never emerged from behind it.

Once, I approached her in the corridor of the Old Executive Office Building. She mumbled a question to herself, wondering whether my attitude was "a black thing" or whether it was "just true arrogance." I blinked at her back as she retreated down the hallway, not sure I'd heard her correctly. I heard Mother whispering in my ear, urging dignity and restraint.

After many attempts, I got her on the line.

"Yes, Kristin?" she asked, sounding busy and exasperated. What in the world is she so suddenly busy working on, I thought hotly—besides packing up her bags and boxes and getting the hell out of Dodge City? Why is she being so unresponsive and uncooperative?

"I thought maybe you'd have some time to sit down with me this week," I said, pursing my lips as my mother used to when she was disgusted. "We're running out of time and I'd really like to s—"

"I'm booked the entire week," she answered back before I could finish. I was beginning to understand why she always wore black and never smiled. I made a mental note to paste a smile face on her office door for her last day—either that or a bumper sticker reading, "Last one out of the Reagan White House, please turn out the lights."

I wasn't going to get catty, for I knew I had the upper hand: She and the rest of the Reaganites were relinquishing their power. We were gaining it. I tried again.

"Maybe I could come down to your office for five minutes. I'd like to at least meet with—"

"I can't do it," she said. "I'm just out of commission this entire week," she said. "No offense, of course."

None taken, I thought to myself. You just better hope the unemployment officer doesn't feed you that same line when you queue up at the window next week.

Several days later, I did sit down with two other Reagan staffers who were much more helpful. They provided a comprehensive overview of what their jobs entailed and the nature of their overall responsibilities; they even had files they were going to let me borrow to study as historical reference. During our meeting, the intercom buzzed. One assistant got up to answer it, then nodded somberly into the phone.

"Yes, yes," she whispered. "Okay, no, we won't. I understand." One of the women continued talking to me while the other finished her telephone conversation. My previous years at the White House had taught me to listen to two conversations simultaneously—especially if one sounded particularly sensitive. I asked questions, but my other ear was trained on the phone conversation.

"Not much longer," the assistant continued. "No, I won't," she finished, and she finally hung up. The hair at the nape of my neck began to rise ever so slightly. The arches of my feet began to throb, a sure sign that something was amiss.

I wasn't surprised to find out later that the woman had called during our meeting. I also wasn't surprised that she was ordering her assistants to withhold from me all of the most important files; she wanted to hand-deliver those herself, directly to Demarest, rather than dally around with the likes of me.

At Demarest's request, several members of Reagan's staff remained with the Bush team for one or two weeks to ensure a smooth, easy transition. She'd poked her head into my office from time to time, but I never invited her in. I felt catty and immature, but in my heart or in my office, she was not welcome.

"Beautiful roses," she said to me of the dozen roses Lonnie sent me during the first week of the Bush administration. "From an admirer?"

"You could say that," I answered, looking through my files and refusing to glance up in her direction. "These days, I need all the admirers I can get. Lord knows I can't afford to have any enemies in a place like this. I'm sure you understand that, don't you?"

She turned and left, looking slightly puzzled. One thing we didn't need in the White House was a bunch of women biting each other in the face and in the back; it detracted from our professionalism. I was glad when she left for good.

· · · · ·

THE TRANSITION OF POWER continued. More and more presidential appointments and cabinet posts were being announced. I bristled a little at Jack Kemp being appointed Secretary of Housing and Urban Development. I knew he enjoyed enormous popularity—particularly with blacks (thanks to his strong civil rights record and outspoken commitment to "empower" more blacks by making the dream of homeownership a more easily attainable reality). I also knew that he was perhaps the most dazzling and energetic Republican visionary the party had to offer, but still, only months before, he had been whipping our collective asses up and down the campaign trail, trying his level best to beat George Bush to a bloody stump. I felt a fierce protectiveness toward George Bush; it sometimes clouded my judgment.

The announcement of Colin Powell as chairman of the Joint Chiefs of Staff had both Lonnie and me puffed with pride. We went to a cocktail party that evening, and many of our white friends came up to congratulate us on Powell's appointment. We accepted the congratulations with pride and warmth. We, too, felt as if we had enjoyed a personal accomplishment. Bush's choice of Powell, the first black man ever to hold the title, told me more about Bush's character than perhaps anything else he'd ever done. It was a wonderful, supportive, appropriate decision. Powell had become the pride of black America, and the darling of the black media.

As we moved deeper into the transition phase, attention turned toward The Big Day: the inauguration. All of us busied ourselves with the festivities surrounding the upcoming ball— the grandest, fanciest, most prestigious party in the Free World, the hottest ticket in town, bar none. The women in the White House compared notes: Rent a gown or buy? Elbow-length gloves or bare hands? Organza or velvet? Rented limo or Lincoln Town Car?

Lonnie and I spent an entire Saturday pampering ourselves in preparation for the big ball. We spent the morning in the fine gown section of I. Magnin in Bethesda. Lonnie browsed the racks carefully, sending gown after gown into the dressing room for me to try on. His taste was impeccable; he leaned toward simple elegance rather than busy, bold fashion statements. And he knew exactly what complemented my features, what he considers my "beautiful brownness."

I could hear him just outside the fitting room, rifling through the racks on a mission to find That Perfect Look. Every few minutes, he'd stop, remove a gown from the rack, and hold it up to the light to imagine me in it. If he liked it, he'd hand it politely to the saleslady standing attentively at his side: "Would you mind asking my wife to try this one on?" he'd ask. "And does this style come in a black velvet? She looks very, very nice in black velvet."

After ten or eleven gowns, I was growing tired. It was getting harder and harder to find clothes that would fit over my bulging tummy without revealing what we wanted to keep quiet for a while longer. After a while, I simply sat in the fitting room, my back against the mirror, waiting for the salesclerk to bring back a fresh armful of Lonnie's newest selections. I didn't want to search anymore.

Finally, we struck gold. I emerged from the fitting room and turned slowly for my husband, who watched carefully as I moved.

"Move more into the light over here," Lonnie said, guiding me gently to a corner of the salon. I moved obediently, tired but turning so he could see the full effect. I was standing on my toes to simulate what I'd look like in heels.

My sweet husband turned to the salesclerk: "Could I bother you to get her some heels, please? She's tired of standing on her toes. Don't you have some in the back? Or can you bring a pair over from the shoe salon?" Lonnie was always more demanding with salesclerks than I. He expected attentive service and one-stop shopping.

The gown was indeed beautiful, and it didn't emphasize my tummy. It was strapless and quite elegant—black velvet with a deep, sexy slit up the back.

"What do you think?" I asked, turning slowly, feeling a little like a chicken roasting on a skewer. But I loved the gown. I loved the way it made me feel: grown up, sexy, proud to be the first African-American woman in history to have been appointed to my White House post, proud that the country's new President-elect had personally made a place for me in his administration. My energy was suddenly revitalized; I no longer

215

felt tired. I felt like partying—like dancing until dawn with the man I loved, celebrating our victory and the beginning of an exciting new phase of our lives.

As soon as the salesclerk disappeared to attend to another client, I did a half step of the Watussi—the very step I'd watched my sisters do so often in the basement of our home in Detroit so many years ago. I snapped my fingers softly, finishing with a quick, dramatic spin. Lonnie smiled, watching me with what looked like a mixture of love and wonder.

"You like?" I asked, bopping and sliding quietly across the salon floor, looking out of the corner of my eye to make sure we were still alone. I would have died with embarrassment if I'd been caught jammin' in the stuffy, high-priced fashion salon of I. Magnin.

"I think I *love* it," he said finally. "You look gorgeous."

The salesclerk appeared from the dressing room as if from thin air: I wondered if she'd been spying on our secret dance.

"Ma'am, we're going to need your help selecting the rest of the ensemble, please: gloves, shoes, and a wrap of some sort to go with this gown," Lonnie said politely and confidently. And then, as if remembering an important afterthought, he added, "And an evening bag, too, of course."

For an evening, I would be Cinderella. And Lonnie would be my handsome prince.

I was famished by the time we left the store. We stopped for Chinese food, split an order of mou-shu pork and fried rice, and then made our way down Wisconsin Avenue toward D.C.—on the prowl, now, for Lonnie's tuxedo. We were going all the way: no rent-a-tux this time but a real-life purchase. We would now be going to our fair share of Big Bashes with the new Administration in power. It was invigorating. I had been catapulted into a festive mood.

Now it was my turn. At Neiman Marcus, I rifled through the tuxedoes. Lonnie is a tall, handsome man with a commanding presence and a great body—the kind of man who looks solid and sexy in the right tuxedo. He tried on several, and finally we again struck gold. He turned slowly for me, holding his arms out from his sides. Lord, did he look handsome. We fitted him up with shoes and cummerbund—even silk socks, mother-of-pearl tux buttons, and matching cufflinks. Lonnie's mood changed, too. It had finally hit us that George Bush was soon to become the next President of the United States and that we would play a role in the continuing Republican administration. We belonged to the party in power; we represented a personal, direct link to this new man who was going to lead the country. The country had been blessed with sense enough to elect George Bush, and we were all going to benefit. By the time we left the store, we were both euphoric.

Two other couples—close friends of ours from Philadelphia—were coming to Washington to attend the inaugural festivities, including the swearing-in ceremony in the afternoon and the ball later that evening. They, too, were excited.

As the six of us walked toward the Capitol that morning for the afternoon ceremony, I thought about all the hard work that had gone into getting Bush elected. I reflected on how much I'd grown and how blessed I was to have come as far as I had.

I sat in my folding chair on the lawn of the U.S. Capitol beneath a cold, cloudy sky, my hands folded and my eyes closed, and spoke to my Lord God. I knew that within a matter of seconds I was to witness, firsthand, George Herbert Walker Bush become the country's forty-first President. I prayed that the Lord would impart upon him the spirit, the drive, and the wisdom to move our country in the right direction. I also prayed for the child growing inside of me.

Listening to Bush recite the oath of office, which was administered by Chief Justice William Rehnquist, I began to cry. I suppose they were tears of pride. Feeling more like his mother than his staffer, I thought I'd burst with pride watching Bush stand tall and handsome and sure, his hand resting firmly on his mother's worn Bible, being sworn into the highest office in the land. I was proud to represent a tiny part of what it took to make it happen.

But as much as I tried, I couldn't stop the tears. Lonnie leaned close, surprised and concerned by my sudden emotional outpouring. He gave my shoulder a comforting squeeze with one hand; with the other, he pulled out a handkerchief and leaned over to wipe away my tears—which didn't stop flowing until shortly after Bush finished reciting the oath of office.

They were tears of relief: relief that the campaign was now behind us, that the winning result had suddenly, magically been transformed from a vague abstraction into a pleasing reality—and we had emerged on the winning side, stepping victoriously into our place in the sunshine. They were tears of sadness, too. More than anything, I missed Mother at that moment. I regretted that she could not be sitting right there beside me, holding my hand, witnessing with her baby girl this historic, emotion-packed event. Lord knows she would have been proud and very, very happy.

· · · · ·

THE INAUGURAL BALL later that evening held none of the same emotional symbolism. In comparison, actually, it was anticlimactic. When we entered, we were greeted by a swarming mass of nameless faces—hundreds of people who didn't look at all familiar and who seemed, suddenly, to have emerged from the woodwork.

Lonnie and I got dressed at his mother's house so she could watch as her son and daughter-in-law left for the ball. Two of his sisters, Rita and Magadalene, and two of his brothers, LeRoy and David, were there to see us off, too, and to take pictures. It felt like a grown-up version of leaving for the prom. We were excited, even giddy. I was glad to have family close around me before we left for the ball. They centered me and kept me calm.

But after four and a half hours of dancing and mingling with friends and soon-to-be presidential colleagues, my poor feet were screaming for mercy. They hurt more than they've ever hurt in their lives.

The highlight of the evening, of course, was the arrival of the President and Mrs. Bush. But even that was anticlimactic. Positioned on a stage several feet above the crowd, the new First Couple already seemed more insulated from the world around them. Mrs. Bush shimmered in her Arnold Scaasi gown; the President looked dapper and handsome in his tux. But in a flash, they were gone, having spent all of about ten minutes with the hundreds of people in the ballroom who had waited all night to greet and cheer their new President. They were to spend the evening rotating around to several different inaugural balls, all located in various places throughout the city.

It was late when we left the ball, and well below zero outside. The wind whipped around and through us. But I

219

couldn't stand it anymore. After a few steps, I stopped in the middle of the street and removed my shoes.

"What in the world are you doing?" Lonnie asked in shock. "It's below zero. You're going to catch a death of cold. Put your shoes back on!" But it was too late. I was beyond rational. My brain wasn't working anymore. It couldn't; my toes hurt too much. They needed relief—quick, fast, and in a hurry. Handing my deadly three-inch heels over to Lonnie, I quickly removed my elbow-length gloves and slipped one over each of my feet. I pulled them on as far as they would go. It looked ridiculous—wearing black satin gloves on my feet as we walked down the street in formal evening wear—but it was far preferable to keeping those deadly shoes on. If they hadn't been so ridiculously expensive, I would have probably thrown them straight into the Potomac River. Lord knows they had given me the blues that night. What a funny thing, I thought later: My aching toes had actually contributed to my disappointment with the 1989 presidential Inaugural Ball.

CHAPTER 13

· · · · ·

A New Breeze Blowing: The Mark of the New Bush White House

· · · · ·

Out of necessity, I came to know the things which relaxed George Bush (and a relaxed George Bush, of course, was a more effective interview). First Dog Millie was one, which presented minor problems for me. Bush loved having her around, and occasionally he even asked staff members to find her. Not only was I a little scared of Millie (and scared of most dogs, for that matter), I was allergic to her as well. Dog hair sometimes made my asthma kick in; direct contact with certain kinds of dogs caused little reddish bumps to appear on my skin. What's more, I just don't like dogs that much.

Unfortunately for me, she followed Bush everywhere. She even had a little wicker bed just behind Bush's desk in the Oval Office (she usually napped quietly, thank God, during most of our prebriefings).

Millie and Ranger were the pride of the White House. On many a day, I'd see Mrs. Bush sitting out on the grass with a big wicker basket full of Millie's newborn puppies. She'd dump them gently onto the soft ground, then pat them and nuzzle her nose into their soft hair. (If I'd nuzzled my nose directly into dog hair like that, my face would have turned into one big, pulsating red splotch, then my head would have probably exploded.)

Bush loved the fact that both Millie and Ranger were purebred hunting dogs. Maybe it was a macho thing. Or maybe it was a throwback to his blue-blooded days of quail hunting, polo matches, and country clubs. If there was one person in the world who enjoyed the thrill of the hunt, it was George Bush, without a doubt.

But it made my stomach hurt.

During my first meeting with Bush shortly after he became President, I walked into the Oval Office and was suddenly overcome with pride and emotion. I told him how proud I was to see him standing there—the country's new President. But he was preoccupied.

"You'll never guess what happened the other day," Bush said excitedly. "Ranger caught a bird and dragged it into the Oval Office. Blood was everywhere. I couldn't make out what it was at first—you know, hanging from her mouth. But when I looked closer, I realized it was a dead animal."

My stomach turned. I was repulsed.

"One of the agents pried it out of her mouth," he continued. "Pretty messy scene. She loves the squirrels around here, too—and, quiet as it's kept, the rats, too."

How revolting, I thought to myself, smiling weakly. I had so wanted my first visit with Bush in the Oval Office to be steeped in symbolism. Instead, all he gabbed about was blood and dead birds and that blasted dog. (From that moment forward, I kept a keen eye peeled for rats and other disgusting rodents when walking close to underbrush or across the South Lawn. We actually had quite a problem with the varmints during the warmer months; a big, fat rat actually fell into the water in the White House pool while Mrs. Bush was swimming. I would have died twice.)

Puppies and birddogs represented the warm, down-home aura of the Bush White House. But within the corridors of the West Wing, more serious business was also being conducted: The layers of power were immediately and clearly defined. With the exception of all but a few of the President's top men —Fitzwater, Demarest, and Domestic Policy Advisor Roger Porter, to name a few—the senior staff rarely acknowledged my existence. Even as we sometimes sat together in the Oval Office or walked with the President through the narrow corridors of the West Wing, they seemed to look over, through, and around me. They weren't being rude or racist; I simply didn't register on their radar screen. I was not senior enough for them to engage in meaningful discourse with me—at least not in the presence of their senior colleagues. It was irritating, but what certainly mattered more in my mind was whether The Man himself continued to acknowledge my presence. He did. I gave less than a hoot about his merry men excluding me from their close-knit circle. My primary client remained satisfied.

The social structure of the White House staff could easily be likened to that of a large, prominent law firm or Fortune 500 corporation, where the seniormost members—those who'd "made partner" or corporate officer, if you will—rotate exclusively within their own power circles and spheres of influence. Similarly, these same people control the flow of access to their big boss, whether that boss is the founding partner of a firm, the CEO of a blue-chip corporation, or, as in our case, the President of the United States.

In the White House, access was power. And power was doled out in tiny bits and pieces—never too much to one person, and always a sprinkling (if only as a matter of courtesy and camaraderie) to those at the top layers.

Perhaps more than any other person inside the Bush White House, John Sununu carefully controlled outside access to the President. His memory was selective and precise: If a senator had voted against Bush on an important bill, the member's access to the Oval Office was quickly reduced (usually only temporarily, just to prove a point). Sununu remembered those who had rallied against or, in his mind, mistreated the President—and he knew how to exact revenge.

In June of 1989, only five months after the inauguration, I proposed a presidential luncheon for a small group of editorial cartoonists. I thought it would be a good way to introduce our new President to those cartoonists who'd drawn his likeness throughout the campaign. Several days before the event, the press discovered that cartoonist Garry Trudeau, who lampooned Bush mercilessly during the 1988 campaign in his "Doonesbury" strip, had not been invited. We were being accused of playing "payback" with Trudeau for depicting Bush as imbecilic and invisible, goaded on by his secret, evil twin brother, "Skippy," who took care of the nasty side of politics. On the day of the luncheon, Marlin was asked in the daily press briefing why Trudeau was being snubbed by the White House. Reporters asked Marlin whether Trudeau would ever be invited in. Marlin's response only helped fuel the fire: "Not in my lifetime," he answered in his pink, boyish grin. *The Washington Post* picked up the story, as did the Associated Press, *USA Today,* and several other newspapers.

Noticeably Absent, one paper said of Trudeau. Bush Invited Cartoonists for Lunch, but Garry Trudeau Isn't on List, said another. I decided to mention it to Sununu.

"You've probably heard we're getting grief from the media about not inviting Trudeau to this upcoming luncheon with the President," I said. "They think we're playing an immature, vindictive game of political payback."

"Aren't we?" Sununu asked, his eyes glinting.

"I just wanted you to be aware of th—"

"Fuck 'em," he whispered simply. *"Now* who feels invisible?" he said with a Grinch-who-stole-Christmas smile. Then he turned to wobble through the narrow West Wing corridors. Access was his final trump card.

The unwritten, unspoken rule was that sustained and regular access to the inner sanctum—the Oval Office, the apex of privileged domain—was reserved exclusively for the Big Boys. And I do mean boys. Yes, there were women in the White House who held powerful, responsible positions: Chriss Winston, deputy assistant to the President and director of speechwriting; Bonnie Newman, assistant to the President for administration; and David Bates' successor, Ede Holiday, assistant to the President for cabinet affairs, to name but a few. But when it came time for the President to call together his exclusive group of "inner circle" advisors—and I'm not talking about merely members of his senior staff, but the people who make up his most trusted advisors—the picture was still made up only of white males. Yes, many women in the White House had a considerable amount of political power. They were even trusted advisors to the President. But some crucial element was still missing: We hadn't yet squeezed into the rarefied air within the President's impenetrable inner circle. Our growing influence was certainly seen on the organizational charts and dotted-line reporting structures within the White House. But in real life that world was still dominated and driven by white males. The President surrounded himself with men whom he knew well: James Baker, a lifelong friend and prep school chum; Marlin Fitzwater, his trusted advisor dating back to Bush's vice presidential tenure and a proven veteran in his field; John Sununu, who pulled him back from the brink of political disaster in New Hampshire; David Bates, who'd worked with him long ago during his days as a U.S. congressman.

I was proud of the women in the White House who did have the President's ear. They were trailblazers, setting the standard for those women who will, I hope, follow in our footsteps. I admired them and what they represented: progress for women everywhere. Even so, we still have a ways to go.

The same limitations held true for African-Americans. Those few of us who made it in were simply unable to penetrate upward, beyond the glass ceiling. Yes, there were the isolated success stories: Fred McClure, assistant to the President for legislative affairs, was the sole black staffer—male or female —on the White House senior staff. I tremendously respected him and all that he represented—particularly to black youth. He was, in a sense, our standard-bearer.

But being a standard-bearer doesn't lend itself, really, to partisan politics. In the same way I was grateful to McClure for sending such a strong, positive message to our black children and our young political aspirants, I was equally grateful to yet another black man from an entirely different political sphere, a man who paved brave new territory and had even rallied hard in direct opposition to the President I served: Jesse Jackson. Although I disagree with Jackson on just about every one of his political beliefs, I still feel tremendous personal pride and grati- tude for all that he has accomplished and all that he represents to our black children. As a Republican, I certainly bristled at his frequent, vocal attacks against my party and George Bush. But as a mother, I am thankful for the real-life message which he sent to my son and all black children in 1988: that a black man can, indeed, seek the highest office in the land. Jackson and I are obviously light-years away from each other on the political spectrum. But regardless of our disparate political be- liefs, I remain thankful for and proud of the positive role model he has become for young black people everywhere.

It saddens me that there aren't more such role models. It frustrates me that even men as powerful as Fred McClure were unable to slip through the buffer zone which had been erected around the President. Within Bush's all-white, all-male inner sanctum, there were simply no extra seats at the table.

This is the thing which I regret most about George Bush's political legacy: that throughout his political career, he never found the need to surround himself with more people of color

227

and more women. His world was made up of white males who saw the world as he saw it, had traveled along the same roads, and tasted the same fine wines—white men who handily and effortlessly leapfrogged over the ugly battles of sexism, racism, and cultural isolation. Inviting more people of color into his inner circle would have made Bush a stronger politician. It would have sensitized our campaign; it would have expanded and sharpened not only our overall political vision, but Bush's personal perception of people of color as well.

· · · · ·

I, TOO, CERTAINLY FELL SHORT of landing inside the President's inner circle. I was by no means considered a member of the President's "key" staff. I wasn't even a commissioned officer. I believe it was extreme luck and divine providence, coupled with the very nature of my job, which afforded me an unusually high level of access to Bush's inner sanctum.

Demarest could have easily denied me entry into the Oval Office (as so many of his senior colleagues did with their staff) and saved the glory all for himself, but he was secure enough not to even want to. He was also smart: He knew that many of the media availabilities I planned for the President were weeks and even months in the making, and that I was intimately familiar with every detail and nuance of the events I planned—more so than him. Rather than risk the embarrassment of being unable to answer a detailed question posed by the President on, say, the intended media audience or a specific reporter or publication who might be present, Demarest allowed me to pull up a chair and join that highly coveted, exclusive group:

the powerful semicircle of presidential aides who sat before the President, always ready to offer counsel.

These were usually sensitive briefings. In them, Bush was totally at ease (he'd make jokes occasionally, use mild profanity, ask silly questions, and generally behave in a way that he never could in the public eye); they were private moments with the members of his staff. I considered myself lucky that Demarest didn't feel threatened or undermined by my presence. If he had, I wouldn't have been allowed in.

It never mattered to me personally that most of the senior staff moved exclusively within their own power circles. It didn't matter that half of them remembered my face but couldn't seem to remember my name. What did matter, though, was that the most important person out of all of them—the President of the United States—actively continued to seek my advice and listen when I spoke. Not only did he listen, but he learned.

I had once arranged an Oval Office meeting between the President and John Johnson, chairman of Johnson Publishing Company (which publishes, among other things, *Ebony* and *Jet* magazines). Accompanying Johnson would be Robert Johnson, *Jet*'s executive editor, and Simeon Booker, an old friend and longtime Washington bureau chief for *Jet* magazine. The resulting article was to run in *Ebony*'s April 1990 edition.

During the prebrief, the conversation moved toward John Johnson himself. Again, Bush's interest in matters financial arose: Leaning back in his chair, he looked at me and said, "John Johnson is one of the wealthiest black men in America, isn't he? I've always had a tremendous amount of respect for him; he started his business from the ground up, worked his keister off for decades, and is now sitting on one of the largest, most successful minority-owned companies in the country. He's making money hand over fist. How much do you think he's worth?"

"I couldn't guess at his net worth, sir," I answered. "But I do think it's important to realize that not only is Mr. Johnson the founder and chairman of one of the largest minority-owned corporations, but he's one of the most successful and highly regarded businessmen in the country, period. Black or white."

It was important for me to convey this message while I had his ear. I wanted Bush to expand his vision of Johnson—and indeed of all successful black entrepreneurs—and place them, finally, where they needed to be: on a level playing field with their white counterparts. Bush meant well with his praise, but Johnson deserved the President's respect and admiration not only because he was a black man struggling against the odds, but because he was, indeed, one of the country's greatest financial successes. To pigeonhole him exclusively as a black rags-to-riches success story did not do him justice. His universe was much, much wider than that.

"Point well made," Bush responded, nodding in approval. "Point well made." I got the feeling he knew he'd received sound feedback and was glad for it. I, too, was equally glad to have been able to provide it.

·　·　·　·　·

ALTHOUGH THE WARMTH and informality previously associated with Bush's vice presidential staff had been cooled somewhat by the no-nonsense seriousness of the Office of the Presidency itself, the Bush White House was still warmer than the Reagan White House had been. As Steve Hart once said to me, "Gone are the days of the imperial presidency."

The Bushes fostered a sense of family closeness which did, thankfully, carry over into the new Administration. There were no more shoulder rides for Lonnie Paul or intimate Christmas parties as we experienced during the campaign, but the warmth was still there. And George Bush was still as genuine and down-to-earth as he'd been when he was Vice President. He was still a master at adding that special, human touch to an interview session, for instance, and he never allowed himself to become too closely choreographed by his handlers. For all of that, I respected him tremendously.

During one interview session in May of 1990—a lengthy, in-depth session with author Joe Hyams, who was working on an exhaustive book about Bush's war years—a question was asked about the nature of some of Bush's written correspondence during that time. The President turned to his longtime aide, Don Rhodes, who kept close track of all of Bush's personal affairs, and asked him to go scrounge up some of the letters he'd written—and saved—from decades before. Ol' Don knew exactly where to go. He returned minutes later, to the absolute delight and surprise of the author, holding a handful of old, yellowed envelopes. As we stood in the hallway of the Residence about to bring the interview to a close, Hyams sifted through several pieces of Bush's correspondence from his heroic war years. The spontaneous gesture on Bush's part added depth and warmth to a fine interview and "humanized" the President in the eyes of the author. Spontaneity was one of the characteristics he'd happily retained—one which blew over into our new White House like a warm summer breeze.

I was glad and relieved that the warm climate of the vice presidency had carried over to the Bush administration. That climate made it easier to establish and nurture genuine friendships—and having good, close friends was a much needed emotional fortifier in a place like that.

Thankfully, Steve Hart and Sean Walsh had both been placed in good jobs on Bush's presidential staff, in Fitzwater's press office. I felt somewhat comforted that they were still close, but I would miss having daily contact with them.

My newly hired assistant, Cheryl Kienel, would come to be a close friend. I liked her quiet manner; she wasn't a hardened White House type. She was almost fresh out of college and had worked on the inaugural staff for several months during the transition.

In fact, it was Tom Gibson who'd first called to tell me about Cheryl. "Consider her as you build your staff, Taylor," he said. Tom was always, always looking out for his friends. I knew that if it hadn't been for him encouraging and supporting me for that first job, I wouldn't have been sitting in my big new office in the White House at all. Since I had an opening, I called her in for an interview; I was impressed by her determination and her admiration for George Bush. Tom's blessings clinched the deal.

Hiring Cheryl was one of the smartest things I ever did. She was wonderful. She, too, found strength and comfort in her spiritual and religious faith. Like me, she let it guide her through each day. Bible verses hung on her office wall. Spiritual, uplifting messages were mounted in small, delicate frames on her desktop. I would let her leave early once a week to attend her weekly Bible study class. What I liked about Cheryl was that she never suffocated others with her spirituality; it simply flowed through her like a calm, gentle river. In it, I found comfort—and, I suppose, a sense of quiet Christian bonding. We laughed together often.

I saw Cheryl's relationships with others mature and ripen. One particularly special friendship began to blossom into romance—and from romance toward matrimony. She was as tickled to tell me about the news as I was to hear it.

"I'm getting married," she said softly one day as she stood in my office. I had suspected as much. "Lonni and I are officially engaged."

At that moment, I felt more like her mother than her boss. I wanted her to know that I approved of Lonni, that I thought he would make her very happy. (Besides, anyone with the same sweet name as my own husband's couldn't be all bad.)

She was to be married in California, her birthplace and family home. I was a little disappointed; I wanted to share at least a small part of her Big Day with her, to sense her joy and excitement. I wanted to be an invited guest sitting in the wedding chapel, eager to turn and stand when it was finally time for the beautiful bride to make that march down the aisle. I wanted to see her in her wedding dress.

Holly Williamson, associate director of White House public affairs, and my deputy Maria Sheehan were two other very close friends in the Bush White House. The four of us, including Cheryl, formed a strong, close bond which helped reduce the everyday tensions and pressures that hung in the White House air. We were friends outside of the White House gates. We'd have dinner together often; our husbands knew each other and got along well. I sensed that our husbands found great pride, individually and collectively, in their wives; we were exceptional—ambitious trailblazers who were exploring the previously uncharted territory of an all-male domain. We were their "White House wives," as they affectionately called us. Our friendship extended far beyond the black iron gates of the White House.

Several weeks before Cheryl's wedding, the four of us sat in my office picking through limp taco salads. We were excited about her upcoming Big Day, but disappointed that we wouldn't be there to witness it.

Cheryl came up with an idea which made us all smile.

The next day, right around lunchtime, Holly, Maria, Cheryl, and I reconvened in my office—and Cheryl set to work. She locked and even barricaded my office doors, pulling a heavy table in front of one door and two chairs against the other. Then, after closing the window shades and repositioning the heavy drapery, she slipped behind one of the closed curtains, as nimble as a dancer.

I buzzed my assistant on the intercom from my office phone. "I don't want to be disturbed for the next fifteen or twenty minutes, please," I said officially. Then, we waited. The three of us sat on my long white sofa, as if waiting for a Broadway show to begin. We were pretty excited.

All that could be heard in my office was the rustling of heavy fabric and material. The only movement came from the human figure hiding behind my curtains, wiggling, readjusting, and squirming.

"Close your eyes," we heard a muffled voice say from behind the thickness of the curtains. The three of us immediately obeyed, our eyes squeezed shut tightly.

After a moment, we heard Cheryl again, with a voice this time clear and strong. She had emerged from her hiding place.

There she suddenly stood in the middle of my office, a beautiful blur of white and pearls and yards and yards of sparkling material. Her presence seemed to fill my office. We all inhaled audibly. I fought tears. Maria groped for her camera. Holly stood for a better look.

For a moment none of us could speak. I think we were all struck not only by Cheryl's physical beauty, but by the incongruity of the scene; the last thing I ever expected to see standing in the White House—in that macho-maddened, male-dominated citadel of political power—was a blushing bride covered in pearls and lace. Cheryl even climbed up onto a chair and turned around slowly as we oohed and aahed. We wanted to absorb every pearl, every detailed puff of her sleeves, and the precise cut of her neckline. She sparkled and shimmered and sparkled some more, reminding me of my childhood jewel box with the pink ballerina inside which pirouetted slowly the second I opened it.

One of my office assistants knocked at the door, then tried to open it. Finding it jammed, he yelled through the door into my office.

"Is everything okay in ther—"

"Get out!" we all yelled together, quickly dissolving into laughter. No one else could see Cheryl's wedding gown; it was for the four of us only. It was our special preview, and the moment cemented our friendship. For those fifteen minutes with my three close and trusted friends, the White House felt like a slumber party instead of the center of the world's power. Cheryl had opened a tiny window for us, an intimate preview into some very special scene, and we watched eagerly, like small children watching a circus. Our friendship transcended the stuffy formality of the White House. Friends knew nothing about protocol and political correctness, nor were they supposed to.

Being able to have someone I could trust—someone I could laugh or cry with—was one of the most effective pressure valves I had. Fortunately, true friendship doesn't lend itself to partisan politics. I made some of my closest friends during those years, and I came to realize while I worked there that you can't go through life distrusting everyone around you. Friends made my White House years enjoyable and multidimensional. Looking back, I realize how much the experience changed my life in very wonderful, positive ways. I am stronger for it, sharper, more committed to my political ideologies. I am a more devoted friend, and, yes, perhaps the tiniest bit tougher.

CHAPTER 14

· · · · ·

Breathe! Breathe!
Breathe!

· · · · ·

I CONTINUED TO KEEP THE NEWS of my pregnancy quiet, but it wasn't a secret to be kept quiet for too long. I knew I'd better say something to someone pretty soon: My stomach was about to betray me.

Again, the personality of the entire Bush family made my pregnancy easier to handle within the White House. It made an incredible difference to me that Bush was a devoted and loving family man.

Once the news was made public, I sometimes got the distinct feeling that folks in the White House didn't know quite how to react, or quite what to do with their eyes when they saw me waddling down the halls of the OEOB. Either their conversation centered exclusively on my pregnancy, or they didn't bring it up at all. There was no happy medium.

I felt as if I were being judged. I began to imagine that the innocent statements of my colleagues—"Kristin! Congratulations on your pregnancy!"—really translated into "So, you been making whoopee, huh? A little turn in the hay? A little bun in the oven? Tiger in the tank? Get it on, Fertile Myrtle!"

Since I was one of the first pregnant women on the President's staff, it was clear that folks hadn't yet figured out how to deal with this delicate dynamic. It was interesting to watch people's reactions.

"When's that baby of yours going to pop?" White House Domestic Policy Advisor Roger Porter once asked me on the way to the West Wing. "You know we just had another one, too," he said. "My wife just seems to spit them out like seeds and keep right on going. I admire the heck out of her."

I bit my tongue. If Lonnie ever said something about seeds and babies popping out of my womb, I'd kill him twice.

Bush's reaction was much more subtle. He took his time in acknowledging my pregnancy. I must have been five or six months pregnant—quite visibly showing—before he even made mention of it. I somehow didn't feel comfortable broaching the subject myself.

One afternoon as I was briefing him for an upcoming television interview, he swiveled his chair toward the window and gazed out onto the South Lawn. Was it my imagination, or was he embarrassed to face me as he broached this fairly sensitive topic?

"So, we're having a little bambino, are we?" he asked. He never used the word "pregnant." I wanted to smile. "How's everything going?" he asked. "You feelin' okay?"

"Thank you, sir, I'm feeling fine," I answered. I wondered briefly if he'd confirmed the news with Marlin or Demarest or someone else beforehand.

"And I don't know about this 'we' stuff," I continued, trying to cut through my anxiety, "but I do know for a fact that *I'm* having a baby at the beginning of August."

"Well, congratulations, Kristin," he said warmly. "You'd better be taking good care of yourself."

I felt slightly uncomfortable. Bush was rarely required to directly confront the personal, gender-related situations of his staffers. And the fact that he surrounded himself with men (more often than not) only exacerbated the situation.

In my mind, the very topic of pregnancy dripped with sexuality. No matter what else is said or not said about the issue, the underlying, unspoken acknowledgment is always that passionate, sheet-tearing, skin-burning, supersteamy lovemaking had to have taken place (and was obviously enjoyed) to get the job done. No two ways about it: Pregnancy was a public acknowledgment of the ultimate loss of innocence.

As my pregnancy progressed, Bush became more inquisitive about my condition and a little more protective. After our initial conversation, he inquired about my health and well-being almost every time he saw me.

Toward the end of the eighth month, Bush finally asked me, "How much longer are you going to work? It looks like you might just have this baby right here in the White House."

I wasn't feeling well that day. My back muscles hurt. My Braxton Hicks contractions were starting up. And, because the baby displaced and pushed aside all of my internal organs, including my stomach, I burped constantly. I wasn't in the mood for any talk about babies or pregnancy. I stifled a burp and responded.

"I'm working right up until I have this baby," I said with determination. "There's no reason in the world for me to be sitting at home twiddling my thumbs. I'm just fine, thanks."

I might have snapped, but I couldn't tell. I was in no mood to interpret conversations or read between the lines. My feet hurt.

Bush remained ever mindful of my condition. When I walked with his entourage, he'd automatically slow his normally fast pace to accommodate my extra load. I sensed that the men surrounding him couldn't have cared less about whether or not I could keep up with them as they walked: I think they considered my pregnancy a slightly uncomfortable abstraction. Their primary concern was keeping up with The Main Man as he moved, remaining in his direct line of vision, scurrying after and around him like nervous jackrabbits. But once Bush altered his pace to accommodate mine, the entire entourage slowed down, more out of necessity than desire. It made me smile.

Bush is the loving father of five children, and that fact made my pregnancy easier to handle inside the White House. He seemed to understand when to back off, when to inquire, and when to slow his pace if I was having trouble keeping up. Either he was an instinctively considerate husband during each of Mrs. Bush's pregnancies, or the woman really whipped him into shape and taught him to be mindful of a woman with child. Whatever the case, I really did appreciate his thoughtfulness.

At one point during my pregnancy, Lonnie and I went to the doctor for a sonogram. Lonnie accompanied me to every doctor's visit and asked more questions than I did. The man is a gift from the good Lord. Ken Blank, our wonderful ob-gyn, stared at the screen in the darkened room while running what felt like a squeegee over and across my stomach. Lonnie and I had decided earlier that week that we wanted to be told the sex of the baby if it could be determined from the sonogram. We'd already discussed it with Ken.

"You ready for your answer?" Ken asked, still squeegeeing my stomach. "You certain you want to know the sex? Because I can tell you with almost 100 percent certainty right here and now."

I never want to forget how the moment felt. Lonnie and I looked at each other and nodded. I held my breath. All bets were on that our second child would be a girl. Whatever it was, we had decided to keep the news a secret. We wanted to savor the knowledge between us until the very moment our child sprang forth into the world.

"It's a girl," Ken said, as if he'd just delivered a kicking, screaming baby from my womb. The miracles of medical science. Lonnie and I went for chocolate sundaes afterward to celebrate.

I gulped down my sundae quickly because I had to get back to the White House. I had a presidential event scheduled for later that afternoon. Prizewinning photographer Eddie Adams was shooting President Bush for the cover of *Parade* magazine. I'd given him fifteen minutes for the shoot, and one of my staffers had already cleared him into the West Wing. All I had to do, really, was show up and preside over the Oval Office shoot.

When everything was ready, I gave the thumbs-up sign to Tim McBride, who escorted Bush into the Oval Office from his private study. After introducing Bush to Adams and readjusting Bush's pocket handkerchief, I moved to the side of the room. Fifteen minutes wasn't much time to shoot.

The nature of the event allowed for quite a bit of uninterrupted conversation between Bush and me. It was a rare opportunity. There were long pauses as Adams loaded film, changed cameras, or adjusted lighting. I stood over in the corner, watching Adams' expert technique. Between shots, Bush looked over at me.

"You feeling okay today?" he asked.

"I'm fine, sir. Just came from a doctor's appointment, in fact. Everything's just fine, thanks," I answered. With slight hesitation, I added yet one more detail. I was still giddy with the news. I wanted to talk to someone about it, and Bush was just as good a person as any.

"I had a sonogram today. Everything's great," I said.

"A sonogram? Isn't that like ultrasound?" Bush asked. The man was sharp. "What exactly does a sonogram do?"

I realized too late that I had backed myself into a corner.

"Its primary function, I guess, is to see if everything's where it should be—if the baby has all its arms and legs and internal organs," I ventured. Keep it simple, I thought to myself. Don't go too much further down that road if you want to keep your secret.

It was too late. He was a step ahead of me. "That means that you found out, then, if it's a girl or a boy?"

I'm surprised the man hadn't been a trial lawyer in his earlier days. He had a mind like a steel trap.

"What is it?" he asked. "Girl or boy?"

Damn.

I paused. Eddie Adams kept on working as if he hadn't

heard a word. One of my staffers lingered near the lighting equipment, trying not to look as though he was listening. I knew he was. I swear, having a private conversation with the man was next to impossible.

"Well, sir . . ." I answered. I didn't know quite what to say. "We really don't know for sure," I lied.

He'd changed his pose and was standing in front of his desk with his arms hanging stiffly at his sides, a wooden smile on his face. I considered whether to interrupt Adams to suggest a change in pose.

And then, the line I'll never forget:

"You're a terrible liar, Kristin," he said. "Come on. Tell me."

"I can't," I said simply. I didn't want to dig myself into a deeper hole, and I didn't feel comfortable lying to the President of the United States.

"You can't," he echoed. "Why not?"

"Because Lonnie and I want to keep it a secret for a while," I said. I realized that Bush might not have understood. When Mrs. Bush was pregnant with their five children, the world was light-years away from sonograms and ultrasounds. The entire concept might have gone right over his head.

He kept pushing, gently. "You mean you're going to keep me in suspense?" he asked. "I promise I won't tell a soul. You know I'm good on my promises."

If the other two people hadn't been in the room, I would have told him without hesitation. I knew the man was honorable enough to keep his mouth shut—who really would have cared anyway?—and part of me really wanted to share our exciting secret. I made a quick decision and whispered across the Oval Office, "It's a girl!"

I felt elated as I said it, almost as though I were floating somewhere high above the lighting equipment and the softly rounded walls and the potted palms sitting serenely behind his desk. Certainly Lonnie would have understood if I told the President.

Bush kept looking into the camera, but now with a warm, genuine smile on his face. Adams clicked and whirred away. "I promise I won't tell a soul," he said under his breath. "Congratulations."

After the shoot, I went home early. It had been a long day, and I was feeling some new, stronger pulling in my lower abdomen. I made it through the door of our house, let Lonnie Paul spend a minute or two running his little brown hands over my moving, kicking stomach, then fell into a deep, deep sleep.

. . . . .

MANY WEEKS LATER, the contractions were still coming on strong. Ken had already warned me that I was categorized as a high-risk pregnancy because of the complications during Lonnie Paul's birth. And Lonnie Paul's prematurity increased the chances of my having another preemie. The last thing I wanted was another premature delivery. And I certainly didn't want another caesarean.

I had begun visualization techniques months before. I pictured myself carrying my baby girl inside of me until she was completely full term; being in complete control over my labor and delivery; and squeezing Lonnie's hand while I leaned forward to watch as her shiny black hair emerged from my body, followed by her tiny brown shoulders, and then, finally, the rest of her squirming brown body. I was going to go full term and have a vaginal delivery if it was the last thing I did. (Lonnie called it the "Clark-women syndrome": stubborn as all get-out and determined to beat all the odds.)

But my contractions kept coming, like waves. I tried to figure out what to do. Should I call Lonnie? Call Ken? Go home and get in bed? Alert a staffer? I walked across the hall to see Chriss Winston, deputy assistant to the President and director of speechwriting. Chriss knew about these things. She'd had a baby boy before she joined the White House staff. We were fellow mothers of firstborn sons, both of whom were close to the same age. I felt a kinship with Chriss. And we'd nurtured our friendship from day one of the Administration.

Speechwriters and other staffers usually formed a line about a mile long outside her office, waiting to get in to see her. But I waddled right in. I was in no mood for waiting. She looked up from a speech she was editing.

"You don't look so good," she said gently. "Everything okay?"

"Everything's okay if you think okay is having fairly regular contractions throughout the night and most of this morning," I said. I suddenly felt very tired, as though I shouldn't be in that place. I wanted to lie down.

She put down her Mont Blanc pen (Chriss always edited the President's speeches with heavy, expensive-looking pens) and looked at me, alarmed. "Kristin, you're *kidding!*" she said, moving toward me from behind her desk. "It's not *time!*" she said in a loud voice.

No-*duh,* I thought, in the words of my young niece Kianna.

Her next expression told me she thought I was playing a joke. She knew it wasn't beyond me: I'd walked into her office

245

several weeks before, announcing that my water had just broken and that I needed to go immediately to the hospital. It was a stupid prank to pull, but it got a rise out of people.

"I know you're shittin' me," she said. If only the outside world knew that the President's director of speechwriting used words like "shittin'." She was such a kick. But she was genuinely worried, and I was beginning to feel guilty for bringing it up at all.

"I'm okay," I said. "I just wanted to let somebody know in case something crazy happens." I turned on my fat heels to leave. Suddenly, I wanted to get back to my office. I really wanted to lie down.

"Don't worry," I said to her over my shoulder. "I'll buzz you on the intercom if my water breaks." I waddled back across the hall to lie down momentarily on the sofa in my office. I only had a minute or two before my next presidential event. I was fed up. I was tired of being stared at by the beautiful, bow-headed females gliding gracefully up and down the halls of the OEOB. I was tired of being overweight, tired of wobbling around the White House.

I had been warned earlier by a colleague that Rose Zamaria, the administrative operations officer in the White House, was on the prowl for women with bare legs. A few of the women on staff had nicknamed her The Stocking Police because she'd turn away any female trying to get into the West Wing with bare legs—without pantyhose. "Go back and put some stockings on those legs," she'd say, sounding like somebody's mother superior. She was a small, slight woman with gray hair and very small feet, but she had the presence and reputation of a burly bouncer at the local bar. Her style didn't intimidate me at all; in fact, it rather irritated me. People should find joy and excitement in working in the White House —not frustration. I was in no mood to spar with the woman, and since Christian Dior didn't make maternity hose, the best I could do in my condition was opaque knee-his from People's drugstore—take it or leave it.

About thirty seconds later, Chriss walked through my door with two more female staffers in tow. I was slightly annoyed at the sight of the other two headband-wearing women. "Any more contractions?" Chriss asked, worry on her face. Everything had been fairly quiet since.

"Nope," I answered calmly. "All quiet on the western front."

Chriss shook her bobbed cut and adjusted her headband. Maria stepped into my office too, looking worried, along with Holly and Cheryl. I was glad to have my three friends close. Holly, Maria, and Cheryl seemed to calm my frazzled nerves. I hoped they wouldn't leave. But the room was getting crowded. You'd think I was about to have quadruplets or something, the way everyone was overreacting.

The ladies held a conference in my office. Eventually they broke from their huddle: "We think you should either call Lonnie immediately or have a White House driver take you to the hospital," Chriss said definitively.

"Good night nurse," I shot back. It was a phrase Mother used to love. I'd been thinking about her a lot lately, as I drew closer to the end of my pregnancy. She was constantly on my mind. I desperately missed not being able to call her on the telephone with questions, tears, concerns about my pregnancy. She wasn't there for me this time around.

"I'll be damned if I'm going to have a White House driver take me to the hospital," I said. "That's not official business anyway. Sununu would have this baby for me if he found out," I said. The laughter helped ease the tension, but it brought on another contraction, the strongest one of all.

"All right, I'll call Lonnie," I finally said, struggling to get up.

"It's all right; I already have," Maria said sweetly. "He wants you to meet him at the doctor's office immediately."

"Mary Kate's going to drive you there," Chriss added.

I'd asked Mary Kate Grant, one of the President's speech-writers, to be my designated driver in the event I went into labor at the White House. She'd readily agreed to the assignment the moment I'd asked, and she had stocked the trunk of her car with a pillow, a blanket, and a list of important phone numbers.

"Not the hospital," Chriss interjected before I could complain, "just the doctor. You need to be checked out."

Mary Kate bounced into my office minutes later. She was always perky, always smiling, as energetic as an Olympic sprinter. She was one of the fortunate ones: Her bob cut bounced when she walked. She had "the White House look," but she was also smart as a whip. My office was full to the brim with ladies. Thank goodness my office was huge (it was four or five times the size of my office during the vice presidential days). I felt as if I were suffocating. Although I really wanted Holly, Maria, and Cheryl to stay close for a few more minutes, I'd have been glad to have everybody else clear out—even though they meant well.

As it turned out, I wasn't in labor, but I did take the next few days off. And something in me just wouldn't let me begin my maternity leave early. I wanted to work right up until the very day, if possible. I wanted to prove to myself that I could do it. (That "Clark syndrome" thing again.) If my mother could do it with every one of her seven children, I could certainly do it with both of mine.

My colleagues were shocked to see me waddle back into the office a few days later. The White House office of communications had started a pool. A chart was posted on my office door. To win the pool, you had to guess the precise date of my delivery, the time, and the sex. Lots of people had signed up. You'd think White House staffers would have more important things to do than sit around guessing delivery dates, but I appreciated their concern.

My visualization exercises actually worked: Our baby's due date came and went. Not only was she not premature, but she was now overdue. Accomplishing my "full term" goal gave me renewed energy and self-confidence: It affirmed that I was still in control of the process. Toward the end, I began feeling quite tired; I always just wanted to lie down.

My grandmother called from Detroit, concerned that I was still working. In her day, women just didn't do that. "Child," she said to me over the phone, "you better quit running all over creation and just settle yourself down," she warned. "You've got no business getting up and going to work every day. The baby's overdue, and you should be home in bed."

Cookie called, too, with words much less gentle. "Listen here, superwoman," she hissed at me from Woodland Street in Detroit. I could feel her hand on her hip as she spoke. "Don't go trying to set any records for doing the most things in the world that a woman can do," she said. "Get off those big boats of yours and prop them up on a pillow somewhere. Let that fine man of yours rub those boats the way only a man can— you know, in between your toes, up and down the arch." She was hilarious. "Nah, that's okay," she said on second thought. "That's probably how you got pregnant in the first place." She knew how to make me laugh. "Uh-huh. Keep laughin', sister," she said, trying hard not to laugh herself. "Laugh yourself all the way to the hospital and give birth to that baby. You're stubborn as a drunken jackass, and you're workin' my last nerve," she said, and then hung up.

I loved Cookie. She was my anchor. She was one of the only people in the world who knew me well enough to cut through the bullshit and get to the point.

Even Bush began voicing some concern that I was still around. But I wanted to complete one last project before I left. We were preparing the President for an important videotaped address (which would air nationally for a full month). It was high visibility, and he needed to look just right. We were about ready to roll. The camera crew was in place, and the room was full of technicians: sound technicians, engineers, lighting directors.

I stood just outside the Library, where the taping was going to be conducted. It was entirely too hot inside the room. I'd move inside the second I received word that Bush was en route. I wasn't feeling well at all, and I assumed it was from all the heat and excitement.

After a minute or two, the Uniformed Division guard sitting down the hall gave me a thumbs-up. Translated: Bush was on his way. Sure enough, after about twenty seconds, Bush appeared down the hall, his long legs taking great strides toward the Library. I could tell from his face that he wanted to get this over with. Television was never his thing.

"Holy cow," Bush said as he entered the Library. "Sure is hot in here." We should have kicked the air conditioning up to high gear hours before the lights were set up. That was basic, elementary White House Production 101. For the first time, I'd let something slip. Maybe it *was* time to get the hell out of Dodge City.

Maria had saved a seat for me in the crowded room. After reviewing the script with the President and making sure he was comfortable with the TelePrompTer, I moved to the side, my portfolio resting on my stomach. I didn't want to sit down because I knew I wouldn't want to get back up.

"Okay, Mr. President. Anytime," I said quietly. It was plenty hot.

"Aren't you going to sit down?" the President said, looking at me.

"I'm fine, Mr. President," I said with formality. I didn't want to get into a debate. "I'd rather stand."

"I think you'd better sit down," he said. He was serious. His face told me he wasn't joking. Maybe he was a little perturbed at having to walk into such a steamy room. Maybe he was genuinely concerned about my being in the advanced stages of pregnancy in such a hot, crowded room.

"I'm really fine. May we begin?" I was losing patience, too. My muscles hurt. I could feel something was about to begin within my body. I prayed that my water wouldn't break all over the beautiful, handmade Oriental rugs in the White House Library.

"I'm not starting until you sit down," he said.

251

A stubborn mule he was. And so bossy.

I didn't want to risk getting him into a bad mood, because that would surely wreck his performance. I sat down. He'd won the battle.

After the taping, he made a beeline for the door. Before he left the room, he turned to me.

"This will be the last time I see you before you have this baby, little mother," he said. "You know I'm on my way to Kennebunkport, and I trust someone will let me know up there when the big moment actually happens," he said. "You're about this close to having that baby right here in this room," he said, holding up his thumb and index finger through a smile. He gave me a big, warm hug. "Good luck. You'll be just fine. See you soon."

And then he was gone.

As usual, Bush had been right. I went into full labor several hours later. The serious, face-distorting contractions began as I walked back to the OEOB after the taping. My water hadn't broken, but I left the office early. I must have known I wouldn't be back for a while, because I packed up the photos on my desk. This was the real thing, all right.

I went home, crawled in bed, and waited. I wanted to stay within the comfort of my own home until the very last minute. Daddy and my sister Ingrid had already flown in from Detroit a few days before in anticipation of the baby's arrival. Lonnie hovered close, rubbing my aching back and pulling out his stopwatch every now and then to time the contractions. After a few hours at home, he made the pronouncement: "It's time to go," he said.

Labor and delivery this time around were a completely different experience. Praise the Lord for visualization exercises.

Ken, Lonnie, and I were in complete control. And even when the pain started, an anesthesiologist came right in and shot some serious drugs into my spine. Ken didn't believe in making folks suffer. And as his patient, neither did I.

My labor was almost precisely how I had visualized it. "I see her hair!" Lonnie announced excitedly after about nine hours in the labor room. He left my side only once during the entire process—to go to the bathroom and get a drink of water. He was with me every step of the way.

"*Push!*" Ken said beside him. "*Push!*" Lonnie and Ken yelled together. Another physician, Julian Safran, who was also part of Ken's team, even stayed past his normal shift to offer moral support and witness The Big Moment. They were a wonderful, rare group of doctors—more like friends than physicians. "*Push!*" the three men yelled together.

"*You* push, goddamnit!" I hissed under my breath. What was this all of a sudden—as the going got the roughest—a participatory pregnancy and delivery?

"Breathe!" Ken said at my side. "Don't forget to breathe, Kristin!" And then, again, the three of them together and their sorry chorus: "Breathe! Breathe! Breathe!"

If I had had the energy, I would have reached out and socked all three of them square in the nose. I was shocked at the intensity of the pain, and I was angry that no one had warned me it would be *this* unbelievably difficult. I'd never experienced anything like it in my life. I felt that if I pushed one more time, I was going to lose consciousness, wipe out completely. Ironically, it would have been the second time in my lifetime: when Mother died, and as our daughter was being born.

Finally, Ken announced what I'd been waiting all night to

hear: "Let's move you into the delivery room! This baby's about one minute away from being born!" The final stage, the crowning glory. I fought tears of relief, of joy, of profound pride in myself for having withstood the ordeal. The tears could flow later. All I wanted was to concentrate on giving birth. About two minutes after they wheeled me into the delivery room—Lonnie still with me every step of the way—our baby girl slipped into her new world.

At that precise moment, I felt Mother's presence more strongly than I had since her death. I don't mean to sound Shirley MacLaine–ish, but I looked and I actually saw Mother, standing in the corner of the delivery room, smiling softly into my eyes. For the next few seconds, the room was completely quiet as the doctors suctioned phlegm and fluid from our daughter's nose and mouth. I held Mother's gaze, not wanting to move an inch, afraid that if I blinked or moved, her presence would lift away or dissipate. And then, suddenly, the room was filled with my daughter's first cries, and it was time to cut the umbilical cord. Ken allowed Lonnie the honors. I wanted to— needed to—see my husband do this, and I looked down for a half-second to watch. After the umbilical cord had been cut, I looked back up, searching for Mother. She was gone.

Lonnie leaned down to kiss my forehead, removing his mask. "Congratulations, dear," he whispered, tears in his eyes. "We have a baby girl."

At that moment, the anger that I still harbored toward Mother for abandoning me began to dissipate. The bitterness lifted from me like a rising cloud. I was no longer hostile. My baby daughter, only seconds old, had blown away forever the last vestiges of anger. In that instant, I understood: Mother's dying was just as much a part of life's cyclical pattern as our baby girl's birth. I had finally been brought face-to-face with life's complete cycle, and I was overwhelmed. I had been praying for months for my Lord God to move me away from the bitterness and anger I still felt toward Mother for leaving me. And He answered my prayers that morning in the delivery room.

We immediately agreed to name our child Mary Elizabeth —after Mother (and after Mother's mother, too). It was a beautiful way of fulfilling the promise I'd made to her less than a year earlier as she herself lay in the hospital: that I would help her live forever through her progeny. And I knew—because I saw—that she had been there to witness it.

The most powerful element of womanhood, for me at least, is my ability to bring forth life into the world. Twice I have been made a living link. I love being a bearer of life. I love being part of the miracle of procreation. I believe it is a woman's single most important overall function while she is here on this earth. I am proud and so blessed to have created life—to have been chosen to be part of the universal chain of continuity. I am emotionally and spiritually committed to doing it again. I only hope that I'll do as fine a job with my children as my own mother did with hers.

· · · · ·

AFTER THE PREGNANCY, I struggled mightily with my hefty hips and my bountiful backside. They were my enemies. I wanted—absolutely *had*—to get rid of them, once and for all. I didn't like the way I looked—I was more displeased with my appearance after I'd given birth than while I was pregnant. (At least while I was pregnant, I had an excuse.)

And in the White House, there was a certain visual standard beneath which one could not descend. To be perfectly honest, there weren't many fat people in the White House. Everybody pretty much watched their weight—not only including, but especially, the men.

Arnold Schwarzenegger helped me realize that fact.

May of 1990 was being recognized as National Physical Fitness and Sports Month. Folks inside the White House wanted to give a big collective push to public health and fitness. As part of the communications plan, I'd proposed a media interview with President Bush and a handful of the nation's leading health and fitness writers. I'd also proposed that Schwarzenegger, who chaired the President's Council on Physical Fitness and Sports, fly to Washington to actively participate in the interview.

He readily accepted—and even joined us for the Oval Office prebriefing immediately before the interview. He was wearing purple socks that just knocked me out. Anybody who had chutzpah enough to wear purple socks to the White House couldn't be all bad. What a hoot. I made a mental note to see his next movie.

Bush was sitting at his desk writing as we all filed into his office to begin the prebrief. (The man was always writing.) Seeing The Great Terminator, he rose from his chair and crossed the room to greet him.

"Arnold, good to see ya again. Good to *see* ya," Bush said, arm outstretched. Schwarzenegger pumped the President's poor hand pretty solidly. Bush looked down at his hand after the handshake and winced dramatically, shaking it in pain like a wet, limp rag. The sound of uninhibited laughter reverberated off the Oval Office walls. It was an unfamiliar sound. In that room, people usually laughed in tiny tee-hees at best.

Folks were definitely affected by Schwarzenegger's presence. I tried several times, unsuccessfully, to steer the conversation into a rehearsal mode, to begin the process of getting the President mentally prepared for his upcoming interview, but no one was interested. Everyone was excited and a bit distracted. Schwarzenegger had brought the Bright Lights of Hollywood into the serious, sophisticated seclusion of the Oval Office. For the moment, the handsome, rock-solid star overpowered the normally muted, dimly lit environment of the White House. I have to admit that the fresh breeze did feel good. Hollywood's razzle-dazzle brought a certain sexiness to the Oval. It was a much needed shot in the arm.

Bush and Fitzwater wanted to engage Schwarzenegger in a conversation about diets, exercise regimens, and personal eating habits. Their concentration level had been shot to hell. Suddenly, macho madness crowded the air.

"How much weight ya pressin' these days, Arnold?" the President asked. He wanted to talk personal fitness, and there was no stopping him. Bush patted his stomach with a frown. "I tell ya, I've been trying forever to get these five or so extra pounds off."

Bush's eyes rested on Marlin's portly figure and zeroed in. I knew what was coming.

"You still on that diet of yours, Marlin?" Bush asked. "Refresh my memory. Which diet is it this time? The liquid one?" he asked with a mischievous smile, winking in my general direction.

And then, turning toward Schwarzenegger with a smirk,

257

Bush said, "You know, my press secretary's lost a considerable amount of weight recently. How much ya lost, Marlin?" the President asked, egging him on. The room grew quiet. Marlin fidgeted on the arm of the sofa. It was true. He was always experimenting with a fad diet to get rid of his considerable, cuddly-looking girth. But this time it had worked. He'd lost quite a bit of weight, and he looked great.

For my part, I'm proud to say, I had lost about thirty-five pounds. It had been nine months since Mary Elizabeth was born, and it had taken me that full nine months to get my expandable hips back down to a reasonable size. But I'd die twice and stick needles in my eyes before I engaged myself in an Oval Office conversation about personal weight loss with Bush, Fitzwater, and Arnold Schwarzenegger.

"I have no official comment for you on that question, Mr. President," Fitzwater said through laughter. He was turning pink. He was adorable.

So much for the rehearsal. I sat back in my chair and listened.

"What do you think of those liquid diets, Arnold? How fast a mile can you run, Arnold? What's your daily caloric intake, Arnold?" I was getting dizzy. I thought I smelled the faint odor of body sweat.

I looked at my watch. By now, my staff had already cleared every reporter into the West Wing lobby. If she was on schedule—and she always was—Maria had already seated them around the table according to the seating chart and had briefed them on the ground rules for the interview. It was time to rock and roll.

I sat forward, uncrossing my legs. I fingered my gold Cross

pen. In the midst of all the macho conversation about calories, weight pressing, and diets, I felt acutely aware of my body and slightly self-conscious. I began to speak. Lord God Almighty, I thought: I'm actually holding in my stomach muscles. Part of me wished I'd squeezed myself into my Playtex that morning as I dressed.

Sitting in the Oval Office that afternoon made me realize that we've all gone slightly insane with the disproportionate emphasis we place on physical appearance. Everybody and their mother is trying their damnedest to find "the look"—whatever that is—and I mean *everybody*. There I was, sitting across from a President who was gingerly patting his midsection, whining about a five-pound weight gain; a White House press secretary on a liquid diet; and a rock-jawed, purple-sock-wearing hunk of a man who could have easily, with two or three curls of his biceps, saved my grandmother the fifteen dollars she paid one summer to have four grown men drag her deep freezer from the dusty depths of her basement and haul it away to the junk-yard. Nor am I above the craze: Even though I'd lost thirty-five pounds, I was still starving myself and exercising like a crazy woman. I was going to get into my prepregnancy clothes if it was the last thing I did.

We'd all be up the river without a paddle, I thought as I looked around the Oval Office, if these men had to face for a day what many women have to face periodically throughout their lives: monthly water weight gain; distended, strained muscles that develop with advanced pregnancy; stretch marks; varicose veins; cellulite; and, as Cookie would say, "thunder thighs big enough to choke a horse." It would have been too much for the men to handle.

"Gentlemen," I said through the din, "the reporters have arrived and are waiting for us in the Roosevelt Room." I hoped that holding in my stomach muscles so tightly hadn't affected the sound of my voice. "Mr. President, why don't we spend just a minute or two reviewing the possible line of questioning?"

Momentary silence. Party pooper, I could feel them thinking. I thought I heard a sigh, maybe even a hiss. The arm of the sofa groaned under Marlin's weight. That poor sofa had had its share of heavier-than-average white men sitting on it improperly—resting their weight on the arms, rather than on the seat cushions. Those sofa arms were the favorite resting place for both Fitzwater and Sununu. You'd think they'd know better.

Bush looked down at the folder on his desk. "That's right. Get us on track, Kristin," he said with a mischievous smile. He swiveled around in his chair and sat back, crossing his legs, ready to begin work.

"Mr. President," I began, my stomach muscles going to town. "You'll be meeting with twelve health and fitness writers for a thirty-minute roundtable in the Roosevelt Room." I spent a few seconds outlining the nature of the event, what he should expect, and what we hoped to accomplish from the interview. It was basically a spoken version of the briefing papers I'd sent the day before.

As I was talking, the President picked up the red folder which contained all of my prepared material: the prebriefing memo, the detailed background information on each publication which would be present during the interview, a seating diagram identifying the precise location of each reporter around the table, an alphabetical listing of each publication, a thirty-second, three-paragraph opening statement to be read upon his arrival into the room (this was also on index cards, which he actually preferred, because he could stick them in his suit pocket and take them out just as he was arriving), and a list of possible questions for his review to be rehearsed during the prebrief—all on thick bond paper, as he liked it. (I was told it felt better in his hands than lighter-weight paper; of course, it looked better.)

I finished speaking, letting him flick through the papers uninterrupted. The room was silent. I watched his face. The moment I saw the familiar lip nibbling begin, I knew that at least he'd begun to concentrate.

I continued speaking. This event could be characterized as fairly softball, I said. It wasn't a major, high-risk interview, and my estimate was that most of the questions would be more about his personal health and fitness than about the Administration's health policy. But it was a good hit, and a wise investment of his time: a simple, noncontroversial topic. In thirty minutes, we'd reach a reading audience of many millions, and we'd maximize an opportunity to convey the message that the President is not only actively concerned about physical fitness, but physically fit himself. And the press would get all this in time to publish it during National Physical Fitness Month. Plus, Schwarzenegger's presence provided great color, a wonderful photo opportunity, and a fresh new dimension to the interview itself.

"Okay," Bush said. "I'm ready to get through the questions. Fire away."

We all sat up in our chairs. The smell of body sweat began

261

to disappear. It was almost showtime. The President sailed through the questions as I knew he would. Schwarzenegger provided valuable input and sound advice during the session. I was quite impressed.

"Are there any other questions you have, Mr. President?" I asked, moving to conclude the meeting. "Anything else you c—" Something fell from my portfolio as I reshuffled papers. I looked down at the thick Oval Office carpet: There on the carpet, a few feet away from my feet, lay a bright orange plastic letter M. It was probably the first time in the history of the world that an orange letter M had landed on the floor of the Oval Office. I squinted to make sure I wasn't seeing things. No one else in the room seemed to notice.

I realized in an instant: Lonnie Paul had been playing in my things again, and he had probably left his "M for Mommy" refrigerator magnet inside my portfolio as a surprise. I bent quickly to recover it, snatching up my prized gift. Wouldn't it just figure, I thought—especially with all the machismo flying around the room that afternoon—that the only woman present in the Oval Office is dropping plastic baby toys from her portfolio? But instead of being embarrassed, I was actually comforted by the warm reminder of the two beautiful, bright children I had waiting for me at home—of how much life and love they brought into my life in unexpected ways. In the same way that I'd sometimes see Colin Powell strutting around the White House like a proud peacock, suited up in full military dress complete with a chestful of medals, I, too, saw my letter M as a medal of Motherhood.

Throughout the interview, Schwarzenegger was comfortable, professional, and in complete command. Although he didn't know me from Adam's dying house cat, I still felt proud of him and his performance. And I felt proud of myself, too, for having given birth to two such wonderful, loving children: I fingered my plastic letter M throughout the entire interview. It's the best gift I've ever received.

CHAPTER 15

. . . . .

The Character
of the Man

. . . . .

I WAS ALWAYS AWARE that, no matter how kind and caring George Bush was, he was also the President of the
United States. I was ever mindful of overstepping my bounds,
never wanting to reveal an inappropriate amount about the
personal conflicts in my life or the problems I was facing at
any given moment. It wasn't appropriate, nor was it fair.
There wasn't much room left on his shoulders for other people's burdens, nor should there be. The man had a country to
run.

But some intangible element about Bush's very nature was
comforting and reassuring. He beckoned people to come and
seek solace—just as he did when he made the way for me to
share my burden about Mother's sickness that afternoon in his
office.

A new conflict had arisen and was weighing on me. And I didn't know quite how to react.

It was shortly after my return to the White House from my twelve-week maternity leave with Mary Elizabeth. Demarest and I had come to an impasse. While I was away, the decision had been made to "redefine" some of my job responsibilities—and the redefinition, to me, was unacceptable. Demarest assured me that these job changes were not a result of poor performance; indeed, he emphasized, my performance continued to be superb. It was just that while I was gone, he came to realize that several operational functions within the staff could be "streamlined"—which, unfortunately, meant cutting me out of a lot of the action. Among other things, Demarest wanted me to relinquish responsibility for all presidential videotaped addresses; these represented a large portion of the time I spent with Bush. Something in me told me that perhaps my access to Bush was being intentionally curtailed; perhaps people were threatened by my seeing him as often as I did. Access to the President, after all, was the primary source of power within the White House. It was simply "time for a change," as Demarest explained—a weak, wimpy definition, in my mind, that was much too loosely woven for my taste. I felt as though I was being penalized for my absence—particularly since these proposed changes would not be occurring as a result of poor performance. It stood to reason, then, that if performance was not the issue, something else was: Had I not been out for twelve weeks, things would have probably purred along as usual.

Demarest's unwillingness to discuss or compromise on the matter only fueled my frustration. I momentarily considered leaving the staff. But I didn't want my tenure at the White House to end like this; it had been too positive an experience.

On December 19, 1989, we were preparing for a video-taping session in the Map Room. Because one of the President's messages would be televised nationally, a light makeup application would be required. As he sat in the Diplomatic Reception Room being fussed over by the makeup artist, I decided the time was right. He had no papers to study, no briefings to listen to; his attention would not be diverted. He was leaving shortly for Kennebunkport to be with his family for the Christmas holidays.

"Mr. President," I said softly.

I was close to making the decision to leave, but not quite there yet. I felt as though I needed to share with him the options I was considering before I actually made the decision. I felt I owed him that.

"While we have this rare free moment, I just wanted to let you know that I'm considering leaving soon," I said.

"Where you off to, Kristin? Somewhere warm, I hope, for the holidays!"

He didn't understand. I tried again.

"No, sir, I don't mean a vacation. I mean that I might well be leaving the staff some time soon. Not immediately, of course, but soon. I wanted you to know it now, rather than after the fact. And I wanted you to hear it from me."

He turned to look at me. The makeup artist had to stop her work momentarily.

"What?" he asked. "Have you gotten another job offer?" He didn't sound angry or upset, only surprised.

"No, sir," I responded.

I had decided beforehand not to drag him down into any of the minutiae; he was the President of the United States. He certainly didn't need to know all the supergory goings-on of his midlevel staffers. All I wanted to do was tell him that I might not be there much longer.

I didn't want or expect him to intervene. I simply wanted to tell him myself. I'd been with him in the White House longer than any of the people on his communications staff, Demarest included. And this would probably be the last opportunity to speak with him face-to-face before we all left for the holidays.

"Then what is it?" he asked. We were running out of time. "Has something happened to make you unhappy here?"

Again, he had made the way for me to share my burden— or at least part of it.

"A little, yes. But I'm not going to bore you with the nitty-gritty details. There are some staff-related things going on that I'm just not thrilled with."

"What kind of 'staff-related' things?" he asked. He wanted to know. I hesitated.

"Some decisions some folk have made recently are ones with which I . . . I don't want to get into th—"

"This is just great," he said. He was halfway joking as he attempted to throw his arms up in exasperation. But because the makeup apron he was wearing confined his movements, his forearms flew up at the elbow. It looked funny, but I didn't laugh. I wasn't in the mood.

"I'm about to leave for Christmas vacation and you spring something like this on me," he said. No laughs from me.

"Kristin," he said. "If you're not happy here any longer, I'm certainly not going to get in your way if you want to leave. But which 'folks' are you talking about? Who?" he asked.

I decided not to play games or beat around the bush. We

were both too busy for that. But I also didn't want to sound like a whining tattletale. But he had asked me, so I told him.

"Demarest is proposing some changes—some of which directly involve me—that I'm simply not happy about," I said. "I'm frustrated because the decisions were made while I was away on maternity leave. I feel like I have no control or influence over what's happening, and it's been made clear that the matter is not—and never has been—open for discussion." I paused momentarily, then continued. Bush was listening. "In my mind, and on general principle, I feel like I almost have no other choice but to consider leaving."

"Do me a favor," he said as the makeup artist completed her work and began putting away her things.

"Don't make any rash decisions right away. If you want to leave, I'm not going to stand in your way. And I'm certainly not going to get in between whatever's going on between you and Dave. Dave's a good man, and I respect his judgment. But why don't you at least mull it over during the holidays. Think before you act," he said.

And then, as an afterthought, he added, "I would be sorry to see you go."

After the videotaping segment, which went very well, Bush exited the room more swiftly than usual, bidding me and the crew happy, safe holidays. He seemed as though he had urgent business to attend to.

"See you when I get back," he said to me pointedly as he breezed out of the room.

Back in my office about an hour later, my phone rang. It was Demarest. Relations lately had been chilly between us. He was essentially a gentle, smart man, but I was disappointed with how he was handling this entire "job reassignment" issue.

"I need to see you in my office," he said into the phone. "Come over right away."

Demarest didn't often act with urgency; his voice told me that something was wrong. As I walked toward his West Wing office, I visualized the possible scenario: Maybe he was tired of all the back and forth and was actually going to ask me to leave. I thought of how I would react.

Inside his office, we both sat on the couch. He came right to the point.

"The President just called me," he said with slight irritation. What's so unusual about that? I thought to myself. What does this have to do with me?

"And?" I asked. I was growing weary myself.

"He wanted to know what was happening with you," Demarest said. "He was quite concerned."

Damn. Maybe Demarest is just pulling my leg, I thought. But he wasn't.

He continued, "He said that you'd just said something to him about resigning and that, while he would certainly never presume to micromanage my staff, he was concerned that you were, for some reason, unhappy here," Demarest said.

I listened with a hodgepodge of emotions. The last thing I expected was for the President to take this matter up directly with Demarest—or with anyone. All I'd wanted to do was make him aware of what I was considering. I was shocked and, admittedly, quite flattered; I still thought Demarest might be joking.

But at the same time, Bush's direct intervention could even have worked against me: Demarest could have felt undermined and (perhaps justifiably) angry by my leapfrogging over him directly to the big boss. But if he was angry, he didn't show it. Overall, I always believed (and still do) that Demarest was a fair man of strong, solid character. We were just at a professional impasse.

"Dave," I explained, "I felt like I had to tell him that I was thinking about leaving. You know we have a history together. I couldn't leave without telling him first myself. But please know that I *never* broached the subject thinking he would call you on it directly. I had no idea. I am sorry."

I was, too. This had taken me by complete surprise.

I continued, "I didn't dare drag him down into all of the minutiae, but I did want him to know my probable intentions. And I wanted to tell him myself."

Dave studied me carefully. Something had changed in his eyes. The President had intervened directly on my behalf. While Bush had made no mandates of Demarest, he had at least expressed his concern with my unhappiness. And he had implied that he didn't want me to leave the staff. In him, I had found a protector.

"You're not really still thinking of leaving just because of this disagreement, are you?" Demarest asked. The dynamics had indeed changed.

"Dave, I just don't know," I answered. I really was confused. I hadn't necessarily wanted to introduce this new element into the debate. It made me even more confused.

"Look," he said. "You've been with Bush longer than I have—longer than just about everybody in communications. You do have a history with George Bush. The final decision, of course, is yours, but why walk away when you're doing such a great job?"

I looked at him.

"At least think about it over the holidays," he said. "I

don't think it has to come to a resignation. We can work something out.''

Of course, I didn't resign. The problems somehow dissolved, and Demarest and I even returned to an even keel. I hadn't wanted to leave the White House; more importantly, I hadn't wanted to leave George Bush on those terms.

But it had been an emotionally tumultuous day.

As I made my way home that same evening, a special news bulletin on the car radio caught my attention: The United States had just invaded Panama. President Bush had just launched U.S. military forces into Panama City to seize the country's leader, General Manuel Noriega.

I sat in my car in amazement and shock: Even with the weight of an imminent invasion on his shoulders, Bush had taken the time—if only a moment—to address the concerns of one of his midlevel assistants.

Had I known he was literally preparing this military move, I certainly would never have brought up the issue. I immediately understood why he'd rushed out of the room and quickly departed. I hadn't been able to put two and two together until the special news bulletin did it for me.

That the President took the time at all while in the midst of such a major military action spoke volumes to me about his character and compassion. He was forever going the extra mile to ensure another's happiness. God really had made a special man when he created George Bush.

But kind, caring, and generous were not Bush's only character traits. The man could get as mad as a wet hen. It was a side of him that the public rarely saw.

· · · · ·

JULY 17, 1990.

Something about the day. From the moment I opened my eyes that morning, something just didn't feel quite right. I awoke with a throbbing headache—rare in itself. Our radio alarm jolted us awake with Janis Joplin screaming "Crah, crah, bay-bay!" into my left ear—telltale evidence of Lonnie Paul's busy little fingers readjusting the radio the night before. Mary Elizabeth had developed a slight fever overnight and threw up into her bowl of oatmeal at breakfast.

I was normally a little tense on days when I was to brief the President, but I didn't mind such tension at all—I actually even welcomed it. Slight tension kept me on my toes. I never allowed it to get heavy enough to weigh me down. But today was different, and my worry fed more worry: Had I overlooked some critically important detail for this afternoon's event? Had I omitted some important piece of material from the briefing package I'd submitted to the President the day before?

I put it out of my mind. Unnecessary worry would blur my focus; I needed to feel sharp during my meeting with Bush. Besides, I thought to myself, I'll only be with the man for a total of thirty minutes—ten minutes for the Oval Office prebrief and a simple twenty-minute press availability with about eighty magazine publishers. I had all my bases covered, as usual. What could go wrong in half an hour?

First off, I was late for the prebrief—the first time I had *ever* been late for a meeting with the President. My crazy watch had generously granted me twelve additional nonexistent minutes, and thinking I had the extra time, I spent a few minutes going over the ground rules with the publishers, who were already convened in Room 450 of the Old Executive Office Building and were eagerly awaiting the President's arrival. I

273

even had the nerve to "amble" over to the West Wing, making my way toward the Oval Office at a leisurely pace and stopping to chat with John the mailman in the West Wing stairwell.

"How's that odometer working, John?" I asked him casually. I'd given him an odometer for Christmas. I was pleased to see that he wore it almost every day. John McGinnis probably got more exercise than anyone else in the White House complex, bar none. He was always walking—on his way here to deliver this document, on his way there to pick one up.

"I'm at about twelve miles already," he answered proudly, looking down to check the tiny apparatus attached to his belt. "And I haven't even started goin' good yet!"

I made my way up the stairs, through the West Wing lobby, past the Roosevelt Room, and finally into the Oval Office reception area. To my surprise, none of my usual briefing partners were lingering outside—Marlin Fitzwater was almost always there. The first twinges of "something ain't right" slapped at the nape of my neck, causing the hair at the back of my neck to stand at attention.

I looked at Bruce Caughman, Bush's newly appointed personal assistant, and realized immediately: The prebriefing had already begun. One thing you don't do—you *never* do—is walk into the Oval Office late. Not even a minute late. I looked at the clock. I was about six or seven minutes late. Bruce looked at me without his usual warm smile. He seemed to be asking, "Do you still want to go in?" I shrugged and gestured toward the closed door. Bruce turned for a final look into the peephole and quietly swung it open, allowing me to enter.

The President sat at his desk, red-faced and going to town on his inner lip. Fitzwater and several other aides sat in a semicircle around his desk, looking unusually dour. No one even turned to acknowledge my presence. I wasn't expecting the entire room to rise and salute, but a simple acknowledgment or a slight turn of the head would have been nice. Something was terribly wrong.

Bush picked up his conversation where he had apparently left off before I entered. He was angry. Very angry. Good night, nurse, I thought to myself. What in the hell has happened?

"I'm still not understanding this," Bush said with mounting impatience. "Can someone please explain how this happened?"

His voice was loud, his skin splotched red. A small sprig of hair fell over his forehead, as it often does when he's outdoors or exercising. Today, it made him look wild. He pushed it back into place.

Thick quiet stuffed the Oval Office like cotton. All I could hear was the grandfather clock ticking away, the President's fingers drumming on his desk, and my ears ringing as I struggled to make sense of what was happening.

Within the softly rounded walls of the Oval Office, grown men usually clambered all over each other—politely, of course —to not only answer but anticipate Bush's every question. These were, after all, The President's Gray Matter Men.

But today, all mouths were strangely mute.

And then, to my horror, every gaze—including the President's—turned to rest upon me. At that moment, whatever happened had become my fault. I was the action officer for this event, and I'd just damned well *better* be prepared with an answer—no matter what the question—'cause the shit had most assuredly hit the fan.

"Maybe you can clear this mess up, Kristin," Bush said, swiveling his chair slightly in my direction. I'd never heard him use a word like "mess" before. This was most definitely some serious business.

"Did you compose the list of participants for this press availability I'm about to do?" Bush asked.

"I did, Mr. President," I answered, resisting the urge to finish the sentence with "But this man sitting right across from you—David Demarest, your communications director—approves each and every document I send to you before it goes out, including guest lists. Demarest and I discussed this list; he gave it the thumbs-up, signed off on it, and even complimented me for a fine, thorough briefing package. So why he's sitting here acting like he doesn't know what's going on is beyond me."

But I didn't say any of that.

"What seems to be the problem, Mr. President?" I asked.

"The *problem* is that this is my home, not just my office. Who you so casually decide to invite into this place is a direct reflection of the character of this White House." He was hot.

"Take another look at your list," he said angrily. Oh, I thought, so it's *my* list now, huh? Everybody's pawning it off on me now, is that it? I swear, everybody scurries like roaches when the going gets tough.

Bush continued, "You've invited *Playboy* magazine into this White House. What kind of judgment is that? How does that make me look? Did you stop to think what the media will do with this when they get their hands on this list of invitees and see Christie Hefner's name?"

He asked again, to the room in general, "Didn't you stop

to think what this will mean?" If he hadn't been so mad, it would have sounded like pleading.

Everyone in the room was completely silent. You could have heard a pin drop. What a courageous group, those President's men.

Fitzwater was wearing his "it's-Demarest's-event,-not-mine" look on his face. And not even Demarest made a peep.

"Mr. President," I tried to explain, "the Magazine Publishers Association had been trying for months to get an audience with you. I proposed the event; it came back approved— from scheduling, Governor Sununu, and you—so I moved forward with coordination." Bush's fingers drummed hard against his wood desk. But he was listening.

"The event which was approved was a White House briefing for the entire group—for the entire association—because that's who initiated the invitation. We didn't think—I didn't think—it was wise for the White House to start censoring their membership or refusing entry to certain members while admitting others." I looked over at Demarest, who looked as though he wanted to say something.

"Sir," Demarest finally said, "this *is* an event with the Magazine Publishers Association. We approved the event, gave them a certain number of seats, and left it up to them to decide which of their members would get to attend. Since we'd already approved the event itself, we thought that was their call to make."

"What you've done shows an incredible lapse in judgment," Bush said angrily. I assumed he was directing his comment to me.

"It's a personal and professional embarrassment—and a

significant risk. Worse, it calls my character into question," he said.

Silence. Much rustling of Brooks Brothers suits. Someone in the room attempted a tasteless one-liner about centerfolds and cotton bunny tails.

I sat there wishing I was somewhere else—at the grocery store, maybe, or even across the street, sitting on a bench in Lafayette Park. Anywhere but there in the Oval Office.

A voice brought me back down to earth. "Where is Christie Hefner sitting in the room?" someone asked. I'd already visually blocked the shot in my mind as we spoke, and I knew that by now the White House press corps was positioned in the room, waiting to cover Bush's remarks. (During events like these, the press corps was allowed to cover his remarks but was precluded from actually participating directly in the Q&A.) Depending on the position of the cutaway camera (the camera which "cuts away" from the main action to get a wide shot of the participating audience), Ms. Hefner could easily appear. I knew exactly where she sat: toward the upper middle portion of the room, close to the aisle.

"It might seem a minor oversight to those of you who help plan my day-to-day activities, but I won't tolerate it," Bush said. "I don't see how this could have happened, people. What were you thinking?"

I decided to try one more time.

"Sir, we discussed *Playboy*'s presence more than once between ourselves. We finally decided that allowing the association the freedom to choose their own attendees was preferable to White House censorship of their list.

"By saying yes to the group itself, we *got* the whole group —lock, stock, and barrel."

But as I spoke, I, too, was beginning to question the correctness of the decision. In retrospect, we probably would have been wiser—and safer—censoring MPA's guest list ourselves rather than allowing *Playboy* to come into the White House. But hindsight is always twenty-twenty. And I knew that in the CYA department (translated: Cover Your Ass), I had already raised the possible red flag with both Demarest and Chriss Winston (both of whom paused momentarily as I showed them the guest list, considered the implications, then waved the list off as approved and signed my briefing memo).

Bush pushed away from his desk, preparing to depart. He was finished talking.

"Let's get this goddamned thing over with and hope like hell Christie Hefner doesn't decide to stand up and ask me a question on national television."

In the President's eyes, I had clearly threatened to publicly undermine his moral and professional integrity. In my eyes, I threatened not only his, but my own. His reaction in the Oval Office that afternoon made me realize that moral fortitude is his yardstick, with which he measures his every action. Exposing him to the stench of impropriety was the worst of all errors. To him, there was nothing more egregious. He is a man of uncompromising character; in his mind, there are no murky gray areas between right and wrong. He was justifiably angry that someone or something had threatened to undermine his integrity. And he also fully recognized the power of the media should they decide to make an issue of it.

I was angry at Demarest for not having come to my rescue sooner, but I was grateful, still, for his coming to my defense at all. I didn't expect the other men in the room to make a peep; I knew they would not. This event wasn't their show; in no way did they want to be associated, directly or indirectly, with the President's vehement anger. What would they get out of defending a principle which they had nothing to do with violating? Absolutely nothing—except, perhaps, the wrath of the President himself, and Lord knows nobody ever wanted to have to face that. But since Demarest was my boss, his simple statement to the President in my defense at least showed a sign of solidarity.

It did nothing, however, to impress the President.

Suddenly, he rose, stretched, then strode toward the door and flung it open. Bruce Caughman, surprised by the sudden movement as he relaxed on the other side of the door, sprung into action, almost running, while two agents slipped into position as smoothly as mercury. We all filed out behind him, looking somewhat apologetic and dog-eared. My mind raced toward solutions, but at this late moment there simply were none.

As we walked, I began composing my letter of resignation: I'd need it if Christie Hefner stood up and asked the President a question. I calculated the minutes I had left, accounting for the fact that Bush would want to stop in the private anteroom adjoining the auditorium immediately upon his arrival to review last-minute questions. I also knew that Commerce Secretary Robert Mosbacher, who had addressed the MPA only minutes before, would be waiting in the anteroom to give the President a brief assessment of the nature of the group itself and their line of questioning. By my calculations, I had about three or four minutes before the press conference actually began. There was one thing left to do.

Once our entourage arrived in the anteroom, I excused myself momentarily and made my way through the back hallway toward the ladies' room. There, in the safety and privacy of a bathroom stall, I closed my eyes and prayed to my Lord God to help me remember that none of us are invincible or perfect, and that all of us, including me, are at some point vulnerable to error.

Three minutes later, I stood on the podium at the President's immediate right, safely out of camera range, my eyes fixed and frozen on Christie Hefner. I was willing her not to move, daring her to raise her hand, kicking myself for making the President so angry. But I'd been energized and comforted by those few minutes of respite.

I studied Bush's face as he began the press conference to see if his anger had subsided. He was truly a professional; not even the slightest hint of his earlier scowl showed in his expression.

About nineteen minutes into the session, I raised my hand slightly and stepped forward, calling "Last question" to both the President and the working media to bring the press conference to an official close. Bush nodded curtly in acknowledgment, but he had no intention of stopping. Either he was enjoying the press conference so much that he didn't want to stop (which I doubt), or he was sending a signal that he was still pissed off and that my gesture meant nothing to him. He went on and on.

"Here, we've got a couple of more," the President said to several outstretched arms, pointing into the group. "I was late getting over here anyway." (Of *course* you were late getting here, I thought to myself in response. It takes a little extra time to bawl out your staff, doesn't it?) If they only knew.

Then, to top it off, he looked over at me with a smile while the cameras were rolling and the pens were flying and said, "Thank you, Kristin. I don't want to overrule my leader here. She'll *kill* me when we get out of here."

I smiled at the comment. I was slightly embarrassed at suddenly being made the center of attention by having the President of the United States refer to me as his "leader," but I was glad that his anger had subsided.

I thought about the heart attack I'd probably have if Ms. Hefner stood to ask the last question (she didn't). Who's killing who? I thought to myself, breathing a sigh of relief and turning to leave as the press conference ended. My Lord had walked with me yet again, but my heart was still racing like crazy.

Just who's killing who? I thought again with a tired smile.

· · · · ·

IF THERE WAS PRESSURE associated with the incident surrounding *Playboy,* there was certainly equal (if not greater) pressure associated with yet another media interview which occurred that following month, in August. Our timing for this particular interview was (as the spin doctors like to say) most definitely "out of synch."

And that is no exaggeration. Our timing *was* off.

I'd been working with Sig Rogich, one of Bush's senior aides, on coordinating the interview (the writer was a good friend of Sig's), but a sudden and dramatic development almost precluded the session: It was August 6, 1990. The Iraqis had begun their invasion of Kuwait. The invasion held the world's attention; it was major news in every newspaper, on every network.

In Fitzwater's planning meeting that morning, we discussed whether to move forward with the interview as sched-

282

uled or cancel it altogether. Marlin was rightfully concerned about the appearance of the President participating in a frivolous media interview on his love of sports while, underneath his nose, Iraq invaded Kuwait. We decided, in the end, that making major alterations to the President's schedule and canceling all of his previously planned activities might also send the wrong signal; we had to be careful not to raise public panic. We decided to move forward with the interview.

My briefing package to the President was fairly succinct (a two-page briefing memo), and our prebrief lasted for only five or six minutes. On that particular day, brevity seemed to be the name of the game. Bush was understandably distracted by other events, and he seemed to want to get through the interview— and the prebriefing—as quickly as possible. General Colin Powell, Defense Secretary Dick Cheney, and a smattering of other top military brass were everywhere; news of the invasion dominated every conversation inside the White House. Our office of media relations had no direct role to play in responding to the invasion; we were essentially waiting and watching like the rest of the world.

Bush looked tired. His face reflected the tremendous pressure he was under.

But when Rogich escorted the reporter into the Oval Office and the talk of baseball, fishing, and tennis began, an element of tension seemed to fall from Bush's face. The interview that afternoon proved a much needed momentary distraction. There was nothing President Bush loved more than to talk sports. It was his true passion. And as I moved to conclude the session, the look on the President's face told me he wasn't ready to stop.

I braced myself for surprise.

Bush leaned across the desk toward the reporter.

"Listen, do you want me to show you this?" Bush asked, gesturing toward the door and outside. "Have you seen the setup we have out here?" He was like a schoolboy showing off his new set of pencils.

The reporter, not even knowing exactly to what Bush was referring, nodded eagerly like a small puppy. He was going someplace, unscheduled, with the President. We all got up to leave together. Bush must have realized he was going overboard —doing too much during such a critically important time— but it was too late. "We do have a war going on, but . . . ," he said, somewhat absently. I could see him mulling it over in his mind. Cut it short or continue the interview? Hell, he'd made the offer. He would stick to it.

We filed through Bush's private study just off of the Oval Office and made our way toward a small hideaway several yards away. The President escorted us into a small room that looked something like a poolside gazebo: It was a workout room, filled with his private exercise equipment. (I hadn't even seen this before.) Bush proudly pointed out a feature or two—like his "running machine," as he called it, which he said he loved. "In the winter I use it a lot," he explained. "It's good. You can fast-walk, and it elevates."

Great stuff, I thought to myself. What else you got in that black bag of yours, Mr. Wizard? I thought. Bush was reading my mind. He showed us a few more pieces of equipment, then ducked back outside, walking several yards away to his prized horseshoe pit. God, how he loved that thing. He was particularly proud of the new clay.

"There's our horseshoe pit," he said with a smile, pointing. "It's a marvelous thing. It's got this new clay that's impervious to water. All you do is sweep the water off and you can start playing," he said. The reporter was scribbling furiously. He couldn't have asked for a greater "inside" story.

"It's been great for the White House," Bush continued. He talked about how he played against everybody within the complex—the furniture men, the Uniformed Division guards, several individual White House staffers.

After a few minutes, Bush himself finally moved to close the interview. I'm glad he did: I didn't have the heart to call for last question. He was enjoying it far too much. By the look on his face, though, it was clear that the weight of the world was again upon him. He had a war to get back to, and although the United States was not yet directly involved, the time had come to get back to the serious business. But the break had been fun. And the reporter was more than satisfied.

· · · · ·

THROUGH CHANNELS LIKE THESE, I came to know George Bush—through the temper tantrums over *Playboy* and the impromptu tours of the horseshoe pit. It was through crisis, particularly during the illness and death of my mother, that our relationship evolved into a true friendship. And through everything else in between—the pregnancy, the transition of power, and the countless media-related activities—I came to know his kind heart.

CHAPTER 16

. . . . .

The Visit

. . . . .

AS DIRECTOR OF MEDIA RELATIONS, one of my tasks was to enhance Oval Office access for members of the non-White House press corps. I wanted Bush to meet with members of the African-American media—especially during February, Black History Month. I'd received a call from a black newspaper publisher in Baltimore weeks before, strongly urging the President to make himself available.

I carefully developed the proposal with a strong personal recommendation, and to my delight, it was almost immediately approved. The proposal first went before the scheduling committee, and once approved by the committee, it then went on to Governor Sununu. Once Sununu gave it his blessing, it was then sent to the President himself for his final approval.

Not only was it important for us to get the ink during Black History Month, but it was equally important for these members of the media to be granted access into the Oval Office. Because most of these media representatives were not members of the White House press corps, they were unable to attain White House press credentials. For them, access into the inner sanctum was difficult at best.

It was time for the President to sit down with African-American newspaper publishers. It had been almost a decade since they had been invited into the White House—in my eyes, an embarrassment and a disgrace. For this particular session, creating a comfortable, relaxed atmosphere would be essential; the format was critically important. I visualized the event: It should be a fairly small group, no more than about fifteen in number. Promoting constructive, meaningful dialogue would be more successful with a smaller group, and it would allow for more in-depth follow-up and a closer examination of issues.

The best room in the White House for small group media interviews? Apart from the Oval Office, my preference was most certainly the Roosevelt Room—a comfortable, intimate, yet dignified room immediately across the corridor from the Oval Office. In it, the President seemed to feel at ease—another important consideration for an event of this importance and, yes, which carried an amount of risk.

The event was risky because, for one, it had been so many years since anything with black newspaper publishers had been tried. Also, the Reagan legacy had left a bitter taste in their mouths—and on the tips of their pens. Many black reporters and newspaper publishers considered Reagan a dispassionate, disinterested President; his civil rights policies, in their eyes, had set minorities back many, many years.

But, like many civil rights leaders at the beginning of the Bush administration (John Jacob of the National Urban League and Benjamin Hooks of the NAACP, for example), they seemed at least momentarily willing to give Bush the benefit of the doubt. At the slightest turn, the mood could become combative. But, in the end, the necessity of this event—embarrassingly long overdue in coming—outweighed the risk.

It turned out to be one of the most rewarding, personally fulfilling events I'd ever planned for the President.

We began the event with lunch in the Roosevelt Room— consommé, wild rice, Cobb salad, and, for dessert, sorbet. There seemed to be a slight discomfort as the meeting got under way. Perhaps the publishers felt nervous. Maybe they, too, anticipated a combative, potentially explosive confrontation. For those first five or ten minutes, everyone tiptoed around each other, but shortly thereafter, for some reason, both the publishers and the President dove headlong into substantive, salient issues: the release of Nelson Mandela, the Administration's most recent efforts to fight the War on Drugs, improved race relations, and empowering black businesses.

By the end of the session, much ground had been covered. The President was truly moved by the publishers' strong convictions and eloquent, honest discourse. And they, in turn, seemed genuinely appreciative of the access and the opportunity.

The Afro-American, a black-owned and -operated publication based in Baltimore, reported on the luncheon, "In an extremely relaxed environment, the publishers were given an opportunity to have an in-depth discussion that spanned a wide range of issues . . . While the President defended his position of being against quota programs, he indicated a willingness to reverse several existing pieces of Federal legislation that effectively prevent moves to help the Black businesses they were intended to assist." Cook went on, "While the President did not support all of the stipulations in the Kennedy Civil Rights Bill of 1990 . . . he made clear his willingness to introduce legislation that addressed some of the points suggested by visiting civil rights organizations who previously met with him."

I knew from experience that Bush would not be satisfied concluding the session with a simple goodbye and a handshake. As I called for last question, his expression told me he definitely had something else up his sleeve.

"What I'd really like to do if anyone's interested," Bush said slowly, checking his watch, "is give you a tour of the Residence before you leave. Any takers?"

Our small group moved right across the corridor, directly into the sun-splashed splendor of the Oval Office. I was glad it was a bright, brilliant day; the room seemed even more magical when the sun's rays reached through the bulletproof windows. A few of the publishers wandered quietly around the office, peering at artifacts and examining the artwork. Others stood immobile, the better to completely absorb and appreciate the breathtaking majesty of the place. After a few minutes, I helped the President form an impromptu receiving line in front of the fireplace while David Valdez, the President's ever ready photographer, sprang into action. Bush took an individual photo with each publisher almost every one of which appeared on the front pages of their newspapers immediately afterward, speaking with every one of them for a few minutes in front of the great portrait of George Washington. Throughout his tenure as President, he clearly enjoyed inviting people to share in the splendor of the Oval Office, and he did it often; indeed, he always seemed to feel just as fortunate and awestruck to be in its midst as his visitors.

The President was on a roll. He didn't want to leave it there. I looked at him for some sign of what he had planned next. With mounting excitement, the President led the group outside, ushering them through the Oval Office door and into the bright sunshine. We continued our impromptu journey. The Uniformed Division guards looked shocked; their heads turned and their postures straightened. Much talking into wrists and radios: "Timberwolf" was moving without prior notice—and with a group of black folks following behind him, no less!

Bush, completely wrapped up in the spontaneity of the moment, walked at a fast clip—toward the East Wing, which housed the Residential quarters. More quizzical looks. The public never moved within the Residence; it was the First Family's private living quarters. I hoped all the beds were made. Where exactly were we going?

And suddenly, there we stood. In the Lincoln Bedroom.

It took all of us a second or two to realize the full significance of where we were.

Bush moved slowly around the room, picking up items, explaining their history. We watched as he sat upon Lincoln's bed; we listened as he spoke softly about the portrait of a family of slaves, minutes away from being freed by Lincoln's signing of the Emancipation Proclamation. One by one, the publishers moved closer to examine the original copy of the Emancipation Proclamation, encased in a glass enclosure against the wall. We watched as Bush moved comfortably around the room.

All of us, including me, were profoundly struck by the symbolism of the moment. And I'm sure that Bush, too, recognized that we were all experiencing something which we would never forget; he realized, I think, that he would never feel the depth of the personal symbolism which we were all feeling at that moment.

How far the world had come. But more importantly, how far we had to go. I stood there in the Lincoln Bedroom, my gaze locked on the portrait of the small group of slaves about to be freed.

Standing in his bedroom, I felt great pride—solace, even —that it was Abraham Lincoln, a Republican President, who signed the Emancipation Proclamation, who released my people from the bondages and indignity of slavery. But some other element provoked me that afternoon; maybe it was unrest. Or frustration. Perhaps it was the realization that we have made tremendous strides, certainly—but the road ahead is long and arduous.

As a black Republican woman, I realize that the time for change and growth is upon us. As with fall foliage, the time is *now* for the colors to change within the Republican party. At long last, it is time for the rich browns and yellows and beautiful copper tones to burst into full bloom and be seen. And I know that we, as a party, will be better and stronger for it.

I've spent my entire life living up to other people's expectations and challenges. Now, I want it to be my turn to issue a challenge. I want it to be my turn to challenge someone to do something great.

To the party of Lincoln: Open your doors as wide as they will go. Open your minds and your arms so that we can *truly* practice the politics of inclusion. Do it now, and let us get beyond our own weaknesses and limitations. For as we identify our weaknesses, are we not also identifying our potential strengths?

. . . . .

I GAZED AROUND THE ROOM, tears in my eyes. I heard the birds singing outside. I felt the warmth of the sun on my sleeve. I thanked the Lord God for allowing me to experience this moment, and I vowed to pass it along to my children as soon as they were old enough to recognize the power of its significance.

But the portrait—even its title, *Watch Meeting*—or *Waiting for the Hour*—had stirred something deep within me.

Perhaps it was the realization that we, all of us—particularly women and people of color—are still awaiting our "hour": that one definitive moment (or series of moments) which will capture us all, finally, vividly, in one all-inclusive, multidimensional portrait. *This* is the portrait I want to see— and the portrait which I know my party is capable of creating.

For I am truly weary of this wintry-white landscape.

· · · · ·

CHAPTER 17

Goodbye, with Love

· · · · ·

BY THE FALL OF 1990, I was finally feeling the urge to move on. I knew I would miss the White House, and more importantly, I knew I would miss George Bush and all the friends I'd made over the years. But it was time to go. The White House wasn't a place to set down stakes and stay indefinitely. It was a place where you learned the ropes quickly, worked at a feverish, furious pace for as long as you were there (making substantial personal sacrifices along the way), and eventually departed. And if you allowed yourself to truly grow from the experience (rather than become burned out by it), you left stronger, wiser, and more adequately prepared to face the world.

So much had happened during my tenure; so much good had come of my life as a result having worked there. I had grown emotionally, had come to know my Lord God in a much more intimate, personal way, had served my country, and made many, many close friends. I had come to learn, first-hand—and, yes, even to finally understand—the nature of life's cyclical patterns: the death of Mother, the birth of Mary Elizabeth. I had become tougher without becoming mean or hard-edged; I had hovered at the highest levels of political power.

But the outside world beckoned, and I finally decided to heed its call. After weeks of negotiation, I was about to accept a handsome job offer from BellSouth Corporation, the largest of the Bell operating companies and a giant in the global telecommunications industry. I would be heading the corporation's communications and media relations efforts, with staff in D.C., where I would be based, and in Atlanta, the corporate headquarters. BellSouth was stable and well-managed; a proven leader in its field.

I was ready to make the leap, but I wanted to inform the President before I formally accepted the offer. Demarest agreed to set the stage. This time around, the situation was as it should have been: I was leaving under happy circumstances to accept an exciting job offer in a growing industry.

Demarest was gracious: One afternoon in early October, as Bush, Demarest, and I were preparing to leave the Oval Office on our way to a media interview, he laid the groundwork.

"Mr. President," Demarest said, "Kristin has something she'd like to tell you." I felt, for an instant, like a child, unable to speak up for myself and dependent on someone else to represent my interests. But I appreciated Demarest's support. And I was relieved that this would be a "good-news" announcement. For some reason, I was also glad we were all standing up. It made the atmosphere a little less formal.

Bush regarded me with an exaggerated wary eye. His facial expression told me he wanted to joke around.

"Don't tell me," he said, smirking. "You're pregnant again, right?"

I laughed aloud and stifled the urge to kick him hard in his shins.

"Very, very funny," I answered. I was actually glad he was in a jovial mood. I didn't want to be sad.

"Let's see . . ." he said, venturing another guess. "What on earth could it be?"

"Sir," I said, "I've been offered a job in the private sector, and I'm strongly considering accepting it. I wanted to tell you before I made any final moves. And I want to leave with your blessing."

"Everything okay?" he asked immediately. I wondered if he remembered in any detail the similar conversation we'd had months earlier, when everything wasn't okay. "You happy about the opportunity?" he asked. I realized, more at that moment than at any other, that he had turned into a real friend. You couldn't help but love him.

"I'm happy, yes, and very excited," I responded.

He smiled. "Well, come sit down for a minute and tell me about it," he said, moving back toward his desk. We sat. Demarest lingered across the room, standing near the grandfather clock against the wall. He looked slightly uncomfortable, but I was glad he was there.

"Who's stealing you away?" the President asked. "Who're you going to work for?"

"BellSouth Corporation," I answered, wondering how familiar he was with the company. I should have known better. The man has business in his blood.

Bush smiled. "Great choice; wonderful company," he said. "John Clendenin's the CEO, right? Very good man. If I remember correctly, the company's also very active in improving education, aren't they? Very philanthropic."

We talked for a few minutes about the specifics of the job. He wanted to know more. "They're based in Atlanta, aren't they? You relocating?" he asked. And then, the question I could have predicted. It was just like him: "How're they doing financially? I hear they're growing by leaps and bounds."

As always, the man was intrigued by the financial aspects of business. I should have brought one of BellSouth's annual reports with me into the Oval Office, but I sensed that my answer was enough to satiate his appetite for matters financial.

"Come on," Bush said, getting up. "Let's take a picture together. For your scrapbook. Call it 'The Day I Told the President I Was Quitting.' "

One of the White House photographers lingered outside the Oval Office, ready to accompany us to the media interview. She materialized immediately and shot for several seconds.

Bush put his arm around me as we were about to leave. I could tell he was pretty proud. "You've done a wonderful job here, Kristin," he said, getting serious now. "We'll miss you, but you know our door is always open."

After the interview, I headed back to my office, relieved that the moment was now behind me. But the hardest part was still to come: the final goodbye.

· · · · ·

M<small>Y LAST DAY</small> at the White House was just as difficult as my first, and equally full of emotion.

On that final day, my family joined me for a farewell photo session with the President. Lonnie Paul, bless his soul, marched straight into the Oval Office: Something on the President's desk had caught his eye, and he wanted to see for himself exactly what it was. I had taught my child well: Face power and authority head-on. It pleased me to no end that he was comfortable with his surroundings, even in the Oval Office.

Bush was sitting at his desk finishing up a note (as usual). Lonnie Paul stood inches away from the President, waiting quietly for him to finish. Placing the cap on his pen, Bush swiveled toward Lonnie Paul, regarding him closely.

"What are these things?" Lonnie Paul asked the President, reaching up to his desk. Two red yo-yos sat on the desk, inches away from Lonnie Paul's grasp. They were presidential yo-yos, of course, emblazoned with the presidential seal on one side, a picture of the White House on the other. Very nice.

"They're yo-yos, son," Bush answered, reaching to pick one up. "Believe me, we've got plenty of yo-yos around this place."

Bush looked up at me from his chair with a smirk. But I didn't feel much like laughing. I was sad.

"May I have it?" Lonnie Paul asked politely, reaching forward. I didn't like my children asking people for things, but at least he was polite about it. And at least the word "May" didn't make him sound like he was begging.

Bush handed it over immediately, then reached for the other one. "Here's one for your sister, too," he said. Then he rose, moving toward Lonnie. I reintroduced them briefly. Mary

Elizabeth regarded the entire scene warily and never once left her father's protective arms. The one time Bush reached to hold her, she burst into loud, mournful tears. Her screams reverberated off the Oval Office walls—a rare sound but, for some reason, pleasing to my ears. Maybe her screams cut through my emotions and chopped them up, making them less intense. My daughter wanted nothing to do with this President; she didn't even want to be there, and she made it very clear that she wanted him to keep his distance. And she was cranky because she'd missed her nap.

We took several photos. And then, thankfully, Lonnie Paul again diverted us from having to face The Final Moment. He ambled back over to the President's desk once more. Bush followed, sitting down again in his big leather chair.

"How would you like a goodie?" he asked Lonnie Paul, leaning forward. And then, ever the father, Bush looked up at me for permission: "Okay with you, Mother, if we give the kids some treats?"

I relented, nodding my head.

Bush pulled out several small, white boxes of candy and began helping Lonnie Paul stuff them into the pockets of his little suit jacket. I thought the pockets would burst at the seams.

"That's enough, gentlemen," I said with a warning. "Between all this candy and the Halloween candy we've already got stored away at home, we have plenty enough for some serious stomachaches." Party pooper, I thought to myself. Always the protective mother.

"But this is special candy!" Bush said. "It's White House candy!"

It was, too—even the candy boxes were emblazoned with the presidential seal. They were presidential M & M's.

Finally, there was no more stalling. The moment had come.

Bush turned toward me, serious. "I don't want you to be a stranger," he said. "Keep in contact. You've done a beautiful job the entire time you've been here, and I'm very, very proud of you."

Try as I might, I couldn't stop the tears. As he spoke, I remembered how he'd looked and sounded reciting the oath of office during the inauguration; how he'd so warmly supported me after Mother's death. I remembered the horsie ride he'd given Lonnie Paul years earlier (although I'm sure he'd long since forgotten), and the handwritten note during the transition of power: "She must be placed." I remembered the lady in the tall, white hat at the Vice Presidential Mansion, and the notes he'd sent home to Mother during her last living days. So very much had happened in such a relatively short amount of time. Most people don't experience in a lifetime what I had experienced in my years at the White House. I had truly been smiled upon.

I finally turned to leave, feeling as though I was about to round a corner and walk away from a place—from a moment in history—to which I could never return. I knew I couldn't stay in that room any longer without embarrassing myself.

My words came out in a rush: "You'll never know how much this experience strengthened my life," I said. "I am honored to have w—" I couldn't continue. Lonnie moved in closer. Mary Elizabeth, from her perch in his arms, grabbed a handful of my hair and pulled gently.

Bush, not knowing quite how to react, gave me a hug, then turned to Lonnie. He knew that if he continued with me, I'd end up embarrassing us both.

"Your wife is really something special," he said to Lonnie. Lonnie smiled proudly, nodding in agreement. "Tell her not to be a stranger."

We took one last picture, all of us together. And then it was time to leave. I pushed an envelope into Bush's hands as I left. (Thank goodness I'd had the foresight to write it beforehand.) It said all I wanted to say.

I looked around the Oval one final time, the lump in my throat burning like acid. I made an attempt at a goodbye smile, for all of my words were gone. Bush smiled back, hands clasped in front of him.

As my eyes swept the room, I silently, quickly prayed that more women and people of color would finally be granted the opportunity to enter these doors. It is an experience rich not only in history and politics, but in personal and spiritual development. It is a place where your potential blossoms because it has to. It is a place that demands cultural, racial, and ethnic diversity.

I looked down at Lonnie Paul, who was eyeing the red buttons on the President's secure phone. I thanked God for giving me the opportunity to make this place a normal, acceptable part of his reality. It had already given him a precious, almost imperceptible head start in the world.

Leaving was bittersweet: I knew I wanted and needed to move on, but I shuddered at the thought of actually walking out of those gates forever. I finally consoled myself with the realization that it would still be possible to keep in touch with all of my friends. The White House was only blocks away from my new office. My friends would remain friends forever, no matter where we were or who was in office.

That realization seemed to give me strength. I looked back one last time at the President standing there in front of his desk, smiling at my children. And then, holding my son's hand and my husband's arm, I turned and walked away, newly aware that my journey through life had only really just begun.